Gender, Sex, and Relationship Diversity Therapy

This seminal book is the original and definitive text presenting gender, sex, and relationship diversity (GSRD) therapy as its own therapeutic approach rather than simply a set of techniques or "add on" to other modalities in working with LGBTQ+ clients and other marginalised populations.

This edited volume draws on the expertise of international clinicians who offer contemporary perspectives as well as modernising traditional psychotherapeutic theories. The book introduces the modality by explaining the essence of GSRD therapy: its history, philosophy, and theories, as well as what it is used for and how it is practiced. It sets the landscape for GSRD therapy, centred on its seven core components. It focuses on specific populations and themes that are prevalent in the GSRD communities, yet often not written about or discussed in core clinical training, such as working with queer and trans young people, parenting, working with serious mental health difficulties, and ageing and the end of life. It also covers topics such as neurodivergence, self-harm, and body image.

This book is a critical resource for clinicians worldwide, particularly those working with or interested in working with populations who do not fit the dominant "norm" of heteronormativity and mono-normativity and those who are gender-expansive.

Dominic Davies is the Founder of Pink Therapy, a UK organisation that is committed to improving the mental health of gender, sex, and relationship diversities. He has been working as a psychotherapist, clinical sexologist, and practice consultant for over forty years, pioneering in the UK the development of GSRD therapy as a new specialist field of clinical practice.

Silva Neves is an award-winning, COSRT-accredited, and UKCP-registered psychosexual and relationship psychotherapist and a trauma psychotherapist. He is a Pink Therapy Clinical Associate and works extensively with the LGBTQ+ communities. He speaks internationally.

Antonio Prunas, PhD, is a licensed psychologist, psychotherapist, and sex therapist, living and working in Milan, Italy. He is Pink Therapy Clinical Associate and Associate Professor in Clinical Psychology at the Department of Psychology of Milano-Bicocca State University.

'After reading this book, I am left with a feeling of joy, wanting to read the book again! It offers valuable insights, reflections, and approaches to a group having faced discrimination, devaluation, neglect, shame and fear for so long. This is another step in the affirmative and explorative approach led by Pink Therapy, guiding "therapists in delivering effective and ethical therapy with GSRD clients," applicable to any psychotherapeutic approach, psychodynamic, behavioural or gestalt; they all have their distinctive contributions to the big picture!'

Elsa Almås, *Professor Emerit, University of Agder*

'This collection deconstructs and decolonises therapy; queers the binaries of exploration and affirmation, acceptance and change; challenges paternalism and hierarchies in therapeutic communities and spaces; embraces the ongoing fluidity of selfing; and encourages us to face our personal and collective shadows with kindness and honesty. I'm so grateful to this exceptional group of authors for their thoughtful, tender words, which expand and deepen what GSRD therapy can be, as well as applying it across a wide range of client groups.'

Meg-John Barker, Co-*author of* Graphic Guides *and* 'How to Understand Your ...' *books on GSRD*

'This book provides a bold and excellent insight into the values and benefits of GSRD-oriented therapy and the application of such across the spectrum of therapeutic modalities. Clinicians will find comprehensive resources to embrace discriminated, disadvantaged and often marginalised clients with fluid, diverse experiences whilst working to reduce any impact of heteronormative pathologization with social justice as a key driver. As therapeutic models expand systemically this is an exceptional resource to recommend that should ensure a meaningful impact is evident for both clinicians and clients.'

Professor Kevan Wylie, MD FRCP FECSM, *Past President, World Association for Sexual Health*

'This book is an inspiring and deeply moving journey through the lives and realities of GRSD people. Too often rendered invisible or rejected in society, they are at risk of being re-exposed to similar dynamics within the therapy room. Whether through personal bias or theoretical distortions, therapists may unintentionally replicate those same damaging patterns. This courageous publication – a continuation of the earlier and now iconic Pink Therapy series – offers a powerful opportunity to shift that reality.'

Dr Bartosz Grabski, MD, PhD, FECSM, WPATH-CM, *Sexology Lab, Department of Psychiatry, Medical College, Jagiellonian University*

'Gender, sex, and relationship diversity (GSRD) therapy is an exciting and important new development in the counselling and psychotherapy field: offering a flexible, sophisticated, and de-pathologising approach that is open to all. GSRD therapy aligns with what we know works best in therapy: a knowledgeable, skilled, and deeply affirming therapist who is able to practice with compassion and humility. I thoroughly commend this book as a comprehensive, in depth, and engaging guide to this emerging practice.'

Mick Cooper, *Professor of Counselling Psychology,*
University of Roehampton

Gender, Sex, and Relationship Diversity Therapy

Theory and Practice

Edited by Dominic Davies, Silva Neves, and Antonio Prunas

Routledge
Taylor & Francis Group

LONDON AND NEW YORK

Designed cover image: Hasyim Hasyim © Getty Images

First published 2026
by Routledge
4 Park Square, Milton Park, Abingdon, Oxon OX14 4RN

and by Routledge
605 Third Avenue, New York, NY 10158

Routledge is an imprint of the Taylor & Francis Group, an informa business

British Library Cataloguing-in-Publication Data
A catalogue record for this book is available from the British Library

ISBN: 978-1-032-87082-3 (hbk)
ISBN: 978-1-032-86880-6 (pbk)
ISBN: 978-1-003-53084-8 (ebk)

DOI: 10.4324/9781003530848

Typeset in Sabon
by Deanta Global Publishing Services, Chennai, India

Contents

Acknowledgements   *x*
Biographies   *xii*

Introduction   1
DOMINIC DAVIES

PART I
The Essence of GSRD Therapy   **7**

1 What Is Gender, Sex, and Relationship Diversity Therapy?   9
ANTONIO PRUNAS

2 What Do GSRD Therapists Do?   20
DOMINIC DAVIES

3 Key Elements of GSRD Therapy   37
SILVA NEVES

4 Obligatory, Not Optional, the Development of the
   GSRD Therapist   49
AGATA LOEWE-KURILLA

PART 2
Integrating GSRD Therapy   **67**

5 Integrating GSRD Therapy – Exploration and Affirmation:
   Bridging the Great Divide   69
PAUL C. MOLLITT

 6 Staring at Shadows   86
    KAREN POLLOCK

 7 Distress Directed Towards Our Own Queer Bodies and Lives:
    A Dialectical Behaviour Therapy (DBT) Informed Approach to
    Clinical Work with People Who Identify as GSRD   98
    JAMES LEA AND BRENDAN J DUNLOP

 8 A Figure of the Affirmed Self: Gestalt and GSRD Therapy Meet   116
    DANIEL BĄK

 9 Internal Family Systems (IFS) to Support GSRD People Dealing
    with Body Image Difficulties   128
    ALESSIO RIZZO

10 Biopsychosocial – and Mysterious! A Queer Jungian
    Perspective on the Meaning of GSRD   145
    GEORGE TAXIDIS

11 Mentalising Internalised Stigma   156
    WILSON GALLEGO HOYOS

12 Mirror Ball Encounters – Group Therapy with GSRD
    Communities   167
    NIKI D AND TIM FOSKETT

13 Decolonising the Vision of Wellbeing in Emotional
    Psychosexual and Relational Health for GSRD Clients   183
    RIMA HAWKINS

PART 3
Special Interests in GSRD Therapy   195

14 Working with LGBTQ+ Youth   197
    CAT JOHNSTON AND MARIA KINDSTEDT

15 The Spectrum of Family: Navigating the Challenges and
    Triumphs of Queer Parenting   213
    DANIEL MORRISON

16 Queer Spirituality in Counselling and Psychotherapy   226
    MATT CORMACK

17 Queer Ageing and Endings   239
    CHRISTIAN SCHULZ-QUACH AND MARGO KENNEDY

   Conclusion   261
   DOMINIC DAVIES, SILVA NEVES, AND ANTONIO PRUNAS

   Index   263

Acknowledgements

Dominic says: This is my sixth and final textbook on working with GSRD clients, marking the completion of a transformative journey that has spanned the past four decades of my career. I am profoundly grateful to have played a role in reshaping the therapeutic landscape for all those who find themselves outside society's prescribed 'norm.'

To my supervisees, students, co-editors, and contributors: you continue to inspire me through your dedication and make invaluable contributions to our community's mental health and well-being. I am deeply impressed by the pioneering work you are undertaking and feel immense pride in witnessing how you are changing our world, one therapeutic relationship at a time.

I owe special recognition to the countless GSRD clients who have trusted me with their stories, vulnerabilities, and healing journeys. Your courage in sharing your experiences has not only informed this work but has fundamentally shaped my understanding of what truly affirmative therapy means.

To my colleagues in the field who have challenged, supported, and collaborated with me over the years: your intellectual contributions and professional solidarity have been instrumental in advancing GSRD therapy as a legitimate and essential therapeutic modality.

Finally, and most importantly, I would like to thank my beloved partner, Dodain, for your unwavering support and profound understanding of both my passion for this work and its vital importance. Through the countless long hours, travels, and periods of deep immersion in teaching and writing, your support has been my anchor. Your love, kindness, and quiet generosity remain constant and unshakeable forces in my life, and I am deeply grateful for all that you are and all that you give to make this work possible.

Silva says: First, I would like to acknowledge all the queer people worldwide who died fighting for our human rights. During the AIDS epidemic, many of our queer siblings died alone, shunned by their families. The memories of all the queer lives lost too soon will never be forgotten. I also want to acknowledge the queer people who are alive today and struggling because of political and societal oppression. I hear you, I see you. I want to honour the tireless activism of queer people who came before us and those who will come after us. I love you all.

I want to say a massive thank you to my two co-editors, Dominic Davies and Antonio Prunas. We share a similar passion for our profession, and I have learned so much from both of them while working on this book.

I would like to thank my supervisor, Anne Chilton, who is always a great support. I'm grateful to all my colleagues who are also friends and fantastic, much needed LGBTQ+ allies who walk their talk: Rima Hawkins, Dr Remziye Kunelaki, Dr Angela Wright, Kate Moyle, Dr Roberta Babb, Catherine Knibbs, Lisa Etherson, Niki D, Diana Moffatt, to name a few.

I would like to pay tribute to three excellent practitioners who passed away too soon: David Stuart, Dr Mark Widdowson, and Ronete Cohen. Their significant contribution continues to make ripples of goodness in our profession, forever.

Last but not least, I thank my husband Dr James Rafferty for his ongoing love and support.

Antonio says: This is my first experience as the editor of a volume, and I could not have wished for more, having had the honour of undertaking this task alongside two colleagues for whom I have the deepest admiration.

My professional journey as a clinician and educator can be divided into two distinct eras: before and after my encounter with Dominic Davies. A few years ago, dissatisfied with various trainings that had consistently left me frustrated and unfulfilled, a colleague remarked: 'Perhaps the time has come for you to meet Dominic.' Never was advice more wise. From that experience, the insights and teachings I gained were so numerous and profound that it is difficult for me to believe that what preceded it holds any true significance. What I had long regarded as vulnerability—a wound to be concealed, a limitation to be managed—became the most powerful therapeutic instrument I had ever possessed.

I express my heartfelt gratitude to the countless individuals who, over the years, have inspired my thinking, nurtured my desire for continual learning, and encouraged me to remain curious. In particular, I am grateful to Dr Annalisa Anzani, my colleagues and co-trainers, my students (with their often disarming questions), and all the patients I have had the privilege of meeting throughout my career. Finally, I would like to thank my partner, Davide, for making me feel loved in a way that no one else has done before.

Biographies

Editors

Dominic Davies (he/him) is a leading voice in queer-affirmative psycho-therapy and a trailblazer in Gender, Sexuality and Relationship Diversity (GSRD). A Senior Psychotherapist, Clinical Sexologist, and Founder of Pink Therapy, he has spent over four decades championing inclusive, culturally competent mental health care for LGBTQIA+, kink, and non-monogamous communities. This is his sixth co-edited textbook on LGBTQ+ therapy. Internationally respected as an educator, supervisor, and speaker, he has trained thousands of therapists in creating anti-oppressive, affirming prac-tices grounded in trauma-informed and intersectional approaches. He is a fellow of the National Council of Integrative Psychotherapists (NCIP) and the National Counselling and Psychotherapy Society (NCPS). In 2021, he was awarded the first Liz McElligot Award for outstanding contributions to counselling and psychotherapy. The University of Minnesota named him one of 50 Distinguished Gender and Sexual Health Revolutionaries.

Silva Neves (he/him) is an award-winning, COSRT-accredited and UKCP-registered psychosexual and relationship psychotherapist, as well as a trauma psychotherapist. Silva is also a COSRT-accredited clinical supervisor and a Pink Therapy clinical associate. Silva is a member of the editorial board for the leading international journal *Sexual and Relationship Therapy*. Silva is the author of three books: *Compulsive Sexual Behaviours: A Psycho-Sexual Treatment Guide for Clinicians* (Routledge), *Sexology: The Basics* (Routledge), and *Sexual Diversity* (Karnac). He co-edited two textbooks with Dominic Davies: *Erotically Queer* (Routledge) and *Relationally Queer* (Routledge). He also contributed chapters to various publications and several articles to psychotherapy magazines and peer-reviewed journals, including *New Psychotherapist, Therapy Today, Sexual and Relationship Therapy*, and *The European Journal of Psychotherapy & Counselling*. He speaks internationally. Website: https://www.silvaneves.co.uk

Antonio Prunas (he/him), PhD, is a licensed psychologist and psychotherapist living and working in Milan, Italy. He completed a four-year training in Clinical Sexology and qualified as a Certified psycho-sexologist at the European Federation of Sexology (ECPS). He is also a graduate of the Postgraduate Diploma in GSRD Therapy at Pink Therapy. Antonio currently works in private practice as a psychotherapist and sex therapist, focusing primarily on GSRD clients. His main area of expertise is psychological work with transgender and gender-diverse people of all ages, as well as their families and partners. He is Associate Professor in Clinical Psychology at the Department of Psychology of Milano-Bicocca State University. Since 2019, he has been the scientific director of the postgraduate programme in Clinical Sexology at the University of Milano-Bicocca, one of the very few offered by a public university in the country. He is a member of WPATH and ESSM. Antonio also serves as an associate editor for the *Journal of Sexual Medicine*.

List of Contributors

Daniel Bąk (he/him), PhD, is a gestalt psychotherapist (EAGT accred.) and supervisor and has been recognised as Advanced Accredited Gender, Sex, and Relationship Diversities Therapist by Pink Therapy, London. He is a faculty member at Nederlandse Stichting Gestalt, Amsterdam, and Pink Therapy, as well as a clinical associate at Pink Therapy. He lives and works in Warsaw, Poland.

Matt Cormack (he/him) MSc BSc MBACP (Accred) RegCOSRT is an integrative psychotherapist, supervisor, and psychosexual and relationship therapist. Matt is a Clinical Associate of Pink Therapy and has a private practice. Matt sat on the BACP Spirituality Division Committee and has worked for several LGBT+ organisations. Liminaljourneys.co.uk

Niki D (she/her) is an existential psychotherapist, trainer, and supervisor working with groups, relationships, and individuals. Having worked with therapy groups for over 20 years, she holds ongoing GSRD therapy groups in London, including one for therapists. She has published other chapters with a GSRD focus and is a co-director of Opening Up CPD. www.rainbowrela tionships.com www.openingupcpd.co.uk

Brendan J Dunlop (he/him), ClinPsyD, is Consultant Clinical Psychologist and Cognitive Behavioural Psychotherapist in the NHS, a Clinical Lecturer at The University of Manchester, and Clinical Director at The Aspen Clinic. He has done extensive research and clinical work with GSRD populations, often with a focus on bisexuality.

Tim Foskett (he/him) is a group psychotherapist and trainer with over 30 years' experience. For many years, he led a pioneering sexual health groupwork programme for gay/bi men in London. He runs psychotherapy and supervision groups, and groupwork training in North London, and facilitates large group experiences with Loving Men+. www.timfoskett.com, www.lovingmen.org

Rima Hawkins (she/her) is a queer British Asian psychotherapist, clinical supervisor, and trainer specialising in GSRD, trauma, and relationship diversity. With 25 years' experience, she is an expert witness, a Survivors UK trustee, and a published author. Her work centres on anti-oppressive practice and cultural trauma. She speaks nationally and internationally on issues related to IPV and GSRD.

Wilson Gallego Hoyos (he/him), PhD, is a clinical psychologist and an alumnus of the PhD programme in the UCL Psychoanalysis Unit. He trained in Psychosexual and Relationship Therapy with Tavistock Relationships, as well as in Gender, Sex and Relationship Diversity Therapy with Pink Therapy. He works within the NHS and in private practice.

Cat Johnston (they/them) is a therapist and supervisor in private practice. They are the founder of Evergreen: Trans Youth Counselling and Support – a non-profit organisation offering affordable support to trans and non-binary youth. They are a Clinical Associate of Pink Therapy and a graduate of the Pink Therapy Post-graduate Advanced Diploma.

Margo Kennedy (she/her) is a Canadian social worker and educator with international expertise in sexual and gender diversity. Her work focuses on inclusive mental health care, trauma-informed practice, and end-of-life support. She integrates queer-affirming approaches into clinical care and education, advancing equity and dignity across diverse communities and healthcare systems.

Maria Kindstedt (she/her) is a clinical psychologist and CBT therapist living and working in Stockholm, Sweden. Maria is an author, university lecturer, and the creator of PRIMA Trans. She is co-founder and head of the Swedish Psychological Association's LGBTQ network. She is a graduate of the Pink Therapy Post-graduate Advanced Diploma.

James Lea (they/he), DClinPsy, is Consultant Clinical Psychologist, Accredited Supervisor and Therapist in Dialectical Behaviour Therapy (DBT), Lecturer, Researcher, and Poet. They have worked in various health settings and universities and have a private practice. James has extensive clinical and research expertise working with people who identify as GSRD.

Agata Loewe-Kurilla (she/her) is a clinical cross-cultural psychologist, systemic family psychotherapist, and PhD in Human Sexuality. Founder of the

Sex Positive Institute, she is a GSRD-affirmative therapist, educator, and activist. She trains professionals in sexology and advocates for sexual justice as a member of the World Association for Sexual Health (WAS).

Paul C. Mollitt (he/him), DPsych, MBACP (Snr Accred) BPC Reg. is a psychodynamic psychotherapist, supervisor, and researcher with fifteen years' experience in the NHS, higher education, and independent practice. He is a Pink Therapy clinical associate with significant experience working with GSRD populations and is currently training to become a group analyst.

Daniel Morrison (he/him) is a psychotherapist, facilitator, speaker, writer, and poet based in Yorkshire. He works in private practice with trauma, neurodivergence, and relationships, integrating EMDR and embodied modalities. He is Clinical Associate of Pink Therapy, and his practice is informed by extensive professional experience, lived experience, and a systemic social justice lens.

Karen Pollock (they/them) is a white, queer, autistic, non-binary psychotherapist, supervisor, and writer from a working-class background living in rural Northumberland. An advanced-accredited GSRD therapist and Pink Therapy Clinical Associate, they believe in radical visibility and dismantling the structures of oppression that keep us in chains.

Alessio Rizzo (he/they), MA, MSc, is Internal Family Systems (IFS) Accredited Psychotherapist, Clinical Supervisor, Trainer, Author and Educational content creator. Their private practice specialises in supporting GSRD and neurodivergent clients worldwide. Alessio is the author of a well-known IFS blog and co-hosts the "Queering IFS" podcast.

Christian Schulz-Quach (he/him) is a German-Canadian psychiatrist, psychoanalyst, and palliative care physician with international expertise in sexual and gender diversity. He integrates hospice and end-of-life care with inclusive mental health practices, advancing global dialogue on queer identities, grief, and dignity in care. His work spans clinical leadership, education, and research.

George Taxidis (he/him) is a Jungian analyst, supervisor, and lecturer in psychodynamic counselling and psychotherapy, and in psychosocial studies at Goldsmiths, University of London. He co-founded the International Queer Jungian Initiative and is currently writing a book on queering Jungian psychology for Routledge's *Jung, Politics and Culture* series.

Introduction

Dominic Davies

As one of the earliest co-developers of this emerging therapy model, I must explain the history and foundations of what we now call Gender, Sex, and Relationship Diversity (GSRD) Therapy.

I began work on the first volume of Pink Therapy (Davies & Neal, 1996) in the late 1980s. I was passionate about sharing the new gay affirmative therapy ideas being written about in the USA during the late 1970s and early 1980s. It wasn't until 1990 that the WHO declassified homosexuality as a mental illness. I began working as an out gay therapist in 1982 when mainstream UK psychiatry would still have classified me as mentally ill.

What inspired me about these earliest pioneers of gay affirmative therapy was the clear information that I wasn't sick, just different. However, the social context of gay life in the USA bore minimal similarity to that in the UK, and one of the key components of working with GSRD clients is a good understanding of the psychosocial contexts in which we live our lives.

Evangelical Christianity hugely influences the USA in churches, each week, congregants are urged to give generously to 'Save Your Child from Sodomy.' Parents would send their children to 're-education camps' to 'cure' lesbian and gay youth, and organisations like the now defunct Exodus International and NARTH (National Association for Research and Therapy of Homosexuality) held conferences and train therapists to convert gay men and women and repair their brokenness. In fact, despite 27 states banning conversion therapy (for minors), recent research showed there were 1300 conversion therapists in practice across the USA, with over 600 of these being state-licensed therapists (Ducharme, 2023).

However, the UK does not subscribe to the religious fervour of the USA. This is not to say Conversion Therapy isn't practised here. UK-based Evangelical Churches are still engaging in these practices, particularly in Northern Ireland, and mainstream counsellors and psychotherapists are also agreeing to work on reducing or eliminating same-sex attraction. A UK study of BACP and UKCP members found that 17% of BACP and UKCP members

DOI: 10.4324/9781003530848-1

had worked with clients to help them reduce their same-sex attractions, and 4% claimed they had agreed to cure them (Bartlett et al., 2009).

Later in 2018, the UK Government's National LGBT survey found that the most impacted group being offered conversion therapy were Asexuals (10%) and that people from all religious groups, from Judaism to Islam, are united in their condemnation of anything other than heterosexuality. The Memorandum of Understanding on Conversion Therapy, signed by a broad coalition of UK mental health organisations, sought to make the practice unethical. Sadly, legal battles diminished its effectiveness.

We also see the influence of Christianity in addiction treatment, where 12 Step programmes, whether professionally run as private inpatient clinics or peer-led self-help groups such as Alcoholics Anonymous (AA) or Crystal Meth Addicts Anonymous (CMA), are built around the idea that people are defective and need to submit to a Higher Power and pray. It is still virtually impossible to find residential treatment programmes that use harm minimisation approaches rather than the 12 Steps. Such clinics also often treat 'porn and sex-addiction' despite there being an absence of research to support the idea of sex being addictive (Prause et al., 2015; Briken et al., 2024), and have both preyed upon and prayed upon gay men for decades.

Back in the 1980s, I often felt like the 'only gay therapist in the village.' However, I was a clinician, not a writer or academic, so writing was slow. I only wrote a chapter each summer during my work at the University of Nottingham Counselling Service. It was only upon meeting Charles Neal in 1992, who founded the *Association for Gay, Lesbian and Bisexual Psychologies* and finding various other pioneering therapists based in London, that the first book came to fruition. I finally found colleagues, many of whom contributed the remaining chapters to what was the first European textbook for therapists working with lesbian, gay and bisexual clients. Therapy with trans and gender non-conforming people wasn't on our radar in the early 1990s; still, by the time our second two textbooks were published in 2000 (Neal & Davies, 2000; Davies & Neal, 2000). I finally met a Dutch gender therapist who contributed a chapter on the importance of gender counselling being independent of the medical pathway, which had various strict requirements to overcome if one were to access medical and surgical gender health care, and the 'treatment' was controlled by a tiny handful of psychiatrists.

What's in a Name?

There have been many different iterations of names for what we do. The earliest, of course, was Gay Affirmative Therapy, a model roundly condemned by Du Plock (1997), almost as soon as Pink Therapy was published, and this caused a rethink. By the time volumes two and three came out, we were using Sexual Minority Therapy (Neal & Davies, 2000; Davies & Neal, 2000). I have struggled to find a more inclusive term than the ever-expanding alphabet of LGBTQIA, etc., and have something that embraces all those people who aren't 'swans' (heterosexuals in lifelong monogamous relationships).

So we moved to Gender, Sex and Relationship Diversity Therapy, where the 'Relationship' was added by Meg-John Barker, and we amended Sexual to Sex to include intersex people, so that 'sex' could be used to mean both biology *and* behaviour. GSRD embraces all forms of consensual sexuality (and asexuality) and all relationship paradigms from monogamy to polyamory and authority transfer relationships.

It's helpful to note that various configurations have occurred during this period. Catherine Butler used Sexual and Gender Minority (SGM) therapy in an early paper on Systemic Therapy (Butler, 2009), and this is also a term widely used by one of the leading American researchers, Dr John Pachankis. More recently, Twist proposed Gender, Sexual, Erotic, Relationship Diversity (GSERD) (Twist, 2018), and down under in Australia, they have started using Diversity in Gender, Body, Kinship, and Sexuality (GBKS) (PACFA, 2025), which I like.

Earliest Pioneers

Some of the earliest pioneers on whose shoulders we're standing are: John Gonsiorek, Eli Coleman, Don Clarke, Betty Berzon, Peggy Kleinplatz, Charles Silverstein, Jack Drescher, Charles Moser, and Dossie Easton, to name a very few.

In my opinion, the USA is at least two decades ahead of the UK regarding vital evidence-based research and clinical thinking. This is primarily due to the research funding and teaching of psychologists in American Universities.

In the UK, there has been a strong tradition of academic lesbian, gay and bisexual psychology, with most of the early pioneers now holding professorial chairs in various universities: Sonia Ellis, Elizabeth Peel, Victoria Clarke, Peter Hegarty, Joanna Semlyen, Roshan das Nair, and Damien Riggs. Some of these psychologists were dual-trained as psychotherapists and have made essential contributions to UK queer therapy, in particular, Meg-John Barker, Darren Langdridge, Lyndsey (Igi) Moon, Alex Iantaffi, Martin Milton, Christina Richards, Ian Hodges, Catherine Butler and Amanda Middleton.

In the UK, it's important to note that the Pink Practice was the first private therapy organisation established in 1990 by Gail Simon and Gwyn Whitfield. It wasn't until a decade later that I set up Pink Therapy. Some of the earliest pioneers in queer therapy contributed to the first three volumes of *Pink Therapy* textbooks (1996, 2000) and supported me in the development of the organisation Pink Therapy. In particular, my dear friend and former co-editor, Charles Neal, and Dr Meg-John Barker, whose input into our conference programming was essential. Professor Darren Langdridge also supported our training programmes as a course consultant.

We have trained over 100 therapists on our one- and two-year programmes, and have an international faculty, as well as around 30 Clinical Associates. Of course, this does not include the many hundreds who have attended one- or two-day training sessions at national and international conferences by me or any of our other faculty, alumni, or clinical associates, etc.

It would be remiss of me to focus only on the UK, when GSRD has now spread worldwide, and it's heartening to see a plethora of queer affirmative therapy texts coming out of Poland, with several of our faculty contributing to these. Daniel Bąk, Bartosz Grabski, and Agata Kurilla-Loewe are prolific despite a social climate which hasn't always been sympathetic to GSRD human rights. In Italy, there is also a hotbed of research being conducted by Antonio Prunas and Annalisa Anzani, especially around Trans and Non-Binary sexualities and relationships. I encourage you to Google all these people for further information!

References

Bartlett, A., Smith, G. and King, M. (2009). The response of mental health professionals to clients seeking help to change or redirect same-sex sexual orientation. *BMC Psychiatry*, 9: 11. https://doi.org/10.1186/1471-244X-9-11

Briken, P., Bőthe, B., Carvalho, J., Coleman, E., Giraldi, A., Kraus, S. W., Lew-Starowicz, M. and Pfaus, J. G. (2024). Assessment and treatment of compulsive sexual behavior disorder: A sexual medicine perspective. *Sexual Medicine Reviews*. https://doi.org/10.1093/sxmrev/qeae014

Butler, C. (2009). Sexual and gender minority therapy and systemic practice. *Journal of Family Therapy*, 31: 338–358. https://doi.org/10.1111/j.1467-6427.2009.00472.x

Davies, D. and Neal, C. (eds.) (1996). *Pink therapy: A guide for counsellors and therapists working with lesbian, gay and bisexual clients*. Buckingham: Open University Press.

Davies, D. and Neal, C. (eds.) (2000). *Therapeutic perspectives on working with lesbian, gay and bisexual clients* (Pink Therapy Vol. 2). Buckingham: Open University Press.

Ducharme, J. (2023). Conversion therapy is still happening in almost every U.S. State. *Time Magazine*. https://time.com/6344824/how-common-is-conversion-therapy-united-states/ accessed online 21 May 2025

Du Plock, S. (1997). Sexual misconceptions: A critique of gay affirmative therapy and some thoughts on an existential-phenomenological theory of sexual orientation. *Journal of the Society for Existential Analysis*, 8: 56–71.

Neal, C. and Davies, D. (eds.) (2000). *Issues in therapy with lesbian, gay and bisexual clients* (Pink Therapy Vol. 3). Buckingham: Open University Press.

Psychotherapy and Counselling Federation of Australia (PACFA), (2025). Diversity in Gender, Body, Kinship and Sexuality Interest Group statement accessed 22 Sept 2025 https://pacfa.org.au/portal/Portal/About/Interest-Grps/GBKS.aspx

Prause, N., Steele, V. R., Staley, C., Sabatinelli, D. and Hajcak, G. (2015, July). Modulation of late positive potentials by sexual images in problem users and controls inconsistent with "porn addiction". *Biological Psychology*, 109: 192–199. doi: 0.1016/j.biopsycho.2015.06.005.

Twist, M. L. C. (2018). *A gender, sexual, erotic, and relational diversity matrix: A tool for exploring intersectional queerness* [Continuing Education Workshop]. Society for Scientific Study of Sexuality Annual Conference, Montreal, Quebec, Canada.

Part 1

The Essence of GSRD Therapy

Chapter 1

What Is Gender, Sex, and Relationship Diversity Therapy?

Antonio Prunas

Introduction

Gender, sex and relationship diversity (GSRD) therapy is an inclusive approach to therapy that questions hegemonic views on identity and mental well-being while exploring new perspectives on gender diversity and relationships using post-modern frameworks to support individuals who do not conform to typical gender identity standards or relationships.

The therapy mainly targets individuals with a variety of gender and sexual orientation identities outside the mainstream dominant conventionalities of binary gender and hetero-monogamy. Its principles can be applied to everyone as it acknowledges that societal norms can impact mental health for all individuals.

GSRD therapy promotes adaptability and inclusivity at its essence by taking on an approach that can blend seamlessly with therapeutic frameworks to tailor sessions toward meeting the distinct needs of GSRD individuals. The open and all-encompassing nature of GSRD therapy sets it apart from methods that could inadvertently perpetuate fixed notions of identity while invalidating those who deviate from the norm.

This chapter delves into the fundamentals of GSRD therapy, its underlying principles, and its goals of challenging normativity while respecting the individuals' freedom and consent.

A Post-modern and Post-structuralist Modality

GSRD therapy sinks its roots in post-modern and post-structuralist ideas, which question and challenge the traditional, rigid, and fixed narratives about identity, gender, sexuality, and relationships.

Post-modernism questions and rejects the idea of objective, absolute truth, particularly regarding identity and societal roles. At the same time, post-structuralism further expands on this by trying to deconstruct established power structures that reinforce these roles.

DOI: 10.4324/9781003530848-3

Post-structural theorists provided insight into how social categories and discourses construct subjectivities (and ultimately personal narratives and identities).

As suggested by Foucault, although same-sex attraction had always existed and been documented, it was only in the 19th century that the joint efforts of psychoanalytic thinkers and medical discourses contributed to the creation of this new social category, i.e. homosexuality.

Interestingly enough, the same applied to transgender identities. Although trans and non-binary people have always existed in all historical eras and cultural contexts, it was not until 1980, with the publication of the DSM-III (APA, 1980), that for the first time in history a clearly described set of criteria to diagnose gender-diverse people of all ages was created (Beek et al., 2015).

Not surprisingly, in that very edition of the *Diagnostic and Statistical Manual of Mental Disorders*, homosexuality was removed from the list of mental illnesses. In a sense, trans people ended up paying the price for the liberation of gay and lesbian people from psychiatric stigma by becoming affected by a mental disorder.

The creation of "medical" and psychiatric labels (like "homosexuality" and "transsexualism" or "gender identity disorder") brought about the establishment of a field in which scientific discourse dictated a "truth" that told individuals who they were and their value in society (Hagai and Zurbriggen, 2022).

These social categories have important implications for the processes through which individuals explore and get to know themselves; self-knowledge is therefore filtered and distorted through the lens of these social categories that are far from being "natural" or "true" (Hagai and Zurbriggen, 2022).

Furthermore, the categorisation of people as part of a non-heterosexual or non-cisgender category contributes to their oppression, as social categories constitute the building blocks of social hierarchy and inequalities.

In short, political, cultural, scientific, and economic institutions create discourses and social categories; people perceive, understand, and act on reality based on these categories. Politics is constructed from these social categories, and political agendas are advanced.

In this context, GSRD therapy critically examines societal expectations regarding gender, sex, and relationships. The therapy does not adhere to a singular, absolute truth about what is "normal" or "healthy" but instead exhorts clients to explore multiple truths and possibilities, elaborating the personal, unique narrative with which they resonate.

Trans-materialism adds another layer, emphasising the fluid and evolving nature of identity and challenging the fixed categories often imposed on gender, sexuality, and relationships. Rather than seeing gender, sexuality, and relationships as fixed entities, GSRD therapy encourages clients to view these aspects of themselves as dynamic, evolving, and constantly shifting. This philosophical grounding allows the therapist and the client to break free from rigid labels and categories, embracing a more expansive and nuanced understanding of the human experience.

By integrating these perspectives, GSRD therapy encourages clients to question and challenge the societal constructs that have shaped their identities and experiences. It invites a systematic process of deconstruction, where clients can examine how external forces, such as cultural norms and power dynamics, have influenced their sense of self and relationships. This exploration empowers individuals to embrace the complexity and fluidity of their identities, moving beyond binary, rigid or fixed categorisations.

A Therapy for Marginalised and Normative Individuals Alike

Crucial to GSRD therapy is the focus on working with individuals whose identities and experiences exist outside the norms.

Queer theories have offered a conceptualisation of normativities, which are the processes that represent the binary, widespread essentialist thinking and support the stigma and marginalisation of minorities.

Nowadays, "queer" generally refers to individuals and communities outside of mainstream sexual behaviours, including lesbian, gay, bisexual, transgender, non-binary, and gender non-conforming individuals, as well as heterosexual individuals who identify with and engage in queer theory (Fangbin Li, 2024).

The term "normativity" refers to societal and cultural expectations about gender, sexuality, and relationships. Normativity encompasses the societal standards that outline what is "normal", appropriate, acceptable, or desirable in that specific social context, particularly regarding gender roles and identities, sexual orientation, sexual practices, and relationship modalities and configurations (Pavanello Decaro, 2025).

The term "heteronormativity" was initially introduced by Michael Warner (1991) to refer to the dominant position of heterosexuality as hegemonic in social relations and the marginal status of sexual minorities.

Like heteronormativity, "cisnormativity" is the pervasive assumption that man and woman are the only possible gender categories and that people will live in either one or the other according to the corresponding gender role behaviour. Cisnormativity privileges people who identify with, embody, and enact gender expressions aligned with the assigned gender at birth.

Heteronormative and cisnormative scripts and expectations constitute the groundwork for homo-bi-trans-negativity and violence, as well as other proximal and distal stressors based on cultural assumptions and ideologies. Furthermore, they can appear at an individual, familial, institutional, and cultural/societal level.

However, another, "darker" side of the coin exists. Not only do cultural standards force LGBTQIA+ (Lesbian, Gay, Bisexual, Transgender, Queer, Intersex, Asexual +) people to live in a hostile context that denies their value, but they also dictate under which conditions a member of a minority group can be assimilated into, "seen" and acknowledged by the majority group. "Homonormativity" and "transnormativity" refer to dominant narratives about the "correct" way to be gay/lesbian or trans (Lindley and Budge, 2024).

By establishing what it means to be "truly" gay/lesbian and "truly" transgender (respectively), these unspoken rules punish the members of sexual and gender minorities who do not assimilate or align to mainstream heteronormative and cisnormative cultural norms.

Transnormativity can be defined as a narrative of a "trans enough" hierarchy that is heavily based on binary assumptions and a medically derived model of transgenderism (Johnson, 2016). This hierarchy includes expectations that all transgender people are "born trans", have a binary identity, conform to a "born in the wrong body narrative", seek and pursue medical and/or surgical treatments, have a gender expression that is stereotypically in line with their experienced gender, and seek to present and be perceived as cisgender (Riggs et al., 2019; Johnson, 2016).

This essentialist model of trans experience, like the "born this way" narrative of lesbian and gay people, hinders any alternative narrative of gender identity (or sexual orientation) as fluid, emergent, processual, or constituted by social norms and influence (Johnson, 2016).

Far from celebrating pluralities and diversity, homonormativity and transnormativity reinforce power dynamics, exert cultural control and function to reassure that sexual and gender minority individuals strictly adhere to the established norms, assimilate, and eventually are "just like" heterosexuals and cisgender people (Robinson, 2016).

The case below provides an example of how the "trans-enough narrative" can impact the well-being and life goals of a trans person by forcing them to question their identity against transnormative assumptions.

Bill is a 32-year-old transman who has been in GAHT (gender-affirming hormone therapy) for over 12 months. At one follow-up session, Bill claims that he wants to discontinue therapy because he is not sure he is "really trans". This discontinuation is very surprising as, in previous sessions, Bill appeared very happy with the results and, for the first time in his life, he had started dating. Bill explains that GAHT has increased his libido to the point that he feels the need to masturbate at least once a day. As he had never masturbated before, he was afraid that getting pleasurable feelings from his genitals might mean that, deep inside, he did not dislike his body. The implication of this, in his eyes, is that he might not be "man enough" to transition.

Granted that a trans person can decide, for a wide variety of reasons, that it is best to discontinue affirmative hormone therapy, in this case, it appears that Bill is acting out of societal forces and pressures he does not seem too aware of.

Rather than defining his path to gender affirmation based on his personal experiences and goals, Bill appears to be conditioned by what his cultural context defines as the "authentic experience of a trans person" (i.e. having to feel contempt and disgust for one's genitals and being unable to derive any pleasure from them). Perceiving himself as different from the dominant narrative implies that he does not feel valid, seen, recognised, and affirmed as a trans person in the eyes of society.

Homonormativity and transnormativity eventually acknowledge only particular specific identities while completely excluding and invisibilising others. This is because queer sexual identities may well fall outside of the categories based on a preference for "the same" or "the other" gender (which leads to heteronormativity and homonormativity, respectively) or based on identifying with the gender assigned at birth or "the other" gender (which leads to cisnormativity and transnormativity, respectively).

GSRD therapy aims to accompany clients in gradually deconstructing all these norms, first by helping them understand their profound impact on their inner world from the very early stages of their psychological development and the psychological price they had to pay to conform to them.

For individuals with marginalised identities, GSRD therapy provides a safe and affirming space to explore their experiences and celebrate their uniqueness and authenticity, regardless of societal expectations. In this way, it is both an affirmative and exploratory therapeutic approach.

Although GSRD therapy was primarily conceived for individuals who identify outside the norms, it is relevant for all people, potentially everyone living in our society and being exposed to mainstream norms.

Many people, even those who may apparently "fit in" within these norms, may struggle with internalised expectations or limitations imposed by these standards. One of the key insights of GSRD therapy is that societal norms, while not always the direct source of distress, can contribute to or exacerbate the client's difficulties. These norms may limit the client's ability to fully understand or express themselves, creating internal conflicts or external pressures (from partners, family, peers, etc.).

Heteronormative scripts and expectations are known to function as obstacles to heterosexual people as well, by not allowing them a variety of personal and sexual expressions (Sale, 2023). For instance, it happens quite often in sexological consultation with heterosexual cisgender men that the very presence of fantasies, desire, or past sexual experiences that do not perfectly fit into the rigidly heterosexual script generates a sense of profound discomfort and threatens their masculinity (i.e. "Am I gay?").

The same applies to cisnormative scripts, making people struggle with what is acceptable and appropriate in terms of traditional gender roles, at the expense of their spontaneity and freedom. These people may benefit from a queer perspective and a GSRD-oriented therapy, as it can offer a framework for exploring how societal pressures influence their behaviour, attitudes, emotions, and relationships.

For LGBTQIA+ people, identifying as outside of the norms already offers the privilege to question and challenge many assumptions around sexuality and relationships that are still widespread in the majority group, and opens the way to embrace other layers of diversity in terms of sexual practices and relationship modalities.

For instance, research has clearly shown that LGB people are more likely to report open relationships than their heterosexual counterparts (Levine et al., 2018), and that LGBTQIA+ individuals are more likely than their cis-het counterparts to be involved in alternative sexual practices such as kink (Sprott, 2023).

A critical aspect of GSRD therapy is ensuring that the therapy remains consensual and affirming for all clients. One of the significant challenges in GSRD therapy is the delicate balance between deconstructing and affirming. While it is essential to critique and dismantle harmful norms, respecting the client's identification, history, and personal experience is equally important.

The GSRD therapist must recognise that normativity is not inherently and necessarily an issue or "the problem" for *every* client. Some individuals may find a sense of safety, inclusion, belonging, self-realisation, or identity within specific normative structures, and it is not the therapist's role to dismantle these, especially without the client's consent or an explicit mandate from their side.

Therapists must avoid the risk of non-consensual "queering" of clients who identify as straight or conform to traditional gender norms. Similarly, it is essential to avoid the opposite—attempting to "straighten" queer clients or force them into normative roles. GSRD therapy prioritises the client's autonomy, recognising that each individual's experience is valid, and the goal is to support their self-exploration rather than impose any particular identity or narrative on them.

The therapist's role is to facilitate exploration and provide tools for clients to understand and deconstruct the elements that have shaped their identity, but always in a way that honours their autonomy and self-determination.

Finally, GSRD therapy requires working at a more "systemic" level, by critically challenging all traditional diagnostic (e.g. DSM-5-TR's (APA, 2022) diagnostic criteria for sexual dysfunctions) and therapeutic approaches, particularly those rooted in heteronormative or cisnormative assumptions. It requires critically examining the theories and frameworks traditionally guiding therapeutic practice. Many therapeutic models are rooted in heteronormative or cisnormative assumptions, often viewing deviations from these norms as problems to be solved or medical (e.g. intersex variations) or psychiatric (e.g. gender dysphoria) pathologies to be treated.

In doing so, it directly confronts and repudiates the pathologisation of gender diversity and non-normative sexualities that have historically been present in the fields of psychology, sexology, psychiatry, and psychotherapy (Prunas, 2019).

To fully embrace GSRD principles, therapists must go beyond simply affirming GSRD clients and actively challenge the theoretical frameworks perpetuating marginalisation. This may involve queering existing therapeutic models, expanding the toolkit of therapeutic techniques and tailoring them to the specific needs of marginalised clients, assuming an intersectional perspective, offering alternative narratives about identity, sexuality, and relationships, and creating a space where diverse experiences and identities are not only accepted but celebrated.

Trans-theoretical: Queering Traditional Modalities

One of the unique aspects of GSRD therapy is its trans-theoretical nature. It can be applied to and integrated with a wide range (potentially all) of therapeutic modalities, including cognitive-behavioural therapy, psychodynamic therapy, humanistic approaches, and more.

What sets GSRD therapy apart is its capacity to "queer" these traditional frameworks—with its commitment to fluidity and diversity, challenging assumptions about gender, sexuality, and relationships, and adapting them to be more inclusive of diverse experiences.

"Queering" therapy involves examining how the modality may reinforce normative assumptions and finding ways to adapt it to better serve clients with diverse identities. This process opens up new possibilities and keys for understanding and addressing the client's concerns, making nuances more visible without pathologising their identity or relationships.

Clients often come to therapy seeking help with specific problems related to their identity, relationships, or broader life challenges. GSRD therapy helps clients identify where these problems may stem from societal norms or expectations that limit their ability to express themselves fully.

"Queering" a therapy implies, first and foremost, the adoption of the seven core components of GSRD therapy.

Such integration is only possible if the modality has space for fluidity. For example, therapeutic approaches that pathologise diversity or treat non-normative identities as problematic and pathological would be utterly incompatible with the core principles of GSRD therapy, and therefore excluded from any effort at integration.

Let us consider this clinical example:

Kwaku is a 34-year-old, Black gay man originally from Ghana, coming to consultation because of problems in finding sexual partners. He works as a security guard and has never had a relationship in his life. In the last few years, Kwaku has been using gay dating apps to get in touch with sexual partners in his area. However, he now feels trapped in a downward spiral of depression, as he is systematically rejected by the very good-looking guys he is attracted to. If he does get any interest at all, the other guys only show morbid curiosity about his penis size.

Any well-trained therapist would see some narcissistic vulnerability in Kwaku, and how his narcissistic needs being systematically frustrated can lead to depression in the long run. With this perspective, we might focus exclusively on intrapsychic variables and minimise the impact of the social context, which plays a pivotal role in Kwaku's case. The whole picture is much more complex and nuanced, and unless we apply the seven core principles of GSRD therapy, we can only have a limited and restricted view.

In Kwaku's case, queering therapy means keeping in mind all the possible axes of oppression that might be at work. Kwaku belongs to an ethnic minority, is gay, lower class, and has a migratory background. This puts him at risk of discrimination and stigma in several social contexts. Even in situations where he might feel included and part of a group (i.e. joining a bunch of Black guys from his own country of origin for dinner), he might feel "different" and excluded because of his other intersectional identities (i.e. being gay).

Kwaku might never have experienced the feeling of being valid, seen, and accepted as a whole individual in all his different facets and identities. He ended up developing a condescending *persona*, a "heterosexual false self" to meet societal expectations at the expense of spontaneity and authenticity.

He might have experienced significant discrimination and a persistent feeling of lack of social safety (Diamond and Alley, 2022) in his country of origin (identifying as LGBTQIA+ is still illegal in Ghana) and possibly traumatic experiences connected to being gay. This has contributed to a persistent and chronic feeling of shame.

Hiding and concealing his sexual identity comes at a very high cost, as he needs to relentlessly monitor his speech, mannerisms, and appearance, and scrutinise other people's language and facial expressions to detect signs of disapproval or safety. All this, daily, can be exhausting in terms of cognitive and emotional resources and immunological functioning; this chronic threat-vigilance fostered by a lack of social safety has detrimental long-term effects on his mental and physical health.

For Kwaku, being in a committed relationship is unimaginable, as it would imply a significant extra amount of stress (i.e. having to come out, running the risk of being seen in public with another man) which, at this point in his life, he does not think he can handle.

Getting in touch with the gay community through dating apps feels like the only viable way now, but it nonetheless exposes him to further discrimination and stigma. Intraminority stress (Pachankis et al., 2020) in the gay community creates pressure for a high status so that only people with specific characteristics (i.e. young, good-looking, able-bodied, White, successful, straight-looking, and sexually skilled and endowed) occupy the top of the social pyramid, while all others are segregated at the bottom. In this sense, aspiring to a partner with a high status (i.e. a handsome, young, White, well-off guy) represents for Kwaku a way to "climb up" the social ladder in his community, gaining a position of greater visibility, recognition, distinction, and power.

It is not infrequent, in gay apps, to be exposed to harsh, discriminatory messages (i.e. "No Blacks", "No femme", "No old") that contribute to perpetuating a sense of loneliness, shame, and not "fitting in" even among one's own people.

Dating apps are venues in which objectification and fetishisation occur very frequently, and Kwaku, besides being rejected and "blocked" by the guys he is attracted to, becomes an object of morbid attention from people who are only interested in his body parts and fetishise him as an exotic "sexual object".

Part of therapy will include proactively getting Kwaku in touch with local resources and helping him establish non-toxic, non-sexualised connections with the local gay community (privileging communities that have worked extensively on their own biases and prejudices) and possibly with people who share other intersectional identities with him.

However, Kwaku might not be ready to get in touch with his community because of the effects of minority stress (i.e. internalised homonegativity), and preliminary clinical work should be directed at removing the hurdles that hinder a full connection.

Through the GSRD lens, we now clearly see that Kwaku's attempt to date very attractive guys can be interpreted as a strategy to repair his wounded self-esteem by gaining social status and visibility in the community, and the narcissistic vulnerabilities any "standard" therapist would have focused on as the primary therapeutic target lose their meaning and move to the background.

GSRD clients come to consultation for any kind of issues, sometimes for problems that have nothing to do with their identity (i.e. anxiety, depression, or personality disorders). Any trained therapist can easily apply their theoretical framework and therapeutic toolbox to support the client in restoring psychological well-being.

However, adding a GSRD lens to their standard clinical work might help provide a social and systemic framework to understand the person's distress, identify new and meaningful targets for our therapeutic intervention, and ultimately find new possible strategies to overcome the blocks that hinder our clients from living their lives to the fullest.

Given the emphasis on society, such strategies may well include direct interventions to change the client's environment (i.e. promoting the creation of a "family of choice", making the context they live in more affirming, and ultimately transforming society at large), as recommended by the guidelines and standards of care of different professional bodies in the field of mental health (i.e. APA, WPATH). In this sense, the therapeutic work is not confined to the walls of the consultation room, and advocacy is intended as an essential component of the mandate of any mental health professional working within a GSRD framework.

From the client's perspective, adopting such a framework is, *per se,* liberating and uplifting, as it clearly locates the origin of distress in the oppressive social environment they live in, thus alleviating their excruciating sense of being faulty, inadequate, hopeless, and broken.

Fluidity and Flexibility

A crucial element of GSRD therapy is emphasising fluidity and flexibility in the therapeutic process and how clients view and experience their identities and relationships. This fluidity extends to the therapist's mindset, where strict adherence to a particular modality or framework is avoided. Instead, the therapist remains open to wherever the therapeutic journey takes the client, allowing space for exploration and change without forcing them into any specific direction. Rather than adhering to a fixed or rigid agenda, therapists remain adaptable, allowing the therapy to evolve naturally based on the client's needs.

This flexible approach acknowledges the complexity of identity, which can shift over time and be influenced by various factors, including social context, relationships, personal experiences, and life events.

In GSRD therapy, identity is not seen as something to be "fixed" or stabilised, but rather as an evolving and dynamic aspect of the individual. The therapist's role is to support the client in navigating these shifts and transitions in a way that feels authentic and affirming to them.

References

APA (American Psychiatric Association) (1980) *Diagnostic and Statistical Manual of Mental Disorders* (3rd ed.). Washington, DC: Author.

APA (American Psychiatric Association) (2022) *Diagnostic and Statistical Manual of Mental Disorders* (5th ed., text revision). Washington, DC: Author.

Beek, T. F., Cohen-Kettenis, P. T. and Kreukels B. P. C. (2015) 'Gender incongruence/gender dysphoria and its classification history', *International Review of Psychiatry.* https://doi.org/10.3109/09540261.2015.1091293

Diamond, L. M. and Alley, J. (2022) 'Rethinking minority stress: A social safety perspective on the health effects of stigma in sexually-diverse and gender-diverse populations', *Neuroscience & Biobehavioral Reviews*, 138, p. 104720.

Fangbin Li (2024) 'What are the strengths and limitations of queer theory for understanding the categories of gender, sexuality and bodies', *International Journal of Social Sciences and Public Administration*, 5(2), pp. 210–215. https://doi.org/10.62051/ijsspa.v5n2.25

Hagai E. B. and Zurbriggen, E. L. (2022) *Queer Theory and Psychology Gender, Sexuality, and Transgender Identities*. Springer.

Johnson, A. H. (2016) 'Transnormativity: A new concept and its validation through documentary film about transgender men', *Sociological Inquiry*, 86(4), 465–491. https://doi.org/10.1111/soin.12127

Levine, E. C., Herbenick, D., Martinez, O., Fu, T. C. and Dodge, B. (2018) 'Open relationships, nonconsensual nonmonogamy, and monogamy among U.S. adults: Findings from the 2012 national survey of sexual health and behavior', *Archives of Sexual Behavior*, 47(5), 1439–1450. https://doi.org/10.1007/s10508-018-1178-7.

Lindley, L. and Budge, S. L. (2024) 'Challenging and understanding gendered narratives: The development and validation of the transnormativity measure (TM)', *International Journal of Transgender Health*, 25(2), 295–312. https://doi.org/10.1080/26895269.2023.2218365

Pachankis, J. E., Clark, K. A., Burton, C. L., Hughto, J. M. W., Bränström, R. and Keene, D. E. (2020) 'Sex, status, competition, and exclusion: Intraminority stress from within the gay community and gay and bisexual men's mental health', *Journal of Personality and Social Psychology*, 119(3), pp. 713–740. https://doi.org/10.1037/pspp0000282

Pavanello Decaro S., (2025) 'Constructing sexual authenticity, deconstructing heteronormative hegemony: Minority stress and queer individuals' sexualities', Doctoral dissertation, University of Milano-Bicocca.

Prunas, A. (2019) 'The pathologization of trans-sexuality: Historical roots and implications for sex counselling with transgender clients', *Sexologies*, 28(3), pp. 54–60. https://doi.org/10.1016/j.sexol.2019.06.002

Riggs, D. W., Pearce, R., Pfeffer, C. A., Hines, S., White, F. and Ruspini, E., (2019) 'Transnormativity in the psy disciplines: Constructing pathology in the diagnostic and statistical manual of mental disorders and standards of care', *American Psychologist*, 74(8), pp. 912–924. https://doi.org/10.1037/amp0000545.

Robinson, B. A. (2016) 'Heteronormativity and homonormativity', in Wong, A, Wickramasinghe, M., Hoogland, R. and Naples, N. A. (eds.) *The Wiley Blackwell Encyclopedia of Gender and Sexuality Studies* (1st ed.). Wiley, pp. 1–3. https://doi.org/10.1002/9781118663219.wbegss013

Sale, J. (2023) 'Exploring erotic diversity in heterosexuality: Keeping a queer eye for the straight guys', in Davies, D. and Neves, S. (eds.) *Erotically Queer*. London: Routledge, pp. 75–88.

Sprott, R. (2023) 'The intersection of LGBTQ+ and kink sexualities: A review of the literature with a focus on empowering/positive aspects of kink involvement for LGBTQ+ individuals', *Current Sexual Health Reports*, 15(2), pp. 1–6. doi: 10.1007/s11930-023-00360-3

Warner, M. (1991) 'Introduction: Fear of a queer planet', *Social Text*, 29, pp. 3–17.

Chapter 2

What Do GSRD Therapists Do?

Dominic Davies

Introduction

This chapter explores the unique approaches and practices of gender, sex, and relationship diverse (GSRD) therapists. It emphasises moving beyond traditional pathologising models to create an affirming, exploratory therapeutic environment. GSRD therapy is rooted in social justice, cultural humility, and intersectionality, recognising the impact of societal stigma and minority stress on clients" mental health.

The chapter outlines the key components of GSRD therapy, including the I-CATCH framework, which encourages therapists to be informed, curious, affirming, trusting, congruent, and flexible in their approach. It discusses the importance of therapist self-disclosure, the creation of safe spaces, and navigating potential dual relationships within GSRD communities.

GSRD therapists are encouraged to embrace authenticity, challenge societal norms, and adapt their therapeutic styles to meet diverse client needs. The chapter also addresses the challenges of maintaining professional boundaries while working within the same community as clients.

Furthermore, the importance of contemporary sexology knowledge is highlighted, enabling therapists to engage comfortably in discussions about sex and relationships. The chapter concludes by emphasising the need for GSRD therapists to balance their roles as professionals and community members while prioritising client well-being and maintaining ethical standards.

In this chapter, we will propose how GSRD therapy differs from and builds upon other modalities. GSRD therapy is an approach or framework. By adopting a GSRD lens with all clients, we can better understand how society, family, and religion have shaped their experiences of shame for being different.

Multiple lenses shape our beliefs in a kaleidoscope. Mononormativity, cisnormativity, hetero- and homo-normativity, and many others create expectations and notions of normalcy, implying that we should all be alike and desire the same things.

DOI: 10.4324/9781003530848-4

The Impact of Heteronormative Pathologisation on GSRD Individuals

Heteronormative pathologisation has profoundly and detrimentally affected GSRD individuals. This practice of labelling GSRD identities and experiences as inherently disordered or pathological has historically held significant weight. It continues to be a root cause of human rights violations against GSRD people. The consequences of such pathologisation are far-reaching and multifaceted:

Mental Health Implications: Pathologisation contributes to an increased risk of emotional problems, suicide attempts, and substance abuse among GSRD individuals. It's crucial to understand that these issues stem from societal stigma and marginalisation rather than from GSRD identities themselves.

Healthcare Barriers: GSRD individuals face significant barriers and inequalities in accessing healthcare. These issues are rooted in structural, interpersonal, and systemic factors that disproportionately affect their health outcomes. They range from a reluctance to seek help and fear of disclosing their identity to healthcare providers, to a lack of knowledge about specific LGBTQ (lesbian, gay, bisexual, transgender, queer) healthcare issues, as well as the considerable delays TGNB (trans and gender non-binary) individuals experience when accessing healthcare. Conversion "therapies" are still practised by

Legal and Social Discrimination: Pathologisation is used to justify the ongoing criminalisation of transgender individuals, the denial of gender identity recognition through self-declaration, and various forms of discrimination in education, employment, and housing. Few cis-het individuals need to worry about being arrested or facing visa restrictions when selecting a holiday destination in another country.

Internalised Stigma: Many GSRD individuals internalise societal prejudices, which can lead to feelings of shame, worthlessness, and a sense of being "broken." This internalised stigma may encourage some to seek harmful practices like conversion therapy in an attempt to "fix" themselves, a process that remains lawful in the UK.

GSRD therapists recognise this historical pathologisation of diverse identities and critically examine traditional diagnostic frameworks. They understand that diagnostic criteria often fail to reflect the experiences of gender and sexual minorities adequately. There is a significant co-occurrence of neurodiversity in GSRD individuals compared to cisgender heterosexuals (George & Stokes, 2018; Warrier et al., 2020; Weir, 2021), and symptoms related to minority stress (Meyer, 2003) can mimic those of other conditions, leading to potential misdiagnosis.

Given the history of the pathologisation of GSRD identities, it is important to critically reflect on the traditional diagnostic taxonomies of the Diagnostic and Statistical Manual of the American Psychiatric Association

(APA, 2013) and the International Classification of Diseases of the World Health Organisation (WHO, 2019), which frequently ignore or fail to adequately reflect the lives and issues of gender and sexual minorities.

> There is a growing tendency in our society to medicalize problems that are not medical [and] to find psychopathology where there is only pathos... [The DSM] is the repository of a strange mix of social values, political compromise, scientific evidence, and material for insurance claim forms.
>
> (Kirk & Kutchins 1997, x)

One example is the need for specialist gender clinicians to diagnose gender dysphoria before they can provide gender-affirming treatment to non-binary people. Not everyone who is TGNC (trans and gender non-conforming) experiences dysphoria (Galupo et al., 2021; Ashley, 2019). Being non-binary or gender non-conforming is not a mental illness. This over-medicalisation of human experience denies bodily autonomy and forces people to have a mental health diagnosis to access treatment. There is no requirement for a psychiatric diagnosis before a cis woman requests breast augmentation or for cis men seeking penis enlargement or testosterone supplementation. Nor is there a requirement to have two psychiatric reports before someone can engage in extreme body modifications such as piercings, implants, or facial tattoos.

Another example of heteronormative bias, particularly relevant to men who have sex with men, is the lack of recognition and appropriate treatment classification for anodyspareunia (painful anal sex), which results in sex therapists often being unaware of how to address this fairly common issue (Morin, 1995; Grabski, 2023).

The lives of GSRD people often intersect with mental health professionals. Aside from the elevated levels of depression, anxiety, and substance use resulting from minority stress, there is also the issue of an over-representation of neurodiversity, which means that GSRD people might want or need a formal diagnosis to access treatment or state support. Others might seek a diagnosis to help them understand what is happening to them.

For the most part, traditional psychiatric diagnosis is highly subjective regarding the potential for differential diagnosis, as the same symptoms can describe something entirely different. It has been noted that symptoms related to Minority Stress Theory (Meyer, 2003), which are altogether understandable within that framework (i.e., rejection sensitivity, emotional reactivity, and suicidal ideation), can mimic those of borderline personality disorder (BPD), placing GSRD individuals at a higher risk of misdiagnosis with BPD (Goldhammer et al., 2019; Rodriguez-Seijas et al., 2021). Specifically, the diagnostic criteria for BPD closely align with the experiences of many bisexual cis-women, a group known to experience significantly elevated mental health issues (Bostwick et al., 2021; Ross et al., 2018). Engaging in sexual relationships with multiple partners (single and dating) or being polyamorous and bisexual has been cited as evidence of "Impulsivity in at least two areas that are potentially self-damaging. Examples include spending, sex, substance abuse, reckless driving, and binge eating" (APA, 2022 DSM-5-TR). Research has shown that bisexual women are also more likely to encounter challenges with alcohol and substance misuse. A meta-analysis revealed that bisexual individuals face the highest risk of suicidality among LGBTIQ subgroups, with odds ratios of 6.71 for suicide attempts, 5.04 for suicidal ideation, and 5.03 for non-suicidal self-injury (King et al., 2008). One can observe the heteronormative and mononormative bias confounding correlation with causation in these examples.

The Co-creation Process

In clinical formulation, therapists and clients work together to develop a shared understanding of the client's challenges. This collaborative process involves:

1. Client's contribution: Individuals share their narratives and lived experiences.
2. Therapist's contribution: Professionals bring their expertise to concepts like minority stress, trauma, adverse childhood events, and other theoretical frameworks that impact clients' mental health systemically.
3. Shared understanding: Together, they explore the client's life through the lens of the four Ps of Psychological Formulation.

The Four P's of Psychological Formulation

This framework aids in structuring the understanding of a client's experiences from a biopsychosocial perspective:

1. Predisposing Factors: Elements that may increase vulnerability to specific difficulties.
2. Precipitating Factors: Recent events or triggers contributing to the current challenges.
3. Perpetuating Factors: Aspects that maintain or exacerbate the problems.
4. Protective Factors: Strengths and resources supporting resilience and well-being.

Dunlop and Lea (2023) have demonstrated the effectiveness of Clinical Formulation for LGBT clients. Their work highlights how this approach can be especially beneficial in addressing the unique experiences and challenges faced by individuals in the LGBT community, particularly considering the systemic oppressions.

By employing clinical formulation, therapists can create a more inclusive, empathetic, and personalised approach to therapy. We can shift away from overly pathologising models and move towards a more nuanced understanding of clients' lives and experiences.

The Therapeutic Relationship

Formulation helps clinicians comprehensively understand client's issues, guiding diagnosis and treatment planning.

The therapeutic relationship is a collaborative partnership that heals trauma by validating feelings, teaching skills for managing dysregulation caused by trauma, and encouraging connections with others who support and affirm us. Whether in online relationships or real-life ones, both are valid.

Having GSRD knowledge fosters an awareness of the external systems that contribute to our internal worlds, both presently and from a developmental perspective.

It is not unusual for therapists to work with a client who presents a tragic and appalling problem-centred narrative, believing they are the creators of their distress. They often overlook the role of external factors—familial, societal, and systemic—in contributing to the client's shame, depression, and isolation.

By fostering an understanding of social justice and anti-oppressive practices, the therapist can create connections between intersectional differences that have contributed to challenges in self-acceptance, forming relationships, and attaining inner peace.

One example of this might be a gay man with undiagnosed autism who has struggled for years to date and form intimate relationships. While most people find dating challenging, it can become even more complex when someone has difficulty reading and understanding social cues.

Dean (35) worked as a senior programmer at a major bank. He earned good money and could buy his house, but struggled immensely to make friends. He tended to avoid bank socials and found it difficult to form friendships with other gay men. He had a few casual hookups in dark rooms while on holiday, but found internet dating back home cruel and awkward. He became depressed and anxious and sought counselling sessions with a gay counsellor through his workplace health insurance. After several sessions, his counsellor asked if he had ever been assessed for autism. He had not considered this before, but after reading about it, he recognised himself in many descriptions and sought an assessment through his health insurance. The diagnosis confirmed the counsellor"s hunch, and together, they explored Dean learning the esoteric arts of gay dating!

Intersectionality

Coined by Black feminist scholar Kimberlé Crenshaw in 1989, intersectionality is a critical framework that explores how multiple aspects of a person"s identity intersect and interact, shaping their lived experiences and access to social opportunities. This concept examines how various social categorisations, such as gender, race, ethnicity, sexuality, class, and disability status, combine to create overlapping systems of discrimination or disadvantage. Understanding the impact of the client's intersectional identities is crucial to GSRD's stance on cultural humility and cultural competence (Turner, 2021).

Therapists should comprehend how their positionality and intersectional identities may align with or differ from those of their clients. Many clients prefer to work with someone who shares at least some of their identities (queer, neurodivergent, trans, and so on). Possessing lived experience can be advantageous, as one may be familiar with some of their clients" social contexts.

However, it is common for clients to actively seek a therapist outside their community, possibly to minimise the chance of social encounters outside the consulting room or due to concerns about therapist bias. Others might benefit from a warm and accepting cis-het therapist to address their internalised shame. We believe there are advantages and disadvantages to therapist matching, but what is perhaps most important is that the therapist has specifically engaged in GSRD training and does not rely solely on their shared membership in the queer or trans communities as their 'qualification.'

Therapist Disclosure of Sexual Orientation (TDSO)

Traditionally, therapists have been taught not to disclose personal information about themselves. Such emotional neutrality is unhelpful and outdated (Danzer, 2018). The concept of a blank screen or neutral therapist is not conducive to effective therapy with GSRD clients, where genuineness, empathy, and social justice are significant. The refusal or avoidance of answering an enquiry from a GSRD client about the therapist's orientation or another essential aspect of their identity can create a considerable rupture or obstacle to psychological contact (Davies & Aykroyd, 2002). While exploring the implications of sharing personal information might be helpful, refusing to share is unethical and unnecessary. The client is assessing whether they can trust the therapist enough to open up. We are not advocating oversharing the details of one's intimate life. Still, the willingness to be open about one's identities and selectively share life experiences with your GSRD client (e.g., kink, cis, queer, trans, neurodivergent, etc.) can be enormously helpful.

GSRD therapy is unapologetically affirmative and exploratory. When clients come for therapy, they have a right to expect their therapist to be genuinely interested in witnessing and affirming their lives and identities amidst all the messiness and fluidity that characterise the human experience. They deserve someone who is on their side and can assist them in exploring the complexities of any emerging identity changes or life goals they may have. GSRD therapists employ a strengths-based approach to help build resilience.

In some circumstances, this may include teaching skills (such as mindfulness), coaching dating skills, and offering feedback on creating online profiles. Psychoeducation can be extremely valuable for a population that may be more familiar with narratives of brokenness, pathology, and perversion. Incorporating microaffirmations—small, often subtle acknowledgements of a person's worth and identity—can further enhance this process by fostering a sense of belonging and validation. Recommending certain books, videos, YouTube channels, and similar resources to help inform and build confidence can also be beneficial. While some of this may feel too radical for therapists who adopt a more austere and less interactive approach, these 'life skills' aspects are routine for therapists trained in third-wave Cognitive Behavioural Therapy (CBT) approaches (see Lea & Dunlop in chapter 7). Our duty of care and therapeutic responsibility is to be a resource for our clients, providing support, affirmation, guidance, and skills in navigating a world that seeks to deny, obfuscate, and restrict them from reaching what Maslow (1943) called Self-Actualisation.

Comfortable with Complexities

Affirmation is combined with exploration, enabling clients to discover their wisdom through the tension between them.

We understand that sexuality may not be fixed for many people, and these changes can sometimes be disconcerting, prompting individuals to seek therapy to explore their sexuality more deeply. We're not talking about gay clients presenting for a 'cure' in sexual orientation change efforts, where the client has an innate wisdom of who and what they are attracted to but feels that this is unacceptable to society, their family, or religion. We mean situations where someone becomes aware of attractions beyond their past experiences.

The GSRD therapist is comfortable exploring the complexities of gender. For example, it can be pretty messy when societal cis-normativity dictates that one, after a psychiatric diagnosis, can transition between only two genders, which are expected to result in heterosexual sexuality and monogamous relationships. However, trans individuals are often not permitted to procreate and have children. Many countries still insist on sterilisation to access gender-affirming healthcare and have their new gender recognised. It is still considered unusual for trans men to become pregnant. Additionally, it's important to remind ourselves of outspoken non-binary gender radicals like Travis Alabanza, Alok Menon, Fox Fisher, and Owl Fisher (Ugla Kristjönudóttir Jónsdóttir), who challenge the hegemony of the gender binary.

Social Justice

As mentioned in this book, social justice is at the heart of GSRD therapy. But how does this play out in practice regarding what therapists do? Many GSRD therapists recognise the economic disparities faced by GSRD communities compared to cis-het communities and offer some form of sliding scale or reduced fee practices. As trans people experience significant economic disadvantages in accessing work, housing, and healthcare, many therapists provide fee reductions to this population.

Some GSRD therapists recognise their role in community activism, involving third-sector organisations, campaigning for trans healthcare, or attending Pride events and community memorial events such as Trans Day of Remembrance or the Candlelit Vigil at Manchester Pride.

The I-CATCH Framework

While the seven core components inform the knowledge and focus of a GSRD therapist, the I-CATCH framework guides what to prioritise when establishing a strong therapeutic relationship. Those trained in the person-centred approach will recognise its influences, as reflected below. However, be cautious and avoid becoming overconfident in your ability to assist your client. The first principle will challenge much of what you've learned!

Let us explain the I-CATCH acronym in more detail:

I—Be knowledgeable and *informed*: This encourages therapists to continually update their professional knowledge and skills to provide the best possible care. A commitment to learning more about the lives of various GSRD identities through self-study, continuous professional development (CPD), and ideally, social friendships with individuals from different backgrounds is an excellent way to remain informed. Additionally, keeping up with emerging research in this flourishing field by reading papers, attending conferences, and having a practice supervisor who has engaged in GSRD-specific training is an effective way to stay informed.

C—*Curiosity* to explore: This reminds therapists to approach each client with genuine interest, asking questions and delving deeper into their experiences and perspectives. By being open and curious to learn about client's experiences, hopes, and goals, therapists can assist them in healing from or overcoming traumas and acquiring the skills and connections to live more fully in the world.

Jane, a 27-year-old non-binary individual, seeks therapy for feelings of isolation and navigating relationships. During the initial session, Jane mentioned growing up in a conservative environment where their gender identity was neither understood nor accepted. They express uncertainty about how to build meaningful connections while remaining true to themselves.

Instead of assuming Jane's experiences, the therapist approaches the conversation with curiosity. They ask open-ended questions like, "Can you tell me more about what connection means to you?" and "What has it been like for you to explore your identity in the context of your relationships?" As Jane shares their story, the therapist listens attentively, affirming their experiences while gently exploring deeper layers of their hopes and challenges.

Through this process, Jane starts to recognise patterns of self-protection that emerged as a response to past rejection. The therapist assists Jane in exploring ways to reframe these patterns and consider new strategies for building trust and intimacy. By staying curious and open, the therapist creates a safe space for Jane to explore her identity further, heal from past traumas, and envision a future filled with authentic connections.

A—Choices and experiences *affirmed*: This reminds therapists to validate and support their clients' decisions and lived experiences while fostering a non-judgmental environment. We believe clients need to know that you have their backs. Your unwavering support and belief in them demonstrate unconditional positive regard. (Rogers, 1951)

Another 'A' here might be the ethical principle of autonomy, which respects people enough to allow them the right to make their own decisions and live their own lives. Therapists hold a powerful position concerning their clients. Our affirmation and validation of their thoughts and feelings can be immensely significant. We cannot know what's best for a client; we need to remain open to the client experimenting and possibly changing their mind. Sexuality and gender can be dynamic and flexible. While some people are comfortable living with fixed and stable identities, others may change under certain circumstances. Sometimes, this occurs due to a significant change in their living situation or unexpectedly falling in love with someone outside their usual norms. For many people, gender and sexuality are not permanently fixed, and 'born that way' narratives are not universally valid or helpful. While some individuals find comfort in the multitude of biological explanations for their sexuality or gender, there are no universal scientific theories that account for what makes someone same-sex attracted or, indeed, transgender.

Jen, a 30-year-old client, comes to therapy expressing confusion about her sexual orientation and gender identity. She shares that she has always identified as a cisgender heterosexual woman but has recently developed romantic feelings for a close female friend. Additionally, Jen has been questioning her comfort with traditional gender roles and experimenting with more androgynous clothing.

In the session, Jen expresses fear of judgment and uncertainty about "what this all means." They ask the therapist, "Do you think this means I'm gay? Or maybe nonbinary? I just feel so lost."

The therapist, guided by the ethical principle of autonomy, responds with empathy and validation: "It sounds like you're exploring some fundamental aspects of yourself right now. It's okay not to have all the answers right away. What feels most authentic to you in this moment?"

Rather than imposing labels or interpretations, the therapist encourages Jen to explore her feelings and experiences at her own pace. They affirm Jen's right to self-determination: "Your identity is yours to define, and it's okay if it evolves. Let's work together to create a space to explore what feels true for you safely."

Over time, Jen experiments with different labels and ways of expressing their identity. Some resonate deeply, while others do not. The therapist remains supportive and non-directive, recognising that Jen's journey is dynamic and personal. When Jen decides to share their evolving identity with loved ones, the therapist helps them navigate these conversations while respecting their autonomy.

T—*Trust* your client with humility: This principle encourages therapists to believe in their clients" capabilities while maintaining a humble stance, recognising that the client is the expert on their own life. This concept is also tied to the resilience we frequently encounter in our clients. Carl Rogers named this the actualising tendency. (Rogers, 1959), a concept familiar to many other modalities by different names.

Andrea, a 35-year-old teacher, came to therapy feeling overwhelmed by anxiety after her recent divorce from her wife. As her therapist, Mike initially wanted to offer solutions or guide her on her path forward. However, he reminded himself to trust Andrea's inner resilience and ability to navigate her life.

Instead of directing her, Mike asked open-ended questions and reflected her emotions. Over time, Andrea began to uncover her strengths—her love for teaching, her deep connection with her children, and her ability to adapt to change. She started to set small goals for herself, such as joining a local book club and reconnecting with old friends.

By trusting Andrea's actualising tendency and remaining humble in his role, the therapist observed her growth unfold naturally. She didn't need him to "fix" her; she needed space and support to rediscover the expert within herself.

C—*Congruent*: This emphasises the importance of being genuine and authentic in therapeutic relationships, including appropriate self-disclosure when beneficial. Answering clients" questions about one's own identity builds an honest and trustworthy relationship.

Laura, a lesbian client, has recently begun counselling and asked her therapist, "Are you gay?" The therapist, recognising the importance of authenticity and the potential impact of their response, replied honestly, "No, I'm heterosexual. However, my brother is gay, and through him, I have gained some understanding of the challenges the LGBTQ+ community can face. I'd like to hear more about your experiences to understand your perspective better."

The therapist demonstrated congruence by responding honestly and sharing a relevant personal connection while focusing on Laura's experiences. This genuine interaction helped build trust and assured Laura that her identity would be respected and understood in the therapeutic space.

H—*Heed* client needs (Flexibility): This principle emphasises the importance of adapting therapeutic approaches to meet individual client needs rather than applying a one-size-fits-all method. While some clients benefit from more passive, client-centred approaches where the therapist observes and accompanies the client as they explore their life, others may require more active psychoeducation or skills training from third-wave CBT approaches. Additionally, it is critical to address past or current traumas. We must also consider flexibility in our methods. Many clients find sitting in a neutrally decorated room, observed by a therapist for 50 minutes, intimidating or unproductive. Therapists who provide walk-and-talk therapy, animal-assisted therapy, or are adaptable regarding duration, seating arrangements, and methods of communication, and this flexibility of approach may suit some clients better.

Jason, a cis-gay man, worked as a nurse in a private hospital. He presented for therapy as his job was under threat for missing too much time. At the weekends, for the past six months, Jason had been engaging in long-duration chemsex sessions, sometimes with one person, at other times with several men. The drugs made him horny, and he felt connected and had tremendous pleasure in having hot sex with his partners. However, the drugs made it virtually impossible to orgasm. His therapist learned to schedule Jason's sessions for a Wednesday or Thursday, as on Monday, Jason could be resting or still high from the weekend, and on Tuesday, he would often be at the lowest point of his self-recriminations and self-hatred.

GSRD therapy challenges the hegemonic ideas of society. It adopts a critical approach to accepted wisdom, which involves being curious and flexible about the timing, duration, location, and therapy setting. Of course, we must protect the confidentiality of our work. However, why insist that the so-called 'therapeutic hour' is 50 minutes? Why not offer two half-hour sessions a week (or perhaps one in person and one online) or schedule asynchronous sessions on a secure messaging system like Signal? Much of our practice and how we operate serve our convenience rather than the client"s benefit. It is also vital to recognise that the formal structure of traditional therapy is not particularly neuroaffirmative.

Being willing to refer clients to various modalities that suit them demonstrates flexibility and a client-centred approach. Some clients may benefit more from drama or art therapy, while others prefer a somatic approach. We owe it to our clients to familiarise ourselves with a broader range of therapy modalities so we can help them heal and live their best lives.

What Else Do We Do Differently?

We strive to be genuine in our vulnerability and treat clients as equals, which means that we may share our vulnerabilities or experiences of shame when appropriate and beneficial for the client, facilitating an authentic, human-to-human connection with individuals from the same community. The therapist is not in a superior position, and power structures are not replicated; instead, there is an encounter at eye level.

Beth is a counsellor and trans woman. Her client, Alice, arrives for her appointment feeling vulnerable and anxious. She explains that on her way to the session, she was misgendered twice: once by a checkout assistant and again by a random passenger on the bus. Beth can share some of her own experiences in responding to these comments.

Queer Therapists Working with Cis-het Clients

While some queer therapists may feel anxious about working with cis-het clients when they come out due to fears of rejection, safety, and homophobia, there are also potential benefits to these situations.

Queer therapists can offer a unique perspective that may be liberating for cis-het clients, informed by their lived experiences.

Challenging Norms: GSRD Therapists introduce alternative dynamics in relationships, including:

Negotiating a broader range of sexual activities instead of assuming default behaviours (i.e., that penis-in-vagina sex is the 'main event' rather than intimacy and mutual pleasure).

Different attitudes toward pornography consumption in relationships; same-sex couples rarely seek to regulate each other's desires or use of porn.

Broadening Horizons: Discussing the differences in queer lifestyles and parenting can be enlightening and liberating for some cis-het clients.

GSRD therapy is an approach that can be helpful for cis-heterosexuals as much as for queer and trans people (Sale, 2023). The performative pressure to meet society's expectations of toughing it out, being the provider, and suppressing feelings of sadness or weakness takes a toll on mental health, in particular. Loneliness and depression can lead to suicide. In the United Kingdom, Canada, and the United States, a significant gender disparity exists in suicide rates, with men accounting for approximately 75-80% of completed suicides (Mental Health Foundation, 2021; Public Health Canada, 2020). This stark statistic highlights a critical public health concern that disproportionately affects male populations in these countries.

Curiosity, not Voyeurism

GSRD therapists strive to approach their clients' lives, stories, and solutions with curiosity, often shaped by shared experiences and challenges. Interestingly, there are times when clients may appear more integrated or confident in aspects of their sexual or relationship identity than their therapists. For instance, a client might seek support regarding their ten-year relationship, while their therapist, for various personal or contextual reasons, may have had fewer or shorter-term relationships. Similarly, some clients might be open with their families and bring partners home for the holidays, while a therapist might navigate a more private or separate approach to family traditions. These contrasts can provide rich ground for reflection, empathy, and mutual growth within the therapeutic relationship.

Some queer and trans clients report feeling self-conscious and protective of themselves and their community when discussing their lives with therapists outside their community. They might feel their cis-het therapist sees them as 'interesting' or as having exciting and exotic sex lives, or, in the case of trans clients, may be curious about what medical and surgical interventions they have had when the client came to talk about living in a transphobic society.

The Reluctant Role Model

Therapists who are also members of the GSRD communities, whether they choose to be or not, are often viewed as role models. They are generally expected to be more integrated and comfortable with their identities than their clients. However, as gender and sexuality are dynamic and relationships change and evolve, a therapist might be experiencing some life transition of their own.

Elliot, a gay therapist, sat across from Liam and Marcus, a couple navigating the uncharted waters of opening up their decade-long relationship. Elliot felt a flicker of recognition as they shared their fears of jealousy and excitement about new possibilities. He and his partner, Carl, were quietly exploring the same path after eight years together. Balancing his professional role with his personal journey, Elliot guided the couple through communication exercises while reflecting on his hesitations and hopes. He found a profound connection in their shared vulnerability—proof that therapists are human, evolving alongside their clients.

Boundaries are Essential: Living and Working in the Same Community and the Challenges of Erotic Transference

Therapists face unique challenges in maintaining professional boundaries, particularly when working with GSRD clients. A critical aspect of this challenge is preparing themselves and their clients for potential encounters outside therapy sessions. This preparation is essential for protecting the integrity of the therapeutic relationship.

A particular concern for GSRD-identified therapists is meeting clients outside the therapeutic space while maintaining their private lives. Clients and therapists will inevitably share the same physical and virtual environments. Some of these contexts are less troubling than others, such as attending Pride events, where large numbers of the community come together. However, other situations can be trickier to navigate, such as sexualised spaces like saunas, play parties, and dating apps (Davies, 2023). It is strongly advised that all therapists create a written professional boundaries statement. This statement serves as a crucial tool to guide interactions and protect the sanctity of the therapeutic relationship, ensuring that both the therapist and the client have clear expectations and guidelines for maintaining appropriate boundaries in various contexts.

It is also vital for therapists to have supervisors who understand the specific GSRD social contexts of their supervisees and can openly discuss any erotic countertransference or transferential issues, along with the dual relationship concerns that can easily lead to boundary violations.

The potential for erotic attraction is something that all therapists need to be mindful of, especially if they are not attending to their own sexual needs. Offering a warm, safe space to discuss sexual themes can elevate the atmosphere for both the therapist and the client. Relational therapy has been compared to being a non-sexual lover. We pay attention to the client with warmth and kindness, offer unconditional positive regard, and affirm them in their lives. It is, therefore, natural for strong loving feelings to arise. These feelings should be considered part of the therapeutic dyad instead of being dismissed as 'transference.' We invite readers to read a convincing and somewhat controversial deconstruction of the concept of *Transference*, where John Shlien explores the idea's genesis from Breuer's consultations with Freud about the formative case of Anna O. (Shlien, 1987).

Therapists must recognise their professional boundaries and ensure they do not actively foster erotic tension by flirting with clients or probing into their sexual lives and fantasies without therapeutic justification. While this guideline should apply to all therapeutic methods, in the context of GSRD therapy, discussions and psychoeducation regarding sexual preferences, activities, and histories may occur more frequently than when working with cis-heterosexual clients.

Our clients are not our friends; we must maintain the balance of being peers within the queer communities and trusted therapists who prioritise their clients" well-being.

One of our trans colleagues described this dilemma as "The tension between being a professional with some objective distance and a member of the same community whose access to bathrooms and own medical treatment is impacted by long waiting lists."

The Importance of Contemporary Sexology

With our understanding of contemporary sexology, GSRD therapists likely feel comfortable discussing sex and porn. We are familiar with peer-reviewed research that challenges the idea that sex and porn are addictive (Ley et al., 2014; Briken et al., 2024).

As part of an intake or assessment interview, we may invite new clients to express any concerns they might have about sex. Conversations about sex do not have to remain the exclusive domain of psychosexual therapists. All therapists should feel comfortable discussing sexual issues and, when necessary, refer appropriately to someone with specific training and expertise.

The PLISSIT models can be beneficial in addressing sexual anxieties and enhancing partner communication. Jack Annon (1976) developed the PLISSIT model, (Permission, Limited Information, Specific Suggestions, and Intensive Therapy). Most therapists can engage in the first three stages. It is only when the client needs Intensive Therapy that a referral to a specialist trained in sexual medicine or psychosexual therapy becomes necessary. However, it is always important to recommend that someone consult a medical doctor to rule out any possible organic causes of sexual problems.

Finally, we conclude this chapter by emphasising the importance of fostering joy in our work with GSRD clients. While we may encounter significant health disparities and challenges, we are more than just a collection of traumas and problems. Discussions about what fosters joy in clients and the significance of celebrating our genders and sexualities are crucial to what GSRD therapists do.

References

American Psychiatric Association (2022). *Diagnostic and Statistical Manual of Mental Disorders, TR* (5th ed.). Arlington, VA: American Psychiatric Publishing.

American Psychiatric Association (2013). *Diagnostic and Statistical Manual of Mental Disorders,* (5th ed.). Arlington, VA: American Psychiatric Publishing.

Annon, J.S. (1976). The PLISSIT model: A proposed conceptual scheme for the behavioral treatment of sexual problems, *Journal of Sex Education and Therapy,* 2(1), pp. 1–15.

Ashley, F. (2019). The misuse of gender dysphoria: Toward greater conceptual clarity in transgender health, *Perspectives on Psychological Science*, 16(6), pp. 1159–1164. https://doi.org/10.1177/1745691619872987

Bostwick, W.B., Smith, A.U., Hequembourg, A.L., Santuzzi, A. and Hughes, T. (2021). Microaggressions and health outcomes among racially and ethnically diverse bisexual women, *Journal of Bisexuality*, 21(3), pp. 285–307.

Briken, P., Bőthe, B., Carvalho, J., Coleman, E., Giraldi, A., Kraus, S. W., Lew-Starowicz, M., & Pfaus, J. G. (2024). Assessment and treatment of compulsive sexual behavior disorder: A sexual medicine perspective. *Sexual Medicine Reviews*, 12(3), 355–370. doi:10.1093/sxmrev/qeae014

Crenshaw, K. (1989). Demarginalizing the intersection of race and sex: A Black feminist critique of antidiscrimination doctrine, feminist theory and antiracist politics, *University of Chicago Legal Forum*, 1989(1), pp. 139–167.

Danzer, G.S. (2018). *Therapist Self-Disclosure: An Evidence-Based Guide for Practitioners* (1st ed.). London: Routledge.

Davies, D. and Aykroyd, M. (2002). Sexual orientation and psychological contact, in Wyatt, G. and Sanders, P. (eds.) *Rogers' Therapeutic Conditions: Evolution, Theory and Practice, Volume 4: Contact and Perception* (pp. 221–233). PCCS Books.

Davies, D. (2023). Living and working within our communities. In Neves, S. and Davies, D. (eds) *Relationally Queer. A Pink Therapy Guide for Practitioners*. Abingdon: Routledge.

Dunlop, B.J. and Lea, J. (2023). Clinical formulation, in Semlyen, J. and Rohleder, P. (eds.) *Sexual Minorities and Mental Health*. Cham: Palgrave Macmillan. https://doi.org/10.1007/978-3-031-37438-8_8

Galupo, M.P., Pulice-Farrow, L. and Pehl, E. (2021). "There is nothing to do about it": Nonbinary Individuals" experience of gender Dysphoria, *Transgender Health*, 6(2), pp. 101–110. https://doi.org/10.1089/trgh.2020.0041

George, R. and Stokes, M.A. (2018). A quantitative analysis of mental health among sexual and gender minority groups in ASD, *Journal of Autism and Developmental Disorders*, 48(6), pp. 2052–2063. https://doi.org/10.1007/s10803-018-3469-1

Goldhammer, H., Crall, C. and Keuroghlian, A.S. (2019). Distinguishing and addressing gender minority stress and borderline personality symptoms, *Harvard Review of Psychiatry*, 27(5), pp. 317–325.

Grabski, B. (2023). Treating Anodyspareunia, in Neves, S. and Davies, D. (eds.) *Erotically Queer: A Pink Therapy Guide for Practitioners* (1st ed.). Routledge. https://doi.org/10.4324/9781003260608

King, M., Semlyen, J., Tai, S., Killaspy, H., Osborn, D., Popelyuk, D. and Nazareth, I. (2008). *Mental Disorders, Suicide, and Deliberate Self Harm in Lesbian, Gay and Bisexual People: A Systematic Review of the Literature*. London: National Institute for Mental Health England.

Kirk, S. and Kutchins, H. (1997). *Making Us Crazy*. Free Press.

Ley, D., Prause, N. and Finn, P. (2014). The emperor has no clothes: A review of the pornography addiction model, *Current Sexual Health Reports*, 6, pp. 94–105.

Maslow, A.H. (1943). A theory of human motivation, *Psychological Review*, 50(4), pp. 370–396.

Mental Health Foundation. (2021). Men and mental health. Available at: https://www.mentalhealth.org.uk/explore-mental-health/a-z-topics/men-and-mental-health (Accessed: 31 January 2025).

Meyer, I.H. (2003). Prejudice, social stress, and mental health in lesbian, gay, and bisexual populations: Conceptual issues and research evidence, *Psychological Bulletin*, 129(5), pp. 674–697. https://doi.org/10.1037/0033-2909.129.5.674

Morin, J. (1995). *The Erotic Mind*. London: Headline.

Public Health Agency of Canada. (2020). *Suicide in Canada: Key Statistics (infographic)*. Government of Canada. Available at: https://www.canada.ca/en/public-health/services/publications/healthy-living/suicide-canada-key-statistics-infographic.html

Rodriguez-Seijas, C., Morgan, T.A. and Zimmerman, M. (2021). A population-based examination of criterion-level disparities in the diagnosis of borderline personality *disorder* among sexual minority adults, *Assessment*, 28(4), pp. 1097–1109. https://doi.org/10.1177/1073191121991922

Rogers, C.R. (1951*) Client-Centered Therapy*. Houghton Mifflin.

Rogers, C.R. (1959) A theory of therapy, personality, and interpersonal relationships as developed in the client-centered framework, reprinted in *The Carl Rogers Reader*. Boston: Houghton Mifflin.

Ross, L.E., Salway, T., Tarasoff, L.A., MacKay, J.M., Hawkins, B.W. and Fehr, C.P. (2018). Prevalence of depression and anxiety among bisexual people compared to gay, lesbian, and heterosexual individuals: A systematic review and meta-analysis, *Journal of Sex Research*, 55(4–5), pp. 435–456. https://doi.org/10.1080/00224499.2017.1387755

Sale, J. (2023). Exploring erotic diversity in heterosexuality: Keeping a queer eye for the straight guys, in Neves, S. and Davies, D. (eds.) *Erotically Queer: A Pink Therapy Guide for Practitioners* (1st ed.). Routledge. https://doi.org/10.4324/9781003260608

Shlien, J.M. (1987). A countertheory of transference, *Person*-Centred Review, 2(1), pp. 15–49. Available at: https://adpca.org/wp-content/uploads/2024/07/PCR21A3-Shlien-J-1987-A-Countertheory-of-Transference.pdf (Accessed: 25 May 2025.

Turner, D. (2021). *Intersections of Privilege and Otherness in Counselling and Psychotherapy: Mockingbird*. Taylor & Francis.

Warrier, V., Greenberg, D.M., Weir, E., Buckingham, C., Smith, P., Lai, M.C., Allison, C. and Baron-Cohen, S. (2020). Elevated rates of autism, other neurodevelopmental and psychiatric diagnoses, and autistic traits in transgender and gender-diverse individuals, *Nature Communications*, 11(1), p. 3959. Available at: https://www.nature.com/articles/s41467-020-17794-1

Weir, E., Allison, C. and Baron-Cohen, S. (2021). The sexual health, orientation, and activity of autistic adolescents and adults, *Autism Research*, 14(11), pp. 2342–2354. https://doi.org/10.1002/aur.2604

World Health Organization (2019). *International Classification of Diseases for Mortality and Morbidity Statistics* (11th Revision). Available at: https://icd.who.int/ (Accessed: 23 May 2025).

Chapter 3

Key Elements of GSRD Therapy

Silva Neves

Introduction

GSRD therapy is now recognised as a therapeutic modality due to its distinct features, which encompass key elements. At the same time, it can easily be integrated with existing modalities. Practitioners from all backgrounds and trained in any therapeutic orientation can deliver GSRD therapy, not by departing from their original modality but by adapting and adding to it.

This chapter explains the key components of GSRD therapy and demonstrates how these components are utilised with diverse GSRD populations and integrated into existing therapeutic modalities.

The Importance of GSRD Therapy Knowledge

As Dominic Davies mentioned in Chapter 2, GSRD therapy is born out of several decades of clinical experience from therapists 'translating' the traditional heteronormative training to make it fit with queer populations. Until recently, gender, sex, and relationship diversities have been absent or ignored in most clinical training programmes and textbooks, other than one brief chapter or one teaching day on populations that are other than heterosexual, monogamous, and '*Vanilla*', usually framed as 'alternative populations'. This has changed since the first Pink Therapy text in 1996 (Davies & Neal, 1996). In more recent years, with more books dedicated to LGBTQ+ clients and GSRD populations, there is still a long way to go for clinical training programmes to properly include diverse populations throughout their curriculum rather than trying to cover this vast subject in one tokenistic day.

Indeed, according to the 2021 census data in England and Wales, 3.2% of the population aged 16 and above identifies as LGB+ (Office for National Statistics, 2023). According to a US-based survey (Jones, 2024), more than one in five Gen Z adults identify as LGBTQ+, which makes it 7.5% of the population. Although it is a minority, it constitutes a significant number of people, and the current statistics are thought to be an underestimate because of societal shame and oppression, which means that many are not 'out'.

DOI: 10.4324/9781003530848-5

Therefore, we can safely assume that most therapists will encounter queer clients during their careers. Not being equipped to work with GSRD means they could unintentionally disappoint or damage these clients. Hubbard (2021) finds that 80% of LGBTQ+ people were satisfied with an LGBTQ+ specific support service compared to 38% of LGBTQ+ people who were satisfied with a generic support service. This highlights the need for GSRD therapy to be integrated into all clinical training.

The well-intentioned position of '*I treat everyone the same*' does not serve our diverse populations because it negates their differences. Indeed, a working-class Black single gay man will have a very different life path than a middle-class white married heterosexual man. Therapy will be different because their lives are entirely different. For example, the topic of holding hands in the streets may be a non-topic for a heterosexual couple. Still, for a same-sex couple, it is a crucial multi-layered consideration involving several aspects such as safety, pride, courage, and threats (Rohleder et al., 2023). The same principle is true for heterosexual people who do not fit in with heteronormativity. For example, a heterosexual couple who choose not to have children may be heavily criticised by friends and family. A heterosexual person who is non-monogamous may be perceived as 'weird', or a kinky heterosexual person may be misunderstood and live in oppression.

The Seven Core Components of GSRD Therapy

Dominic Davies and Silva Neves created the seven components to advance a framework for GSRD therapy as a modality (Davies & Neves, 2023). Initially, we thought of six components, and after consultations with peers in the GSRD therapy field, we realised we had omitted joy! It became our seventh component.

Practising a Commitment to Social Justice

This component encompasses several considerations. Firstly, it is connected to the history of queer movements, which, from their very origin, have held anti-capitalist and anti-racist agendas. GSRD therapy is rooted in Feminist, Black, and other liberatory psychologies, and it is aimed at dismantling state structures that privilege the nuclear family, exploit workers, and discriminate against people of colour. Secondly, the key GSRD therapy knowledge of this component is to situate clients' distress in the world we live in and to formulate mental health problems not only in the self but also in interaction with societal oppression and family dynamics. In this way, this component employs a systemic lens to understand mental well-being. Finally, this component encourages practitioners to be mindful of all the norms that are embedded in our society, unquestioned, that we believe to be true – but are only constructs that often do not serve GSRD populations: binary gender roles, fixed sexualities, patriarchy, misogyny, racism, othering people, etc. Therefore, GSRD therapy is an anti-oppressive practice because of the thorough awareness of the societal norms of heteronormativity, mononormativity, cisnormativity, repronormativity, patriarchy, white, and Western supremacy, neuro-normativity, and ableism.

Demonstrating Cultural Humility and Cultural Competence

Cultural competence involves proactively educating ourselves, rather than waiting for clients to educate us. We must understand and keep learning about the diverse queer cultures and subcultures, such as the kink subcultures, the lives of trans people, polyamorous people, sex workers, etc. We must also remind ourselves that we never know it all, so we must continue learning and not become defensive when we reach the edge of our knowledge. Instead, we should strive to widen our understanding. For example, we must not make assumptions based on what clients look like. A heterosexual-looking couple may not be heterosexual. A femme-presenting client may not identify as a woman and prefers they/them pronouns.

Being clinically arrogant and believing in certainty is one of the most significant mistakes therapists can make. As a therapy tutor, we should be comfortable sharing our mistakes and what we have learned from them to model humility, rather than only teaching the 'perfect' therapies we practise. We also need to be reflexive and understand our positionality, which is often situated in Western thinking, the English language, and frequently a medicalised lens of mental health. Understanding our limitations within the frame we work with, and keeping conscious that our positionality may not serve all populations, is part of maintaining cultural humility and keeping aware of our blind spots.

Understanding the Specific Adverse Effects of Oppression

This key component is congruent with practising a commitment to social justice. Once therapists are fully aware of all the societally constructed norms imposed on us such as heteronormativity, mononormativity, cisnormativity, repronormativity, neuro-normativity, ableism, patriarchy, and white supremacy, we can better identify with clients the level of oppression they face depending on their intersecting identities.

Indeed, some clients will have several layers of oppression if they have several marginalised identities (Dunlop, 2022). In addition to the everyday societal oppression, some clients also face individual circumstances compounding the effects of oppression, such as being employed by a homophobic manager, being in an intimate relationship with an abusive partner, or living with homophobic and transphobic families, etc. Pervasive societal norms can worsen some of those individual circumstances. For example, domestic violence is still seen mainly through a gendered lens, so the authorities may not take a case seriously when it is one woman who abuses another woman (Calton et al., 2015). Having a thorough understanding of all the different ways that oppression shows up in GSRD clients' lives means that therapists can make a better assessment of clients' distress. The specific effects of oppression are often impossible to 'fix' because they are ongoing in our society. This is why therapists need to understand the concept of oppression. Suppose a client is distressed daily because of their specific intersectionalities that make life difficult. In that case, it might be tempting for a therapist without enough knowledge of oppression (or a therapist blind to oppression because of their privileges) to make a diagnosis based on mental health disorders such as 'clinical depression', 'acute anxiety', 'borderline personality disorder', 'highly sensitive person', 'anger issues', 'avoidant attachment style', and so on, which will direct a treatment that is only to do with the self, and not hold space for the adverse effects of the oppressive environment. When GSRD clients don't respond so well to the treatment, therapists might then stick another label on the client: 'therapy resistant', 'client not psychologically minded', or 'client doesn't want to change'. This, in turn, will replicate societal oppression in the consulting room, which can be further damaging to GSRD clients. Of course, the client may not respond to therapeutic interventions focused on the change of self if their distress is a normal response to their environment. Instead, therapists who understand the specific effects of oppression will be able to assess clients' mental health through a more systemic lens and locate their distress where the dysfunction exists: in society and the client's environment. GSRD clients will often feel 'broken', but a good GSRD therapist won't collude with the sense of 'brokenness', and, instead, will help the client understand that their distress is congruent with the oppression they face. This is when therapy becomes anti-oppressive and affirming. With an assessment that incorporates the specific effects of oppression, treatment can be more effective for clients by helping them build resilience and self-care, connect with a supportive social network, and discover moments of joy in their lives, as well as heal past traumas and childhood issues.

Being Trauma, Grief, and Shame Informed

Given that most GSRD clients will encounter ongoing oppression, a significant history of trauma and/or current traumatic situations is likely. The typical history of trauma may be homophobic and transphobic bullying at school, being rejected by parents after coming out, and homophobic and transphobic attacks in the streets. These homophobic and transphobic specific traumas may be in addition to other trauma that is seen in all populations, such as childhood sexual abuse, domestic violence, rape in adulthood, accidents, parental neglect, and so on. Unresolved past trauma may affect clients in the here and now in the form of post-trauma stress symptoms (i.e.

flashbacks, dissociation, hypervigilance), and if the symptoms are so intense that clients are unable to function in life, they may be diagnosed with PTSD (post-traumatic stress disorder) (APA, DSM-5-TR, 2022. p. 303) and complex PTSD (WHO, 2019). In these cases, we can offer clients trauma therapy (it is recommended that all therapists are appropriately trauma-informed).

Grief is also widespread for GSRD clients and comes in different forms. Some clients experience ongoing grief for being rejected by their families. Some clients may grieve the loss of their childhood when they couldn't be as carefree as the other children because they had to be hypervigilant about not being 'found out' as gay or trans, and editing themselves regularly. For those who experienced daily homophobia and transphobia at school, it is the loss of feeling safe and often the inability to concentrate. When heterosexual teenagers experiment freely with their sexuality and intimate relationships, queer people tend to hide and pretend, so there is the loss of that sexual and relational development in adolescence. This is changing now with more queer representation in the media such as Netflix's *Sex Education* and *Heartstopper*. However, the reality of homophobic and transphobic childhood still very much exists today (Frost & Meyer, 2023). Some clients can experience grief even with positive processes. For example, a trans client can feel happy to access gender-affirming surgery, yet they may still grieve the fact that they had to go through that ordeal to feel good about their bodies and wait many years to access the health care they need. In therapy, we can create a space for clients to express their trans joy and grief together. There are various theories of grief and different methods to work with grief, but most of the time, grief is a natural process that does not require treatment to 'get through it'. When a loss is significant, people may feel grief at varying degrees forever. We should not put pressure on clients to 'get through it', but we can help clients learn to live with it through the therapeutic relationship, characterised by the presence of empathy and unconditional positive regard.

Shame is another common feature of the lives of GSRD clients because there are many messages in society and within some families that constantly tell GSRD people they are 'wrong', 'undesirable' or 'bad'. For many, shame is so much a part of their everyday life that it is undetected. Yet, often, shame pulls the strings of some common problems clients present with in therapy (Lyne, 2023). For example, depression and anxiety may be shame-induced. Sexual problems, such as erectile dysfunction or vaginismus, could be protective factors concerning shame. Behavioural problems and suicidal ideations could also have their roots in shame. The literature on shame is somewhat limited, but one current school of thought suggests that shame plays a protective role. It alerts us that actions must be taken to modify behaviours to restore a good self-view. Therefore, shame ensures survival. The quality of early attachment and child development will determine whether shame hinders self-development. Ongoing attachment rupture without repair from caregivers will eventually lead to the 'rupture of self'. Just like grief, we must exercise caution in pathologising shame, because, even though it feels awful, it is a human emotion, not a disorder. If therapists want to 'treat' shame to help clients be 'shame-free' or 'eradicate the shame', we will find that this type of therapy can be relatively unsuccessful. Not only because we can't make a human emotion with evolutionary purposes be an enemy, but also because we can't get rid of human emotions forever. Just like grief, with many GSRD clients, the therapy would be about recognising shame and helping clients have a relationship with it (Etherson, 2023).

Knowing Contemporary Sexology

There is much sexological misinformation because of poor sex education and almost no training in sexology in our core psychotherapy training. Therefore, it is a field where therapists often struggle to distinguish between their personal ideas and what is clinically sound and evidence-based. With GSRD clients, the topic of sex and intimate relationships will come up frequently because much of the marginalisation and societal oppression is about politicising, restricting and pathologising the sexual behaviours of LGBTQ+ people and kinky people.

The sex lives of LGBTQ+ people – and particularly gay men – were deemed to be a perversion, a criminal offence and a mental health disorder, until 1973 in the DSM (Drescher, 2015) and 1990 in the ICD (Cochran et al., 2014). In the 80s, the AIDS epidemic gave rise to another wave of homophobia, and gay men's sex lives were further pathologised, this time under another pseudo-diagnosis of 'sex addiction' (Carnes, 1983). Unfortunately, this pseudo-diagnosis remains widely used, despite its lack of evidence-based support (Ley, 2012; Neves, 2021). The pseudo-diagnosis of 'porn addiction' unduly pathologises heterosexual men who enjoy watching porn, queer people who find watching queer porn affirming of their bodies and sexualities (Droubay & White, 2024), and digisexual people whose primary sexual attraction might be watching porn (McArthur & Twist, 2017). Therefore, those pseudo-diagnoses are not only 'snake oil'; they can be actively harmful to many populations and can encourage conversion practices, as highlighted in a study conducted by the UK Government (2021). Without the knowledge of contemporary sexology, it is easy to believe those pseudo-diagnoses and myths. Although there is progress in de-pathologising some sexual practices that are deemed 'unusual', there is still a long way to go as people with a kink erotic orientation are still misunderstood by our profession and may still be pathologised, assumed that their kink interests have to do with childhood trauma despite no evidence that this is the case (Shahbaz & Chirinos, 2017). Fortunately, a growing body of literature on kink is available to help practitioners become kink-aware and kink-affirmative (Kleinplatz & Moser, 2006; Langdridge & Barker, 2007; Shahbaz & Chirinos, 2017; Goerlich, 2023). It is also imperative for practitioners who work with kinky clients to pay attention to their moral judgements, assumptions, and reactions, as they could get in the way of good therapeutic work (Bisbey, 2023). Other populations within GSRD benefit from the contemporary knowledge of sexology, especially those that tend to be underrepresented in the literature, such as asexuals (Russell, 2023; Kelleher & Murphy, 2022) and lesbians (McCaffrey, 2023; Thorpe et al., 2022).

Another area relevant to the contemporary knowledge of sexology is that therapists may need to engage in psychoeducation to help their clients have better sex. It is crucial that GSRD therapists learn to be comfortable to talk explicitly about sex, for better therapeutic outcome.

Anodyspareunia (pain during receptive anal penetration) is absent from the DSM, yet relevant to gay men who bottom (Grabski, 2023). Gaining a better understanding of anodyspareunia can avoid the internalisation of bottom shaming.

Integrating Core GSRD Theories

A GSRD therapist must be familiar with GSRD theories, some of which have already been discussed in this chapter and will continue to be addressed throughout the book. Some of those core GSRD theories link to the commitment to social justice, developing cultural competence, understanding the effects of oppression, understanding the impact of homophobia, biphobia, transphobia, and all the societal norms that restrict people's sexualities and relationships such as heteronormativity, mononormativity, cisnormativity, amatonormativity, repronormativity. Other core theories (discussed throughout the book) are intersectionality (Dunlop, 2022; Turner, 2021) and understanding minority stress (Meyer, 2003). Pachankis et al. (2020) propose the theory of intra-community minority stress integrating intrasex competition theory (men compete for social and sexual status, with low-status individuals at greater risk for stress and exclusion), sexual field theory (gay and bisexual men evaluate themselves and others by the same standards of desirability, intensifying status concerns) and precarious manhood theory (gay and bisexual men may feel pressure to defend their masculinity, particularly in a context where their manhood is already socially questioned). The authors identified key sources of stress within the gay community, including (1) body image and style demands, (2) socioeconomic status and materialism, (3) racial and sexual stereotypes, (4) hypermasculinity and ageism, (5) hypersexuality and focus on casual sex, and (6) exclusion of diversity (e.g. racism, HIV stigma, and biphobia). Therapists need to pay attention to these key sources of stress in the assessment of gay and bisexual men for a relevant therapeutic focus.

Borgogna et al. (2021) extend the minority stress model to consensually non-monogamous individuals. Hughes and Hammack (2019) also find that stigma, concealment, isolation, and self-pathologisation are sources of stress and negative self-evaluation for people practising BDSM/Kink. The social safety theory (Diamond & Alley, 2022) is also relevant to working with GSRD clients because it extends the minority stress theory in proposing that the cumulative stress caused by social stigma and marginalisation harbours stress-related health problems. It explains the increased risk in terms of medical health (not only mental health) and has significant implications for psychological development.

An essential part of this GSRD therapy component is understanding the theories and how they are integrated. There is so much human diversity in GSRD that having one model for everyone is virtually impossible. It requires the clinician to listen properly to their clients' lived experiences and determine a therapeutic pathway for each, rather than forcing clients to fit our favourite theories or models.

Fostering Joy

Even though it is essential to understand and give space for the psychological pain that oppression, shame, grief, and trauma cause GSRD clients, we must not forget that, within all of that, we have to help our clients access joy. It might be tempting to think that joy is what clients can experience at the end of the therapeutic journey, when they are 'self-actualised', to use a person-centred term (Rogers, 1961). Indeed, it would make sense to have joy at the top of Maslow's hierarchy of needs (Maslow, 1943). However, for our GSRD clients, we might want to consider helping them access joy early in therapy, rather than making it the outcome of therapy. I argue that for marginalised people, fostering joy is part of basic needs, as it can be the one component that makes a difference between someone deciding to keep living and someone deciding to end their life. Fostering joy is vital to GSRD therapy because it acknowledges the unique challenges GSRD clients face while actively cultivating positive experiences and emotional well-being. Fostering joy is essential in therapeutic work with GSRD clients because it

- Counteracts minority stress
- Enhances mental health outcomes
- Affirms identities and experiences
- Builds resilience through gratitude
- Becomes resistant to oppression

Counteracting Minority Stress

Joy acts as an antidote to the adverse effects of minority stress (social discrimination, stigma, anxiety, depression, and other mental health issues) by promoting resilience and emotional balance. Celebrating moments of happiness and success helps clients shift focus from adversity to empowerment

(Eckstrand & Potter, 2017). In the case of trans clients, moving from gender dysphoria to gender euphoria (Beischel, 2021) is an integral part of the therapy. Finding community boosts resilience (Benestad, 2010)

Enhancing Mental Health Outcomes

For GSRD clients, experiencing joy can reduce feelings of isolation and anxiety while boosting self-esteem. Moments of self-expression, such as wearing affirming clothing or attending Pride events, can be transformative and improve overall well-being.

Affirming Identity and Experiences

Celebrating milestones in clients' queer journey – such as coming out, finding community, achieving personal goals, fostering pride in who we are – validates the lived experiences of GSRD individuals. These moments of joy reinforce identity affirmation and provide a sense of belonging. Therapists can amplify this by encouraging clients to acknowledge and celebrate their achievements and strengths (Singh, 2018).

Building Resilience through Gratitude

Practising gratitude is a powerful tool for fostering joy. It helps clients focus on positive aspects of their lives, even amidst struggles. Therapists can guide GSRD clients in identifying sources of gratitude, such as supportive relationships or personal growth, which strengthen their ability to cope with adversity.

Joy as Resistance

In the context of ongoing systemic oppression, joy becomes a form of resistance and liberation for GSRD individuals. Celebrating queer joy challenges narratives of marginalisation and reinforces the inherent value of diverse identities. Therapists can empower clients by framing joy as defiance against societal discrimination.

Conclusion

The key elements of GSRD therapy are the guiding principles that differentiate this modality from others. It is focused on working with diverse clients who fall outside of the dominant societal constructs, yet it is easily integrated into other existing modalities. Paying attention to the seven core components of GSRD therapy will help therapists maintain an anti-oppressive practice that can offer profound healing for marginalised people facing ongoing oppression.

References

Beischel, W.J., Gauvin, S.E.M., & van Anders, S.M. (2021, May 3). "A little shiny gender breakthrough": Community understandings of gender euphoria. *International Journal of Transgender Health*, 23(3), 274–294. doi: 10.1080/26895269.2021.1915223.

Benestad, E.E.P. (2010). From gender dysphoria to gender euphoria: An assisted journey. *Sexologies*, 19(4), 225–231. https://doi.org/10.1016/j.sexol.2010.09.003.

Bisbey, L.B. (2023). Examining therapist bias when working with kink. In S. Neves & D. Davies (Eds.), *Erotically Queer. A Pink Therapy Guide for Practitioners*. Abingdon: Routledge.

Borgogna, N.C., Aita, S.L., & Aita, L.J. (2021). Minority stress in consensually non-monogamous individuals: Mental health implications. *Sexual and Relationship Therapy*, 39(1), 46–65. https://doi.org/10.1080/14681994.2021.1959545

Calton, J.M., Cattaneo, L.B., & Gebhard, K.T. (2015). Barriers to help seeking for lesbian, gay, bisexual, transgender, and queer survivors of intimate partner violence. *Trauma, Violence, & Abuse*, 17(5), 585–600. https://doi.org/10.1177/1524838015585318 (Original work published 2016)

Carnes, P. (1983). *Out of the Shadows: Understanding Sexual Addiction*. CompCare Publications.

Cochran, S.D., Drescher, J., Kismödi, E., Giami, A., García-Moreno, C., Atalla, E., Marais, A., Vieira, E.M., & Reed, G.M. (2014). Proposed declassification of disease categories related to sexual orientation in the International Statistical Classification of Diseases and Related Health Problems (ICD-11). *Bulletin World Health Organization*, 92(9), 672–679. https://doi.org/10.2471/BLT.14.135541

Davies, D., & Neal, C. (1996). *Pink Therapy. A guide for counsellors and therapists working with lesbian, gay and bisexual clients*. Open University Press.

Davies, D., & Neves, S. (2023). Gender, sex and relationship diversity therapy. In T. Hanley & L.A. Winter (Eds.), *The Sage Handbook of Counselling & Psychotherapy* (5th ed., pp. 409–415). London: Sage.

Diamond, L.M., & Alley, J. (2022, July). Rethinking minority stress: A social safety perspective on the health effects of stigma in sexually-diverse and gender-diverse populations. *Neuroscience & Biobehavioral Reviews*, 138, 104720. doi: 10.1016/j.neubiorev.2022.104720.

Drescher, J. (2015). Out of DSM: Depathologizing homosexuality. *Behavioral Sciences*, 5(4), 565–575. https://doi.org/10.3390/bs5040565

Droubay, B.A., & White, A. (2024). Sexual orientation, homophobic attitudes, and self-perceived pornography addiction. *Sexuality Research and Social Policy*, 21, 1567–1583. https://doi.org/10.1007/s13178-023-00846-8

DSM-5 TR. APA. American Psychiatric Association. (2022). *Diagnostic and Statistical Manual of Mental Disorders* (5th ed. Text Revision). https://doi.org/10.1176/appi.books.9780890425596

Dunlop, B.J. (2022). *The Queer Mental Health Workbook. A Creative Self-help Guide Using CBT, CFT and DBT*. London: Jessica Kingsley Publishers.

Eckstrand, K.L., & Potter, J. (2017). *Trauma, Resilience, and Health Promotion in LGBT Patients. What Every Healthcare Provider Should Know*. Cham: Springer International Publishing.

Etherson, L. (2023). Shame containment theory - a new approach to shame. *Attachment*, 17(2):141–154

Frost, D.M., & Meyer, I.H. (2023, June). Minority stress theory: Application, critique, and continued relevance. *Current Opinion in Psychology*, 51, 101579. doi: 10.1016/j.copsyc.2023.101579.

Goerlich, S. (2023). *Kink-affirming Practice: Culturally Competent Therapy from the Leather Chair*. New York: Routledge.

Grabski, B. (2023). Treating Anodyspareunia. In S. Neves & D. Davies (Eds.), *Erotically Queer: A Pink Therapy Guide for Practitioners*. Abingdon: Routledge.

Hubbard, L. (2021). *The Hate Crime Report 2021: Supporting LGBT+ Victims of Hate Crime*. London: Galop.

Hughes, S.D., & Hammack, P.L. (2019). Affirmation, compartmentalization, and isolation: Narratives of identity sentiment among kinky people. *Psychology & Sexuality*, 10(2), 149–168. https://doi.org/10.1080/19419899.2019.1575896

Jones, J.M. (2024). LGBTQ+ identification in US now now at 7.6%. *Gallup*. https://news.gallup.com/poll/611864/lgbtq-identification.aspx

Kelleher, S., & Murphy, M. (2022). Asexual identity development and internalisation: A thematic analysis. *Sexual and Relationship Therapy*, 39(3), 865–893. https://doi.org/10.1080/14681994.2022.2091127

Kleinplatz, P.J. & Moser, C. (Eds.). (2006). *Sadomasochism: Powerful Pleasures*. Routledge

Langdridge, D., & Barker, M. (Eds.). (2007). *Safe, Sane and Consensual: Contemporary Perspectives on Sadomasochism*. Palgrave Macmillan

Ley, D. (2012). *The Myth of Sex Addiction*. Lanham, MD: Rowman & Littlefield Publishers, Inc.

Lyne, S. A. (2023). Working with sexual shame. In Neves, S. & Davies, D. (eds) *Erotically Queer. A Pink Therapy Guide for Practitioners*. Routledge.

Maslow, A.H. (1943). A theory of human motivation. *Psychological Review*, 50(4), 370–396. https://doi.org/10.1037/h0054346

McArthur, N., & Twist, M.L.C. (2017). The rise of digisexuality: Therapeutic challenges and possibilities. *Sexual and Relationship Therapy*, 32(3/4), 334–344. doi:10.1080/14681994.2017.1397950

McCaffrey, J. (2023). Attachment narrative therapy as a tool for sex therapy with lesbian couples. In S. Neves & D. Davies (Eds.), *Erotically Queer: A Pink Therapy Guide for Practitioners*. Abingdon: Routledge.

Meyer, I.H. (2003, September). Prejudice, social stress, and mental health in lesbian, gay, and bisexual populations: conceptual issues and research evidence. *Psychological Bulletin*, 129(5), 674–697. doi: 10.1037/0033-2909.129.5.674.

Neves, S. (2021). *Compulsive Sexual Behaviours: A Psycho-Sexual Treatment Guide for Clinicians*. Abingdon: Routledge.

Office for National Statistics (ONS), released 6 January 2023. https://www.ons.gov.uk/peoplepopulationandcommunity/culturalidentity/sexuality/bulletins/sexualorientationenglandandwales/census2021 (Accessed 17/01/2025)

Pachankis, J.E., Clark, K.A., Burton, C.L., Hughto, J.M.W., Bränström, R., & Keene, D.E. (2020). Sex, status, competition, and exclusion: Intraminority stress from within the gay community and gay and bisexual men's mental health. *Journal of Personality and Social Psychology*, 119(3), 713. doi: 10.1037/pspp0000282

Rogers, C.R. (1961). *On Becoming a Person: A Therapist's View of Psychotherapy.* Houghton Mifflin.

Rohleder, P., Ryan-Flood, R., & Walsh, J. (2023). Holding hands: LGBTQ people's experiences of public displays of affection with their partner(s). *Psychology & Sexuality*, 14(3), 559–571. https://doi.org/10.1080/19419899.2023.2185533

Russell, J. (2023). The sex lives of asexuals. In S. Neves & D. Davies (Eds.), *Erotically Queer. A Pink Therapy Guide for Practitioners*. Abingdon: Routledge.

Shahbaz, C., & Chirinos, P. (2017). *Becoming a Kink Aware Therapist*. New York: Routledge.

Singh, A. (2018). *The Queer & Transgender Resilience Workbook: Skills for Navigating Sexual Orientation & Gender Expression*. Oakland: New Harbinger Publications, Inc.

Thorpe, S., Malone, N., Dogan, J.N., Cineas, M.R., Vigil, K., & Hargons, C.N. (2022). Exploring differences in Black heterosexual and queer women's sexual experiences through a Black queer feminist lens. *Sexual and Relationship Therapy*, 39(2), 403–421. https://doi.org/10.1080/14681994.2022.2077927

Turner, D. (2021). *Intersections of Privilege and Otherness in Counselling and Psychotherapy*. Mockingbird. Abingdon: Routledge.

UK Government. (2021). Conversion therapy: An evidence assessment and qualitative study. https://www.gov.uk/government/publications/conversion-therapy-an-evidence-assessment-and-qualitative-study/conversion-therapy-an-evidence-assessment-and-qualitative-study#what-forms-does-conversion-therapy-take-1

World Health Organization. (2019). ICD-11. International statistical classification of diseases 11th revision. https://icd.who.int/

Chapter 4

Obligatory, Not Optional, the Development of the GSRD Therapist

Agata Loewe-Kurilla

Introduction

Developing as a GSRD-affirmative therapist is not optional but essential for ethical, inclusive, and effective practice. This chapter explores the personal and professional transformation required to support clients with diverse gender, sexual, and relational identities. It emphasises the importance of experiential training, self-reflection, and supervision grounded in cultural humility and anti-oppressive practice. The model outlined draws on Pink Therapy's four-stage framework, integrating lived experience, social context, psychosocial impact, and clinical insight. Through structured exercises—such as identity exploration, hand-holding in public, and the gender, sexuality, and relationships (GSR) lifeline—therapists are invited to examine their values, attitudes, and beliefs (VABs) around sexuality and gender. The chapter also critiques mainstream therapeutic education for its heteronormative and Eurocentric limitations, advocating for an embodied, affirming approach that prioritises safety, visibility, and self-awareness. By cultivating a deeper understanding of their positionality and the lived realities of GSRD clients, therapists can better embody the role of the wounded healer and work towards truly inclusive psychological contact.

Imagine finally enrolling in a course that brings you closer to realising your aspiration of becoming an exceptional therapist. In this role, you support others in healing early childhood trauma, offering a non-judgemental space for growth. You guide them through effective and ineffective coping mechanisms, help establish flexible boundaries, and empower individuals to embrace fuller, more authentic versions of themselves.

Would it not be remarkable to become that therapist for others—an archetype of an optimal caregiver, encourager, and sage? A professional who can ease psychological pain and reignite joy in others' lives, or at the very least, alleviate the existential distress many encounter daily?

However, this raises an important question: how can we embody this role for others when we, as therapists, navigate life, grappling with our own complexities, contradictions, and challenges? Working therapeutically with

DOI: 10.4324/9781003530848-6

others often entails confronting our discomforts, limitations, and blind spots. We enter the archetype of a Wounded Healer, who, just like others, needs to better themselves.

Embarking on a training programme designed to prepare you for therapeutic work demands courage. It takes bravery to challenge yourself and question your own status quo. As you prepare yourself to face real people in face-to-face contact, anxieties often surface: "How can I, as flawed as I am, help others? Don't I also need help?" Sometimes, it feels like this endless cycle of self-reflection, where we constantly challenge, question, and deconstruct to pursue self-awareness.

Many training programmes recommend undergoing personal psychotherapy and clinical supervision as essential components of training.

Supervision in GSRD therapy is crucial to ensuring ethical, competent, and culturally sensitive support for clients with diverse sexual orientations, gender identities, and relationship structures. Supervisors must possess technical and theoretical knowledge, a deep awareness of social and relational dynamics, and a commitment to continuous reflection and learning.

The core requirements of GSRD-affirmative/exploratory supervision are:

Awareness and Knowledge: Supervisors should have an up-to-date understanding of GSRD issues and be self-reflective about their own unconscious biases and identities. Affirmative supervision should actively address power, privilege, and intersectionality.

Relational Approach: As Daniel Bąk emphasises, supervision should be grounded in relational ethics, acknowledging the interconnected identities of supervisors, supervisees, and clients. Creating space to explore GSRD-related dynamics enhances both client care and therapist growth (Bąk, 2023).

Explicit Affirmation/Exploration: Supervisors should help therapists explicitly affirm, explore, and validate GSRD identities, avoiding heteronormative or cisnormative assumptions while giving space for intersectional identities to develop.

Rima Hawkins and Silva Neves (Hawkins & Neves, 2024) propose critically reimagining the traditional 7-eyed supervision model (Hawkins & Shohet, 2012) to support GSRD therapy. They argue that the original model, while valuable, is embedded in heteronormative, mononormative, and Eurocentric assumptions that can limit its effectiveness in diverse clinical contexts. Their queered version encourages supervisors to adopt an anti-oppressive, culturally humble stance—actively addressing systemic power dynamics, integrating GSRD perspectives, and fostering inclusive, affirming environments for supervisees and clients. By reframing each "eye" of the model through this inclusive lens, Hawkins and Neves offer a practical and ethically grounded framework for clinical supervision that better reflects contemporary understandings of identity, sexuality, and relational complexity.

While specialist post-qualifying courses can drain our energy and finances, there always seems to be another layer to peel back, a new theory, a new demographic, or a new challenge to address. Human existence is fragile and perpetually evolving. We swim in a toxic soup of limiting binaries and prejudice; few can escape this (even those who identify as GSRD themselves), and so uncovering our VABs about societal structures and what we've been told about the 'deviants' who co-exist in our soup is crucial to our ability to join in "psychological contact" (Davies & Aykroyd, 2002) with our clients. We have an obligation to our clients to acknowledge and address our unconscious biases and correct the misinformation that some sectors of society perpetuate.

In this chapter, I will share some of the theory and practice of personally exploring these VABs to GSRD people. This seems particularly important since mainstream training programmes rarely offer explicit experiential training.

There are key questions we can ask ourselves and be curious about when we begin the exploration of sexuality:

- What is sex?
- What is sexuality?
- What defines "healthy" sex?
- How is sex performed? What constitutes a "normal" or "normative" sexual experience?
- Is sex a "performance" or an experience?
- When imagining humans having sex, what assumptions do we make about their bodies, abilities, and age?

These questions immediately challenge our VABs about sexuality, which are often deeply ingrained, invisible, and unquestioned. In many societies, sex is still a taboo subject, discussed openly only in professional settings like specialist therapeutic training. Even in such contexts, individuals must often confront internalised shame, stigma, minority stress, and past traumas. Overcoming stereotypes of being perceived as "deviant" or "hypersexual" can also create barriers to open discussions about sexuality.

Reflecting on Sexual Experience

A key element in reflecting on human sexuality involves reconsidering assumptions about sexual experiences. If someone identifies as having "a lot" of sexual experiences, what defines "a lot"? Conversely, if someone feels inexperienced, what metrics are used to classify this? It also circles back to a question on "what counts as sex/sexual experience?"

This reflection ties into early research on human sexuality by Alfred Kinsey et al. (1948), where their landmark study, "*Sexual Behavior in the Human Male,*" Kinsey introduced the concept of "sexual outlets," which included a wide range of sexual experiences—from thoughts and fantasies to physical activities—over a person's lifetime.

Kinsey's findings showed considerable variation in the number of sexual outlets reported by individuals, with some extreme cases involving over 1,000 sexual outlets in a year. While Kinsey's research has faced criticism, particularly regarding methodological flaws such as sample bias, his work continues to be foundational in the study of human sexuality.

By studying these perspectives and research, we can better understand the complexity of human sexuality and challenge normative assumptions about what is "normal" or "healthy" in sexual expression.

It is also necessary to reflect on asexual experience and how to address and navigate language in allosexual-dominated discourse. Practitioners must challenge the assumption that sexual attraction is a universal human experience and, as Russell (2023: 71) notes, "As therapists aiming to work competently with asexual clients, whether they identify as such or not, we can be effective in holding an open space for exploration of what kinds of intimacy and connection clients may find appealing" (Russell, 2023: 71).

GSRD Modality Formation in Experiential Training

Unlike most courses on human sexuality, which tend to centre on procreation, conventional sex and relationship training often emphasises diagnosing 'disorders' that affect penis-in-vagina sex and hinder family creation, typically offering behavioural 'treatment plans' to address these issues.

In contrast, training as a GSRD therapist provides a unique opportunity for self-exploration and reflection on one's own sexual history and how this may shape the therapeutic relationship. It also fosters a deeper understanding of diverse sexual practices and relationship styles, broadening both personal and professional perspectives. It is focused more on sex as pleasure, intimacy, and connection than on helping a male-female dyad procreate through penetration.

Globally, sex education at the middle school level is often absent or heavily influenced by political, cultural, or religious forces. Many of us enter adulthood with a mix of conflicting messages about gender, sex, and relationships, shaped by mainstream media, religious leaders, family dynamics, peer influence, and the internet.

In a heteronormative world, the framework we are handed is typically cisnormative, monosexual, mononormative, allosexual, and largely sex-negative. On a personal level, some of us are fortunate to live in societies that uphold human rights and provide legal and health protections for people of all genders and sexualities. However, public displays of affection (PDAs) remain a site of vulnerability and risk for many LGBTQ individuals. A recent UK study found that 68% of the 100,000 LGBTQ individuals surveyed reported avoiding holding hands with a same-sex partner in public for fear of hostile or violent responses (Government Equalities Office, 2018). This statistic underscores the persistent threat of discrimination in everyday interactions and highlights how visibility can still come at a personal cost, even in societies that claim progress towards inclusion. So many of us still struggle with the effects of minority stress, whether due to chronic abuse, overt homo and trans hate, trauma, or daily life challenges.

From a professional standpoint, too few institutions adequately prepare mental and sexual health professionals to work with clients whose identities intersect across GSRD lines.

When designing GSRD training, it's essential to acknowledge that while many prefer a more cognitive and didactic approach to research and information, it is crucial to help participants explore themselves. The emotional weight of such exercises can be significant. Creating a safe, supportive environment where participants feel prepared for what lies ahead is crucial.

In Pink Therapy, we've developed a four-stage model of training therapists to work with GSRD clients. However long the training is, it's essential to include something from all four stages.

1. Experiential *Learning* is always the first place to start, using exercises that allow participants to explore their VABs.
2. Social *Context* is next: What is life like based on geography, age, race, etc.? What legal rights and freedoms exist to parent, be employed, be safe, and practise one's beliefs?
3. Psychosocial *Implications* - how do these social contexts affect the GSRD group under study (impact on mental, physical and sexual health, suicide and self-harm, neurodivergence, family life and their relationships)
4. Clinical *Issues* - common presenting and frequently occurring issues worked on in therapy (coming out, self-esteem, shame, building resilience, finding community, stigma management, concealment strategies and coping with trauma, both pervasive and PTSD/abuse).

Key steps to support the process of experiential training include the following practices that help establish safety, trust, and clarity from the outset. Where possible, it helps to:

•   Gather background information from participants during recruitment and selection on personal motivation, previous training, lived experience, and connection to GSRD communities. In our experience, it is unusual for participants not to have any connection to GSRD communities through close friendships, family relationships, or personal lived experience.
•   Establishing a clear learning contract, which includes autonomy and mutual respect.
•   Creating a 'safe container' by providing time for team-building activities before diving into the course syllabus.

It's vital to clarify that the purpose of experiential exercises is not therapy. However, they may evoke deep feelings that may need to be addressed in personal therapy. Some exercises may be emotionally stirring, while others may seem uneventful. Regardless, self-observation and presence are critical. Participants will learn about themselves and each other, making confidentiality agreements essential.

Many of us carry educational trauma, where the teacher-student dynamic was rigid and authoritarian, leaving little room for personal boundaries. Experiential training for adults and professionals is an opportunity to assess how individuals manage self-care and participate at their own pace. Participants need to engage as deeply as they feel comfortable while also observing the space they take up within the group dynamic.

We teach and follow the informed consent model to provide the participants with as clear instructions as possible on what they are supposed to pay attention to during the exercise.

Each exercise follows a structure:

• Clear instructions with time for clarification.
• Short time for personal reflection.
• Small group engagement.
• A large group debrief, where participants reflect on:
• The personal impact of the experience.
• How can they apply the experience professionally?

Let's continue with some helpful exercises.

Hand Holding Exercise

Introduction: Many LGBTQ individuals grow up with a sense of being "other" in a heteronormative society. This is not just an internal psychological experience, as many LGBTQ individuals report being recipients of hostility, victimisation, and harassment. Interpersonally, homophobia and transphobia (both actual and fear of) may play out between partners and inhibit partners from commonplace displays of affection (e.g. holding hands in public). Holding hands in public is a taken-for-granted act of interpersonal affection for many heterosexual couples, but it may carry particular anxieties and significance for LGBTQ partners. In same-sex couples, it can be viewed as a political act of queer visibility. A way to show pride in one's identity and relationship, but the risk of actual violence or microaggressions needs to be evaluated. Couples report constantly scanning the environment for safety (Rohleder et. al., 2023).

Instructions

We have used this exercise frequently in in-person courses, and we recommend that you read the instructions as written.

We invite you to participate in a brief, embodied reflection on public intimacy and visibility.

As you head to lunch (or the break), if you feel willing and safe enough, hold hands with someone *who shares a similar gender identity or might be read by others as the same gender as you,* for at least one minute. If same-sex hand-holding is something you're already very familiar with, consider partnering with someone of a different gender and notice what comes up for you.

The exercises are not about attraction or identity but about noticing what it feels like to engage in a gesture that society often codes in particular ways.

As you do this, we invite you to tune into:

- Your internal responses: Do you feel ease, discomfort, pride, tension?
- The social environment: Are you aware of how others might perceive you? Are there reactions?
- Any stories that arise about gender, sexuality, visibility, or belonging.

If you choose not to participate, that's completely valid. You might instead walk alongside someone and reflect on *why* this invitation feels challenging—or even irrelevant—for you. That, too, is valuable data.

This exercise is especially designed for use on GSRD awareness training; it's invaluable with a predominantly cis-het group. It acknowledges that for many bisexual, pansexual, queer, and non-binary people, visibility and legitimacy in public spaces can feel complicated or elusive.

Topics to address beforehand: As many of us identify as non-binary, gender fluid, agender, bigender, free spirit, or gender fuck. Ask the group if there is a way to solve this binary hand-holding concept, where we're asking people to pair up with someone of the same (binary) gender.

As a trainer using this exercise, consider the following issues:

- Physical Safety: Ensure the participants are in a context where the risk of putting themselves in danger of aggression or assault is minimal or relatively low.
- Emotional Safety: For participants who are questioning their gender identity or sexual orientation, this exercise could trigger a mix of feelings from longing and sadness to anger, shame, and immense discomfort. This exercise may cause stress reactions in a minority of individuals, such as hypervigilance.

Reflect on amatonormativity and the expectation that not everyone wants romantic relationships, which can lead to public displays of affection (PDA).

- Responses to Discomfort: It's common for individuals, including cisgender people, to experience discomfort or cognitive dissonance when confronted with the reactions of society.

This exercise is meant to challenge the heterosexual privilege of public displays of affection and status change when in a relationship. Another aspect (in more conservative or religious contexts) would be artefacts of formal commitment, such as wearing rings or clothing informing us of the couple's marital status.

Further Ways to Explore One's Feelings

Here are some suggestions for deepening empathic understanding, which could include doing one (or more) of the following activities, and writing down the details of this experience in a personal journal, describing what the feelings were:

- Purchase a gay or lesbian magazine or book and read it in public.
- Wear a pro-lesbian, gay, bisexual or transgender T-shirt or badge.
- Keep your heterosexuality in the closet for one week by not disclosing it to anyone, i.e. this could mean when talking about what you did at the weekend with your partner, you are careful not to name them or mention their gender.
- Challenge heterosexist or transphobic jokes or comments.
- Initiate a serious discussion on the topic of heterosexism or transphobia.

Exercise: Identity Exploration

We incorporate exercises that connect personal experience with therapeutic insight to deepen self-awareness and promote reflective practice. One fundamental exercise in Pink Therapy training is identity exploration. Participants complete the sentence "I am…" as many times as possible, reflecting on the types of identities they prioritise. This can reveal much about how we view ourselves and what aspects of our identity we express. These could include nationality, gender, profession, or personal characteristics.

> Please finish the sentence below as many times as you can:
> I am…
> I am…
> ….
> …

Exercise: Reflecting on Gender Identity and Expression

Building on the previous self-reflective work around identity, this next exercise invites participants to delve more deeply into one specific and often complex aspect of identity: gender.

This exercise is designed to help participants explore their understanding of gender, focusing on personal experiences and societal perceptions. It invites reflection on gender identity and expression, challenging traditional stereotypes and assumptions.

Instructions

Set a Timer for 10 Minutes

Take the next ten minutes to reflect on the following questions, writing down your thoughts if it helps:

- How do you know what your gender is?
- Is your gender the same as your sex? How do you differentiate between the two?
- When did you first become aware of your gender expression?
- What do you like about your gender expression?
- How do your family and friends react to your gender expression? Do they know your gender identity?
- If you could change anything about your gender expression or identity, what would it be, and why?

Purpose of the Exercise

This exercise is meant to:

- Challenge the assumptions and stereotypes surrounding gender, biology, and cultural roles.
- Encourage a deeper awareness of how gender is expressed and perceived by oneself and others.
- Help participants reflect on the cultural shift that questions binary constructs of "femininity" and "masculinity."

Important Considerations

- Emotional Safety: Ensure the group feels safe sharing and discussing these personal reflections. When working with diverse groups, particularly those with GSRD individuals, be mindful that some may find this exercise challenging or triggering.
- Responses to Discomfort: It's common for individuals, including cisgender people, to experience discomfort or cognitive dissonance when confronted with the complexity of gender. Acknowledge this and create space for open dialogue, without forcing participation.

Discussion (Optional)

After the reflection, participants may share their thoughts with the group. Facilitators should encourage open, non-judgemental dialogue, allowing different perspectives and experiences to be heard.

Gender, Sexuality, and Relationships (GSR) Lifeline

In addition to the above, participants are invited to explore their identities through exercises such as the gender, sexuality, and relationships (GSR) lifeline, which enables them to map their experiences over time. This exercise offers valuable insights into the complex interplay between gender, sexuality, and relationships throughout life.

GSR Lifeline Exercise for Gender, Sexuality, and Relationship Diversity Exploration

This exercise is a part of the personal sexological experience training (PSE) during my practical sexology training. Historically led at the Institute for Advanced Studies in Human Sexuality in San Francisco, it is designed to help individuals explore their sense of belonging within GSRD. It encourages deep reflection on key life milestones related to gender, sexuality, and relationships, to gain a more comprehensive understanding of how these elements intersect in one's life.

Instructions

Materials Needed:

- A large sheet of paper (flip chart or A3).
- Coloured pens or pencils (optional).

1. Identify Key Milestones in Your Sexual History

Begin by reflecting on significant moments in your sexual history. This includes moments related to gender identity, sexual orientation, and relationships. Think about these milestones and their impact on your personal development.

2. Divide Sexuality into Three Dimensions

Break down your broadly understood sexuality into three key factors: gender, sexuality, and relationships. These factors often intersect and influence one another, and visualising them can provide insights into your journey.

3.   Draw the GSR Lifeline

On paper, create a graphical representation of your "Gender-Sexuality-Relationships Life Lines" (GSR). Use colours, symbols, and different line styles to represent your experiences, feelings, and key moments related to the three factors. Each line represents a specific dimension:

Line 1: Gender

Reflect on the history of your gender identity. Consider the influences of genetics, upbringing, social messages, and personal experiences during childhood and adolescence. Consider that you may not identify with a specific gender throughout your life, or you may identify with multiple genders, either situationally or permanently.

Line 2: Sexuality

Explore the history of your sexuality, including sexual identity, preferences, and activity. Think about periods of high and low sexual activity, and how these periods relate to your experiences with gender and relationships. Include all forms of sexual expression, such as self-love, masturbation, fantasising, and consuming sexual content.

Line 3: Relationships

Reflect on the history of your relationships. Consider how you define relationships and how they have shaped your identity (e.g. monogamous/non-monogamous, kinky/vanilla, platonic, or long-distance). Identify key people who have influenced your relationship journey through positive or negative experiences. Also, explore how these relationships intersect with your gender and sexuality.

4.   Analyse Your GSR Lifeline

Once your lifeline is complete, observe patterns, connections, and changes across the three dimensions. Reflect on how periods of change or stability in one area (gender, sexuality, or relationships) influence others.

The Purpose of the GSR Lifeline

The GSR lifeline exercise is a powerful tool for self-reflection. It allows individuals to gain insights into their sexual history through the lenses of gender, sexuality, and relationships. Breaking down sexuality into these three dimensions provides a broader and more nuanced understanding of one's identity and experiences.

This exercise provides a non-invasive way for therapists to explore a client's context, revealing patterns and analogies related to their history. The GSR lifeline can highlight the integration and disconnection between love, sex, relationships, and sexual behaviours, offering rich material for discussion and therapeutic growth.

Further Reflections on the Gender Dimension

In today's sociopolitical climate, gender is often a source of tension and controversy. The concept of gender itself can evoke ambivalence and anxiety, shaped by stereotypes and misinformation perpetuated in the media. The process of drawing the gender line offers an opportunity for psychoeducation and a moment of clarity; everyone has a gender, and it is fundamentally a cultural construct reflecting how we perform our sexual identity in the world.

The gender dimension also opens the door to philosophical reflection on 'performing gender.' (Butler, 1988). In everyday life, we often adopt different strategies for presenting ourselves, adjusting our gender expression to fit societal expectations or personal circumstances. The question arises: is gender a binary spectrum or two distinct and meaningful categories? Many students are surprised to discover that qualities like "strength" can apply to both women and men, blurring the lines of gendered traits.

Cisgender individuals, who may feel consistent in their gender identity, often speak of the pressures to conform or exaggerate certain traits based on societal expectations. This might involve hiding or emphasising specific gender characteristics (e.g. clothing, body structure, or makeup) to align with cultural norms or subcultural identities. These experiences are often shaped by family messages, societal pressures, and internal conflicts about one's body and its characteristics.

Such reflective exercises allow therapists-in-training to confront their biases and assumptions about gender and sexuality, helping them to understand their clients' experiences better.

Ultimately, experiential training challenges us to dig deep personally and professionally. The more we engage with these exercises, the better equipped we become to support others on their journeys. As therapists, our personal growth becomes the foundation for our professional practice.

The GSR lifeline is a powerful tool for self-exploration and reflection, particularly in the context of therapeutic work. By breaking down the concept of sexuality into three dimensions—gender, sexuality, and relationships—this exercise facilitates a more comprehensive and nuanced understanding of an individual's identity. The lifeline will allow clients or participants to reflect on their lived experiences, personal milestones, and the interconnections between these key aspects of their identity.

Therapeutic Value of the Gender, Sexuality, and Relationship Lifeline

The GSR lifeline provides a non-invasive method of exploring one's context for individuals in therapy. It can reveal patterns and analogies in how one navigates love, sex, and relationships over time. By mapping these aspects, individuals may see how they have integrated or separated these dimensions in their personal lives.

Jack Morin (1995) builds on John Money's theory of "lovemaps" (now criticised for its pathologising tone over sexual diversity dimensions) with his exploration of how love and sex can merge or remain distinct in one's experiences.

Eroticism thrives on the unexpected, the forbidden, and the mysterious. It is in the tension between desire and restraint that the erotic mind comes alive (Morin, 1995: 5).

This encapsulates his view that sexual arousal and fulfilment are deeply tied to psychological complexities and emotional connections.

For therapists, the GSR lifeline offers rich insights without the need for direct probing, allowing clients to express themselves in a safe and self-directed manner.

Gender: A Key Dimension in the Current Cultural Climate

Of the three lines—gender, sexuality, and relationships—the gender line often stands out as particularly significant, especially in today's political and cultural context. The term "gender" is increasingly charged, frequently causing ambivalence or even anxiety due to pervasive stereotypes and misinformation. This anxiety is exacerbated by media narratives, such as the so-called "gender monster" or fears about educators "changing" children's gender in classrooms.

Drawing the gender line offers a valuable opportunity for psychoeducation. It provides a moment to pause and reflect on whether everyone has a gender, and whether it conforms to cultural norms. Gender is a cultural construct that reflects how we perform our sexual identity in the world, and this exercise opens up space for individuals to explore how they perform gender throughout different stages of life.

Through the exercise, many participants realise that traits traditionally associated with one gender, such as strength, can apply equally to both men and women. This discovery challenges long-held binary conceptions and encourages more fluid thinking about gender roles.

Navigating Gender Expression

For many cisgender individuals, the gender line reveals internalised pressures to conform to societal expectations. They may share experiences of hiding or emphasising certain traits to align with cultural norms. This could involve wearing oversized clothing to mask their gender, adopting a specific subcultural identity, or emphasising traits deemed desirable by society through clothing, makeup, and accessories. These behaviours are often shaped by early messages about gender and sexuality from family, peers, and society. For example, individuals may recount being told to "hide your breasts" to avoid sexual attention, or conversely, being encouraged to showcase physical attributes.

The exercise also highlights ambivalence about one's own body and gender identity, which may stem from societal norms and personal beliefs about gendered physical characteristics. Many participants reflect on childhood experiences of discomfort with their bodies, whether feeling "too feminine" or "not masculine enough."

Emotional Depth and Group Dynamics

The GSR lifeline is not just an intellectual exercise—it often stirs deep emotions. Participants frequently share personal stories of gender exploration, romantic relationships, and moments of self-realisation. These stories may evoke a range of emotions, including nostalgia, anger, sadness, and even helplessness. Facilitating a safe space where these emotions can be expressed is crucial. After completing and discussing the lifelines, it's essential to create time for processing the intense feelings that may arise.

Equally important is recognising minority stress within the group. Those whose lifelines reflect non-normative experiences, such as LGBT+ individuals, may feel vulnerable, especially if others' lifelines align more closely with societal expectations. Without a sense of safety and mutual respect, some participants may disengage from the exercise entirely, offering excuses such as "I am not good at artistic exercises" or providing minimal, surface-level responses to avoid exposure. For example, a participant might say, "I was born a boy, I feel like a man, my relationship aligns with my sexuality—nothing unusual."

This dynamic highlights the need for therapists and facilitators to be mindful of the group's diversity. LGBT+ individuals, in particular, may carefully observe how others react to the exercise, gauging whether it is safe to share their authentic experiences. The facilitator's role is to ensure that all voices are heard and respected while maintaining an environment free from homo-, bi-, or transphobic comments. A guiding principle could be:

> We are here to learn from each other, inspire each other, and remain curious about our commonalities and differences. In doing so, we reflect not only on the other but also on ourselves, and we confront the shadows that shape our understanding of gender, sexuality, and relationships.

By encouraging open, respectful dialogue, the gender, sexuality, and relationship lifeline becomes a tool for self-discovery and a powerful exercise in empathy and understanding across diverse gender and sexual identities.

SAR Training

Sexual Attitude Reassessment (SAR) is a well-established training method developed in the United States, widely used in sex therapy, counselling, and sexuality education. It combines multimedia presentations, experiential exercises, and group discussions to challenge participants' beliefs and attitudes about human sexuality. The primary goal is to foster self-awareness, empathy, and openness to sexual and relational diversity. In recent years, SAR training has gained growing interest and implementation across Europe (all across Scandinavia, Central, and Eastern Europe, especially in Poland, in the Sex Positive Institute), reflecting increasing demand for inclusive and affirming approaches to sexuality in clinical and educational settings.

The Sexual Attitude Reassessment & Restructuring (SAR) training was developed in the 1970s at the Institute for Advanced Study of Human Sexuality in San Francisco by Peggy Brick and Bill Taverner, among others, as a part of efforts to promote sex-positive education and professional development in the field of sexuality (Stayton, 1998). Many human sexuality courses utilise SAR as a key experiential component for students of sexology. This innovative programme aimed to expand sexologists' awareness of the diversity of human sexual behaviour and expression, fostering greater understanding, acceptance, and tolerance while encouraging a celebration of sexuality in its most whole form.

Today, SAR remains a crucial element of professional training for sexologists. It is required for certification by the American Association of Sexuality Educators, Counselors, and Therapists (AASECT, 2025) and is incorporated into the curriculum of programmes like Sex Coach U (Criss, 2023). Globally recognised, SAR is considered an essential part of professional development for anyone working in the field of human sexuality.

SAR is intended for sexologists—such as relationship psychologists, sex therapists, sex coaches, bodyworkers, and spiritual sex teachers, as well as professionals from allied fields like medicine, therapy, clergy, and social work.

SAR is an experiential, provocative, and emotionally engaging training. It is designed to challenge participants by pushing boundaries and eliciting emotional responses. The training encourages professionals to explore their attitudes, values, and beliefs around sexuality, ultimately enhancing sensitivity and deepening their understanding of human sexual diversity. Through this immersive experience, participants often experience personal breakthroughs, gaining new insights into their boundaries and even sparking curiosity to explore new perspectives on sexuality.

The programme includes media presentations (such as contemporary films, television, and art), guest speakers sharing their experiences, and demonstrations showcasing the wide range of human sexual expression. Participants also have the opportunity to engage in small group discussions, supported by trained facilitators, to process their experiences and reactions.

It's important to note that SAR is not a clinical training in sex therapy, nor is it traditional sex education. Instead, it is designed to foster emotional growth, acceptance, and tolerance of human sexuality in all its diverse dimensions.

Obligatory, Not Optional. Conclusions

Experiential training is not merely a supplementary or optional component in developing a GSRD therapist; it is essential. The nuanced and complex nature of GSRD issues demands more than theoretical understanding or textbook knowledge—it requires an embodied, personal engagement with the material. By participating in experiential exercises, therapists are better equipped to confront their biases, challenge societal norms, and cultivate an authentic empathy for the diverse experiences of those they serve.

Through experiential training, therapists develop deeper self-awareness and gain critical insights into how their identities inform their therapeutic approach. These reflective processes ensure therapists are knowledgeable and attuned to their clients' emotional and psychological landscapes. Furthermore, as GSRD issues evolve in response to cultural shifts and emerging identities, experiential training allows therapists to remain adaptable, open-minded, and sensitive to the ongoing needs of diverse populations.

All Core Components of GSRD therapy, such as

Affirmative and Inclusive Attitude, Cultural Competence and Awareness, Sexual Health and Identity Exploration, Understanding Intersectionality, Affirming Relationships and Non-traditional Family Structures, Self-Reflection and Personal Growth, Trauma-Informed Approach, Therapeutic Alliance and Empowerment, Sexual and Relationship Education, Continuous Professional Development need to be self-tested, processed and reflected upon professionally and personally.

In short, experiential training fosters the personal transformation fundamental to effective and compassionate therapy. Without these immersive, reflective learning experiences, GSRD therapists risk failing to deliver the nuanced, empathetic care that is essential in this critical field.

References

American Association of Sexuality Educators, Counselors and Therapists (AASECT). (2025). *Requirements for Sex Therapist Certification*. AASECT, accessed online 23 May 2025

Bąk, D. (2023). GSRD-affirmative supervision of psychotherapy. In S. Neves & D. Davies (Eds.), *Relationally Queer*. Routledge. https://doi.org/10.4324 /9781003260561-13

Britton, P., & Dunlap, R. (2017). *Designing and Leading a Successful SAR: A Guide for Sex Therapists, Sexuality Educators, and Sexologists* (1st ed.). Routledge. https://doi.org/10.4324/9781315301112

Butler, J. (1988). Performative acts and gender constitution: An essay in phenomenology and feminist theory. *Theatre Journal*, 40(4), 519–531. https://doi .org/10.2307/3207893

Criss, S. (2023). *How Mini-SAR Moments Continuously Expand Your Perspective (and Make You a Better Sex Coach)*. https://sexcoachu.com/sar-training -perspective/ accessed online 23 May 2025

Davies, D., & Aykroyd, M. (2002). Sexual orientation and psychological contact. In G. Wyatt & P. Sanders (Eds.), *Rogers' Therapeutic Conditions: Evolution, Theory and Practice, Volume 4: Contact and Perception* (pp. 221–233). PCCS Books.

Government Equalities Office. (2018). National LGBT survey: Research report. https://www.gov.uk/government/publications/national-lgbt-survey-summary-report on 22 May 2025

Hawkins, P., & Shohet, R. (2012). *Supervision in the Helping Professions* (4th ed.). Open University Press

Hawkins, R., & Neves, S. (2024). Queering the 7-eyed model of clinical supervision. *Sexual and Relationship Therapy*, 40(2), 340–359. https://doi.org/10.1080/14681994.2024.2403347

Kinsey, A.C., Pomeroy, W.B., & Martin, C.E. (1948). *Sexual Behavior in the Human Male*. Indiana: Indiana University Press

Morin, J. (1995). *The Erotic Mind: Unlocking the Inner Sources of Passion and Fulfilment*. HarperCollins.

Rohleder, P., Ryan-Flood, R., & Walsh, J. (2023). Holding hands: LGBTQ people's experiences of public displays of affection with their partner(s). *Psychology & Sexuality*, 14(3), 559–571. https://doi.org/10.1080/19419899.2023.2185533

Russell, J. (2023). The sex lives of asexuals. In S. Neves & D. Davies (Eds.) *Erotically Queer* (pp. 71–72). Routledge.

Stayton, W.R. (1998). A curriculum for training professionals in human sexuality using the sexual attitude restructuring (SAR) model. *Journal of Sex Education and Therapy*, 23(1), 26–32.

Part 2

Integrating GSRD Therapy

Chapter 5

Integrating GSRD Therapy – Exploration and Affirmation

Bridging the Great Divide

Paul C. Mollitt

Introduction

This chapter explores the growing polarisation in therapeutic approaches to work with gender, sexuality, and relationship diversity (GSRD) clients, particularly the perceived divide between affirmative therapy and exploratory therapy. The author argues that this binary is both false and harmful, proposing instead a creative integration that honours both stances. Drawing on psychodynamic training and clinical experience, the chapter outlines the ethical and clinical foundations of affirmative therapy whilst defending the value of exploration when grounded in empathy, curiosity, and minority stress theory. It critiques harmful practices disguised as neutral exploration and highlights the psychosocial dimensions of GSRD distress, including internalised oppression and shame. The chapter advocates for training that equips therapists to attend to both distal and proximal minority stressors and offers a case study to illustrate the transformative potential of integrated GSRD therapy. Ultimately, the chapter makes a call to unite the profession around a more inclusive, reflexive, and socially aware practice that does not see affirmation and exploration as mutually exclusive but as complementary forces in meaningful therapeutic work.

As clinical work with the GSRD community continues to evolve into a hopeful modality in its own right (Davies and Neves, 2023), and therapy training attempts to redress the wrongs of past harms and omissions, a split in the wider profession appears to be growing. It seems we are being asked to choose: Do we want to be affirmative therapists who are passionate about social justice and dismantling oppression, or do we want to be exploratory therapists who are curious about those unconscious processes that shape our lives? You can't be both; some would have you believe. A recent "X" post by a US therapist (Ruffalo, 2024) seems to capture this:

> It is a sad truth that there now exist two types of therapists:
> Those who believe that psychotherapy is a critical self-examination aimed at changing something about the individual person.

DOI: 10.4324/9781003530848-8

Those who believe psychotherapy is simply an exercise in validation. Choose wisely.

Behind this take, dismissing an affirmative stance lies a false dichotomy that, whilst appealing to those on social media looking for in-group validation, does a disservice to the profession, especially those seeking therapy. I don't disagree with his first definition of exploratory psychotherapy, but it's incomplete. I would add: ...*in the context of the world they live in,* which is the affirmative part. In trying to promote exploratory therapies (traditionally those derived from psychoanalysis), this therapist punches down on those affirmative therapies that have proven so vital for the GSRD population. Ironically, he also seems to model one of psychoanalysis' fundamental defensive theories – splitting – by dividing therapists into *all good* and *all bad*. But in today's fractured world, perhaps picking a side often offers over-worked and under-valued therapists some sense of belonging or control – even a sense of superiority over the other. Where affirmative therapists might find meaning through their essential political practices, exploratory therapists may find meaning in the idea that only they are practising *real* psychotherapy.

As an experienced GSRD therapist with a core psychodynamic training, I am in a curious position with this split. Exploration *and* affirmation are essential to my work. Still, I've been disappointed to see purists from both camps attempting to discredit the other, often by caricatured understandings of how they work. These tropes can feed through from our training and supervision, entrenching this unhelpful split. Where I think GSRD therapy is at its most powerful is in its creative fusion of affirmation and exploration, dispelling the belief that they are mutually exclusive. But before that, let's break down these two seemingly incompatible therapeutic stances.

Affirmative Therapy

With its roots in social justice, affirmative therapy grew out of the historic and shameful pathologising of sexual and gender minorities (Drescher, 2015). Over recent decades, it has proven to be a vital and effective intervention for many LGBT people (Burger and Pachankis, 2024). Two decades ago, Pachankis and Goldfried (2004) wrote, "many clinicians think that LGB clients can and ought to be treated in the same manner as their heterosexual counterparts" (p. 230). Much has changed in the profession, but this remains true for many therapists, who fail to recognise the unique issues facing gender and sexual minority individuals and the importance of affirmative work.

Foundational to an ethical affirmative therapy (Langdridge, 2007) is the idea that sexual and gender differences do not represent mental health conditions in themselves, and that they are valued equally with heterosexual and cisgender identities. In a session, an affirmative therapist might offer some psychoeducation on shame or minority stress or express warmth and encouragement when exploring identity to offset prevailing heterosexism. They will want to help the client foster a sense of compassion and joy through an affirmative and compassionate therapeutic relationship that raises self-worth and pride and highlights the importance of community (Davies and Neves, 2023). Affirmative therapy is as much about the therapist's work outside of sessions. The concerted effort that goes into educating oneself about the diversity of sexual and gender identities and relationships, the impact of oppression and shame, and our investigation into personal biases and blind spots are also what makes an affirmative therapist. This personal work will be felt by a GSRD client, often even without it being verbalised. In affirmative therapy, clients are free to define themselves without fear that we might attempt to change them to fit our theories or worldview. As Don Clark (1987) writes, the therapist's "...objective should be to help the person to become more truly themselves... to reinforce integrity by encouraging behavior and attitudes that match inner feelings" (p. 221). Affirmative therapy could be said to be *more* neutral than gender exploratory therapies, often grounded in paternalism and suspicion as they are client-led and "scaffold clients' self-directed and autonomous gender exploration" (Ashley, 2022, p. 477).

However, it must work both ways. A major criticism is the "risk of affirmative therapies restricting a client's power to work through and create their own meaning within the therapeutic relationship" (Langdridge, 2007, p. 33). We must also be comfortable taking a back seat. As Wilfred Bion wrote (1988), we meet clients "without memory or desire" (p. 259) – that is, we attend to the person in front of us without assumption based on what has gone before or what we hope might lie ahead. The tacit stance of the affirmative therapist is *you are welcome as you are*. We invite clients in and, as the relationship deepens and trust develops, we help them to understand themselves in the context of the world they inhabit, and how they might live better, more fulfilling, and more authentic lives. In other words, we explore.

ExploratoryTherapy

Exploratory therapies examine out-of-awareness or unconscious thoughts, feelings, and motivations and trace past relational patterns that might contribute to current difficulties. The therapeutic relationship itself is seen as the agent for change. Exploratory therapies are challenging – they push us to confront ourselves and bring those shadowy, disowned parts back into the light. This is something that many good therapists of all theoretical approaches are already doing – they know the difference between a chat with a supportive friend and the deep relational work of therapy.

However, the legacy of harmful exploratory therapies in the form of conversion therapy (once seen as a legitimate treatment for sexual minorities) has understandably left many distrusting of exploratory work, therapists included. Whilst we live in increasingly tolerant societies, "the effects of prejudice continue to be felt in subtle and more explicit ways by those whose sexuality and gender do not fit within heterosexual norms" (Wadell *et al.*, 2020, p. xii). This is echoed within the profession. The treatment of transgender and gender-expansive people today by some echoes the pathologising of homosexuals of the recent past, where an over-reliance on "longstanding tropes of trans people as confused and mentally ill" (Ashley, 2020, p. 792) is causing untold damage. Those of us working thoughtfully and humanely with LGBTQ+ populations whilst critiquing gender exploratory therapy are taken as "evidence of trans health care's ideological capture" (Ashley, 2022, p. 478). A tactic of right-wing politics is to confect a moral panic over something not actually happening, or at least not in large numbers. A straw man has been created out of affirmation – that it is a dumbed-down, even unethical practice. That "real" therapists have to carry out "Ethical Care in Secret" (Jenkins and Panozzo, 2024) with transgender clients. The group "Thoughtful Therapists" (2024), whose tagline "First do no harm", is made up of a small pool of so-called "gender critical" therapists, some of whom no doubt have real concerns about their clients but are being whipped up by bad-faith actors who are "relying on scientific-sounding language to achieve respectability" (Ashley, 2020, p. 779) such as the "politicised pseudo-diagnostic category of rapid-onset gender dysphoria (ROGD)" (ibid.).

However, whilst most of us believe in the importance of exploration (with an affirmative foundation), such groups do not believe in affirmation, too wedded to their ideological beliefs (heteronormativity, cisgenderism) to accept a middle ground. Whilst a genuinely neutral exploratory therapy could be helpful for trans clients, "gender-exploratory therapy" has as its starting point essentialist theories that come from a position of suspicion and of potential pathology. Ergo, they share "strong conceptual and narrative similarities" (Ashley, 2022, p. 472) with conversion practices. "Although couched in the language of exploration, gender-exploratory therapy seems more akin to interrogation or perhaps even inquisition" (Ashley, 2022, p. 473). "Thoughtful Therapists" is thus revealed to be a misnomer and euphemism: "the positive-sounding language of inquiry and exploration" (Ashley, 2022, p. 476) hides more insidious ideological aims. The use of "thoughtful" and "ethical" aims to diminish and monster affirmative practices whilst obscuring their own role as the intellectual arm of a right-wing political stance that would ban transgender care. Sadly, many well-meaning therapists are being seduced into such circles through the misuse of therapeutic terms: "Appeals to therapeutic neutrality in highly politicized contexts are too often a preemptive rejoinder to potential critics, cynically turning the concept against its very purpose" (Ashley, 2022, p. 477). In their failure to do their exploratory work on their biases, these exploratory therapists harm the profession, acting as a Trojan Horse; they shelter and embolden unapologetic conversion therapists.

For balance, it would also be an exaggeration to say that most exploratory therapists are enacting conversion therapy – again, a caricature that is wielded too freely – most are not (Mollitt, 2022). But a small minority will continue to practise conversion (intentionally or otherwise) and this has led to many LGBTQ+ people understandably turning their backs on exploratory therapy – depriving them of a potentially life-changing therapeutic encounter.

Minority Stress and the Psychosocial

GSRD therapy understands the specific adverse effects of oppression in its various manifestations (interpersonal, societal, internalised) for different marginalised groups (Davies and Neves, 2023), which can be understood using the minority stress framework (Meyer, 1995, 2003). Coming across this theory far too late in my clinical career, I found it to be helpful in bridging the divide between exploration and affirmation. Considered one of the core GSRD theories (along with intersectionality, social safety, and microaggressions), minority stress offers a "bi-focal" understanding of a client's distress. Referring to the additional and unique stress that minority people can face, minority stress comprises distal and proximal stress. Distal stress points to external events such as prejudice, discrimination, and violence based on one's minority status. Proximal stress is our subsequent internal response to these outside events and may include concealing unwanted aspects of ourselves, avoidance of intimacy, and self-hatred, such as internalised homophobia. These defences may initially be helpful and even necessary. Still, when they become fixed ways of perceiving and relating to the world, they paradoxically end up adding to our stress load, creating a vicious cycle that's hard to quit. This can lead to higher incidences of poor mental and physical health in LGBTQ+ populations (Meyer, 2003; Meyer and Frost, 2012).

Think of the impact of Section 28[1] in the UK and the homophobic bullying many young queer people faced up and down the country during the 80s and 90s. It left me achingly self-conscious beyond those awkward teenage years that we all must bear: paranoid about the way I moved my body and expressed myself. Much of my time and energy would be spent hiding those aspects that might draw hostile attention. At the time, this made me slightly less of a target, but at the expense of my capacity for spontaneity, unselfconscious play, and being able to relax in public. It also made me unbelievably angry, with no way to express it except internally – my mind and body often taking the hit by way of depression, chronic pain, or illness.[2]

Exploratory therapy with LGBTQ+ clients often makes a beeline for psychological defences and characterological issues without fully considering the social context or the impact of minority stress. There's a Group Analytic concept known as the *location of disturbance* (Foulkes, 1948, p. 127). Denied and unwanted aspects of a group are projected into a person or persons who are then punished. Bigotry, such as homophobia and transphobia, could be seen as the disowning of the fears and fantasies about one's sexuality and gender. As Malyon (1982) writes about gay men, it is "…homophobia as opposed to homosexuality, as a major pathological variable in the development of certain symptomatic conditions" (p. 26). Minority individuals and communities serve as a convenient location for these disowned shadowy parts of normative society – the disturbance is always *out there*, never within; but it is "society's madness [that] has been denied, not their own" (Haslam, 2000, p. 16). However, so used to being othered we start to identify with the names and labels of societal prejudice and begin to other ourselves and one another, policing our bodies on behalf of the majority through internalised homophobia and transphobia. It follows then that, "if we are met by a therapist who confirms the 'badness' of our desires [or gender identity], we may be angry but all too ready to accept what was already expected" (Newbigin, 2020, p. 36).

For many years, I kept myself apart from the queer community, convincing myself it was a professional decision to protect work boundaries. But I was avoiding that part of myself I had internalised as deviant, identifying with those projections placed on me since I was a child. I shut myself away, keeping my deviance away from polite society. Through these robust projective identifications, we can become what is expected of us – chaotic, shallow, mentally ill, promiscuous, and sick. Society then takes these responses as evidence to confirm its prejudice and pathology. Linked to this is the overdiagnosis of borderline personality disorder in sexual and gender minority people compared to other groups (Rodriguez-Seijas *et al.*, 2021, 2024). Psychological splitting might speak to attempts to fit into a world that accepts us only conditionally, and the resulting behaviours share some common ground with personality disorders (Diamond and Alley, 2022). As clinicians, we must be open-minded as to what indicates psychopathology and what relates to the cumulative trauma of a life of stigma and stress. Such a powerful and often invisible cycle of abuse and trauma is too often missed in work with minorities. Group analyst Stuart Stevenson (2022) writes that therapists should not collude:

> with any oppressive social ideology in the name of 'analytic neutrality'. This is not to say that sexualities should not be explored nor that any sexuality will be free from defensive strategies. Group analysts and psychoanalytic psychotherapists can cause great harm, even today, to those who live outside the safe borders of heteronormativity.
>
> (p. 22)

Working with GSRD populations, an affirmative stance should never be optional because, in our self-protective responses to distal minority stress, we were so often cut off from those affirmative relationships that many others may take for granted.

Introducing a GSRD Lens to Existing Modalities

The GSRD model, including an understanding of minority stress, "combines well alongside many other theoretical approaches, perhaps unsurprisingly with a long tradition of adopting a non-pathologizing stance, such as person-centred therapy" (Davies and Neves, 2023, p. 411), cognitive behavioural therapy (CBT) (Burger and Pachankis, 2024), and contemporary sexology (Contemporary Institute of Clinical Sexology, 2024). GSRD therapy represents a relatively unobtrusive addition to these models. CBT in particular has enjoyed increasing support as an evidence-based manualised therapy due to its replicability in research and relative ease of training. It has, therefore, become one of the most promising approaches to explore the evidence base for affirmative therapy, as explored by Burger and Pachankis (2024) in *State of the Science: LGBTQ-Affirmative Psychotherapy*. CBT has not lived up to its promise within the National Health Service in the UK (Bruun, 2023; Marks, 2018), and so I'd be wary of putting all our eggs into this basket. Burger and Pachankis, in their paper, point to other therapies, such as interpersonal therapy (IPT) and emotion focused therapy (EFT). I would add dynamic interpersonal therapy (DIT) and cognitive analytic therapy (CAT) as other, more exploratory, therapies that might work well with affirmative or GSRD therapy. To help our GSRD clients, a relationship is needed, not manuals. Work now needs to be done to expand the exploratory and psychodynamic therapies evidence base for LGBTQ+ populations, building on existing research (Shedler, 2010) to complement the potential offered by CBT.

Therapists trained in affirmative-friendly models can ensure that they are also exploring in their work (as most do) and that it doesn't become that caricature of "tea and sympathy" expected of us. Whilst an affirmative therapist would artfully acknowledge and work through the impact of a client's distal minority stress, they might be reluctant to address any defensive responses that emerge from proximal minority stress in case they are seen to be pathologising. To truly help our clients, we must address the dual psychosocial aspect of their distress.

Problematic Psychoanalysis

For those of us working within psychodynamic models, a much more intentional shift is needed, as previously explored in *Pink Therapy Volume 2* (Davies and Neal, 2000). If psychoanalytic therapies are to survive – and I want them to – they must evolve from the narrowly psychological to a more expansive psychosocial. This is vital to address the "longstanding tensions between the emancipatory and the conservative impulses within psychoanalysis" (Wadell *et al.*, 2020, p. xii) to seek some middle ground that deconstructs those assumed binaries and pathologies inherent in the theory. Some organisations, institutes, and publications do offer a more contemporary and inclusive exploratory model, if currently from the margins, theorising gender and sexuality as far more fluid than contrived and rigid traditional Oedipal interpretations might allow (Hertzmann and Newbigin, 2020). As GSRD therapists, we need to be knowledgeable about contemporary sexology, including the biopsychosocial processes of sex, and we keep up to date on specialist knowledge of gender, sex, and relationship diversities (Davies and Neves, 2023).

Group analysis, rooted in the psychoanalytic tradition, with emphasis on the social dimension, is a great model for those interested in deep exploratory work that is non-pathologising and particularly suited to minority clients. Jungian therapy too, in non-pathologising hands, has much to offer the GSRD population in its narrative of the brave and creative act of transgressing narrow gender and sexual boundaries on the road to individuation and its unearthing of a hidden shadow – that is, becoming more oneself.

Whilst exploratory therapies have traditionally been very comfortable working with the proximal stressors embedded within a client's personal psychology and nuclear family, they have often neglected the wider interpersonal and structural distal stressors of the social domain. The psychoanalytic tradition has had a "skew towards questions about aetiology (i.e. why is the person gay?) rather than focusing on meanings (i.e. what does it mean for this person to call herself gay?)" (Drescher, 2020, p. 172). I've wondered if psychoanalysis' instinct to pathologise those who don't adhere to essentialist norms of gender, sexuality, and relationships represents an avoidance of those darker, encapsulated elements of its orthodox analysts. Like religion for the child-abusing priest, does the psychoanalyst's chair provide cover for the unspeakable and unthinkable, asking us to "look over there!" at a deviance projected rather than examined? As analyst Collette Chiland wrote of working with transgender patients, "The analyst needs to work on himself or herself as much as on the patient" (2000, p. 33). A heteronormative and cisgender bias looms large in the work of many psychoanalytic clinicians, who, in their judgements on the non-normative, perhaps haven't fully explored their own psychosexuality (Newbigin, 2020).

As Susannah Izzard (2000) writes, "It is tragic that psychoanalysis lacked the capacity to self-reflect upon its attitude in the past, particularly when the intellectual understanding of them is clearly at its elbow" (p. 110). Conflating affirmative practice with non-exploratory work is a lazy and perhaps intentional way for aspects of the psychoanalytic community to undermine based on its perceived higher status in the profession. Rather than a defensive doubling down, some humility and efforts to reach across the aisle might be a better look, and vital if we are to move forward and unite the profession.

It's also true that non-psychodynamic therapists need to stop monstering all of psychoanalysis, given the major strides it has made to modernise. Contemporary psychoanalysis, as well as group analysis, are incredible lenses through which to understand the human experience, particularly in explaining how we might internalise projected transphobia or homophobia and for understanding the shame and self-hatred that is too often our "inheritance of growing up in a homophobic [and transphobic] world" (Izzard, 2000, p. 112). Poul Rohleder (2020) describes shame as

> a deeply painful experience of self-consciousness in the presence of others, where the individual feels exposed as having a real or imagined deficiency in their identity or self... this sense of exposure may leave the person feeling small, undesirable, worthless, fearing rejection, and wanting to hide from others.
>
> (p. 42)

Rohleder points out that psychoanalytic writing often focuses on the intrinsic component of shame without also giving consideration to the impact of "the trauma and damage caused by persistent social hostility and oppression, nor the shame to repeated parental, familial, and social rejection" (pp. 43–44).

A focus on shame can also shed light on why we might paradoxically inflict harm upon those within our own communities too, in the form of intra-community minority stress (Pachankis et al., 2020), and how shame becomes the under-explored shadow of the more visible pride in GSRD communities (McDermott et al., 2008) where, for example, it can be located in effeminate, brown and black, or disabled gay men as undesirable. As Elspeth Probyn (2000) writes, "pride operates as a necessity, an ontology of gay life that cannot admit its other" (p. 19). Psychoanalysis, through a minority stress lens, can help us to unpick and explore the complexity of shame as an intra-psychic, interpersonal, and social phenomenon. As GSRD therapists, we are trauma, grief and shame-informed through an understanding of how individual, collective, and cumulative trauma can manifest psychologically and physiologically, as well as recognising and helping to build resilience (Davies and Neves, 2023).

On Analytic "Neutrality"

One of the main critiques exploratory therapists make of affirmative therapies is that by addressing the political in our work we contaminate the transference or analytic neutrality. And yet, as many have said before, everything is tainted with the political. A therapist can't help but give themselves away – in their manner, clothing, skin colour, wedding ring, office decoration. Modality, even. Writing over thirty years ago, psychoanalyst Richard Isay (1986; in Izzard, 2000) provided a definition for an analytic neutrality that is both exploratory and affirmative. An

> undeviatingly uncritical, accepting therapeutic stance in which thoughtfulness, caring, and regard for the patient are essential. By so doing I am

not underestimating the value of the questioning, uncovering, and usual interpretive work of any analytic or dynamically oriented therapy. Nor am I advocating the unquestioning acceptance of the patient's views and values. Rather, I'm attempting to demonstrate that an attitude of positive regard makes analytic work possible because it enables the patient to express and analyse negative transference distortions from both the past and the present.

(p. 33)

With such a foundation, exploratory therapy arguably is *already* affirmative and doesn't prevent working in the negative transference; it actually supports it: "much can be fruitfully explored in the transference between heterosexual therapists and their gay [and trans] patients about difference and acceptance" (Rohleder, 2020, p. 56). Exploratory therapists working with GSRD populations "balance a commitment to neutrality *alongside* awareness of the impact of the real world" (Izzard, 2000, p. 115). As Bateman and Fonagy (2016) write,

Reassurance and support are necessary components of all therapies. ... These are not the same as agreeing with everything the patient says. ... A quiet nod of encouragement from the clinician may be all that is required. Positive and hopeful questioning provides some reassurance for the patient and demonstrates your desire to know and to understand.

(pp. 238–239)

This is all affirmation. So perhaps the issue is less with the practice and more the nomenclature. *Affirmation signals safety* to potential GSRD clients seeking therapy, but within the profession perhaps it is badly named. Affirmation can sound woolly, antithetical to the challenging work of therapy, and seems to antagonise some orthodox exploratory therapists. "GSRD therapy" is a better fit – it acknowledges that affirmation is foundational to the work, but that it is also so much more than affirmation.

And yet, for many potential clients, knowing the sexuality of their therapists is vitally important; it also can signal safety and a shared understanding. Some of us may advertise our own sexual and gender identities on our websites. Those of us from a psychodynamic background might be more subtle, saying that we work within the community without explicitly disclosing. When asked, many of us will disclose, depending on the work, the person in front of us and the timing. We might work initially with the meaning of the question for the client, but ultimately, withholding this important information is usually unnecessary. The blank screen is a conservative myth, and clinging to it in the name of analytic neutrality is essentially a selfish endeavour.

In Practice

Louis, a gay man in his mid-20s, came to see me wanting to explore his gender identity, having not felt safe to do this in previous attempts at therapy. He was a drag performer and would increasingly become depressed when he'd change out of drag after a show, in contrast to his peers who seemed to enjoy reverting to their gay male identities. Louis had previously had therapy in the NHS where it was suggested that his cross-dressing might be part of a sexual fetish, which was very shaming, and it had taken him years to seek further support. Coming across my website, he said he had felt I might be a better fit given my experience working within the community and had assumed I was a gay man. In the assessment I explained that the therapy I practice explores how past experiences might relate to the present difficulties and how the therapy relationships itself can be a useful way to explore how we relate to others. He seemed curious and keen. "Do you think I'm trans?", he asked me at the end of the first session. "I don't know", I said, "but I'm happy to explore it together".

We did explore how drag had become a relatively safe way for Louis to get in touch with what he felt to be his real self outside of the family home. Despite feeling female from a young age, his family were deeply conservative, and drag had been his compromise. But it had started to not feel enough – he was tired of performing off the stage. He asked me to call him Leila in one session to see how it felt. I could see the fear in his eyes that I might deny his wish. "Of course", I said, and his relief was instant.

Over many weeks, we explored who Leila was beyond the drag persona. As part of her coping mechanism, Leila had leant into a false gay male persona that was excessively affected and shallow. It had worked as a drag queen, but in her daily life it had lost her friends, and she had struggled in relationships. I introduced her to the concept of minority stress. She wept at the implications, and a wave of compassion hit her, as well as grief for time lost not being herself (both as a woman but also as an inauthentic man). By this point, I felt I'd earned enough trust that I was able to draw attention to when her affectations would kick in – she might be critical about my clothing or appearance or sometimes seem petulant and uninterested – which we came to see as a way for her to avoid deeper emotion, especially the shame.

Towards the end of our six months together, she was becoming clearer in her trans identity, beginning a social transition, and started to come out to her friends. She had feared coming out to her drag queen peers, certain that they would reject her. But they were very supportive. She left therapy grateful for the space to explore her gender in all its complexity, recognising how bigotry and discrimination had harmed her but also that her defensive responses to this in the present had been getting in the way of her getting close to others. Acknowledging that this was something she

*needed to continue working on, I referred her to a queer therapy group
to begin to explore some of these interpersonal issues in situ as well as to
build a sense of community.*

Most of the work involved a back-and-forth exploration of her gender in
session, playing with her identity in an iterative process that was unhurried,
deep, and humane. Some days, she would have doubts, and we explored
those too, but it was clear that she knew the final destination. I was simply
there to accompany her, perhaps check in on her thinking or feeling, sometimes to play devil's advocate, or be cast as her parents or peers, knowing she
could rally and rail against me, and I would not be pushed away.

Isn't this how most of us work already? An openness to welcoming the client as they are, without foreclosing on the direction or outcome of therapy. For
an exemplar of an exploratory and affirmative case study, please read *Crossing
Over* by Melanie Suchet (2011) – this moving work with a trans person (25
years ago now and by a clinician inexperienced in working with this population) shows the power of a deeply thoughtful, psychoanalytic therapy:

> [I] resist my urge to read everything I can on the subject, with the fantasy
> that I will understand it all. I know that for now I must stay close to my
> experience in the room with Rebecca. I have to let myself feel the anxiety
> of not knowing, of exploring unfamiliar territory, just as she is.
>
> (p. 217)

Some of you reading this might recognise that the exploratory or affirmative
aspects of your work might have been over-developed at the expense of the
other. I invite you to consider rebalancing this. After many years of assuming my exploratory training was sufficient to work from within the GSRD
community, I knew I had to re-educate myself on the importance of affirmative practice. Those from non-psychodynamic or less exploratory trainings
could enhance their work by seeking out a supervisor in this modality, and
psychodynamic therapists could benefit from additional CPD around minority stress, shame, and internalised oppression, such as with *Pink Therapy*.
To therapy training providers: please think about how to integrate GSRD
therapy within existing courses – it will pay dividends down the line – for
therapists, but more importantly, for GSRD clients needing safe and effective
exploratory and affirmative therapy.

Summary

I hope I have laid out clearly my wish – that we can unite the artificially
opposed tribes of exploration and affirmation and successfully blend them
into our work with GSRD clients. Or that it may affirm many of you already

working in this way. The minority stress framework is particularly helpful in attending to the psychosocial world we inhabit.

In championing exploratory therapy, we must not ignore the threat of the small number of therapists who seek cover for unethical conversion practices. Nor should we avoid exploration out of fear of our work being labelled as such, if we are confident that our work is also affirmative. In Jungian terms, perhaps affirmation and exploration represent the disavowed shadow of the other – projected elements that can be reclaimed to enrich and improve our work with this community.

Psychoanalyst Avgi Saketopoulou (2023) writes,

> Our ethical call is toward metapsychologies and clinical spaces that treat gender and sexual diversity not by simply making room for them or "accepting them", but by delighting in the pleasure of difference.
>
> (pp. 69–70)

As depth therapists working with GSRD clients we may need to move away from the classic conservators of psychoanalytic theories and join "the free thinkers, the agitators, the renegades" (Haslam, 2000, p. 12) in a forward-looking psychodynamic practice. GSRD therapy practices a commitment to social justice through an affirmative stance in line with anti-racism, queer, feminist and LGBTQ+ philosophy (Davies and Neves, 2023). We can represent social justice in actions on the picket line, but we can also be radical in our thinking and in our own introspection. Detractors and critics will say we have been captured by ideology, but theirs is the original ideological capture – binary and essentialist misunderstandings of complex human beings. As Langdridge (2007) writes, "the client's needs must not be subjugated to those of the therapist's particular political framework" (p. 39), regardless of whether they are coming from an exploratory or affirmative perspective. *Let our clients come as they are.*

In my view, therapists should be trained in GSRD therapy as part of initial training and seek a balance in clinical work between affirmation and exploration – *which need not be mutually exclusive* – to attend to both distal and proximal minority stress. Indeed, a truly curious and exploratory therapy *is* affirmative, not because it verbally and effusively validates a patient, in what seems to have become a caricature of affirmation (D'Angelo *et al.*, 2020), but because it takes LGBTQ+ patients as they are, not as seen through normative lenses and theories "that can foreclose further questioning if we allow [them] to take primacy in dictating our understanding of what we see" (Hertzmann and Newbigin, 2020, p. 10). Our role as psychodynamic therapists is to provide room for "the development of a particular kind of attention and reflection in a special setting" (ibid.) – this is the precious offer of psychoanalysis, if we can free it from its orthodox past.

GSRD clients need help to recognise that their experiences of discrimination and bigotry were not their fault, whilst their responses in the present are now their responsibility if they are to avoid further damaging themselves and their communities. GSRD is the creative synthesis of both affirmative and exploratory therapy, and finding a therapist to help us unpick this dual aspect of distress can be life-changing. If therapy training can internalise the message of GSRD therapy, the future of this corner of the profession, and for those brave, creative, and resilient souls it supports, is hopeful and bright.

Notes

1 A series of laws brought in by Prime Minister Margaret Thatcher in the UK in 1988 that banned teachers from "promoting" homosexuality in the classroom. It left many young queer people vulnerable to bullying and isolation (Baker, 2022).
2 In my doctoral thesis, I link my blood cancer to chronic minority stress.

References

Ashley, F. (2020) 'A critical commentary on "rapid-onset gender dysphoria"', *The Sociological Review*, 68(4), pp. 779–799. https://doi.org/10.1177/0038026120934693

Ashley, F. (2022) 'Interrogating gender-exploratory therapy', *Perspectives on Psychological Science*, 18(2), pp. 472–481. https://doi.org/10.1177/17456916221102325

Baker, P. (2022) *Outrageous!: The Story of Section 28 and Britain's Battle for LGBT Education*. London: Reaktion Books.

Bateman, A. and Fonagy, P. (2016) *Mentalization-based Treatment for Personality Disorders: A Practical Guide*. Oxford: Oxford University Press.

Bion, W. R. (1988) 'Notes on memory and desire', in Bott Spillius, E. (Ed.) *Melanie Klein Today: Developments in Theory and Practice, Volume 2: Mainly Practice*. London: Routledge, pp. 17–21.

Bruun, M. K. (2023) '"A factory of therapy": Accountability and the monitoring of psychological therapy in IAPT, *Anthropology & Medicine*, 30(4), pp. 313–329. https://doi.org/10.1080/13648470.2023.2217773

Burger, J. and Pachankis, J. E. (2024) 'State of the science: LGBTQ-affirmative psychotherapy', *Behavior Therapy*, 55(6), pp. 1318–1334. https://doi.org/10.1016/j.beth.2024.02.011

Chiland, C. (2000) 'The psychoanalyst and the transsexual patient', *The International Journal of Psychoanalysis*, 81(1), pp. 21–35. https://doi.org/10.1516/0020757001599483

Clark, D. (1987) *Loving Someone Gay*. Millbrae: Celestial Arts.

Contemporary Institute of Clinical Sexology. (2024) *Why CICS? Why choose the Contemporary Institute of Clinical Sexology?* Available at: https://www.theinstituteofsexology.org/why-cics

D'Angelo, R., Syrulnik, E., Ayad, S., Marchiano, L., Kenny, D. T. and Clarke, P. (2020) 'One size does not fit all: In support of psychotherapy for gender dysphoria',

Archives of Sexual Behavior, 50(1), pp. 7–16. https://doi.org/10.1007/s10508-020
-01844-2

Davies, D., and Neal, C. (Eds.). (1996). Pink therapy: A guide for counsellors and therapists working with lesbian, gay and bisexual clients. Open University Press.

Davies, D. and Neal, C. (2000) *Therapeutic Perspectives on Working with Lesbian, Gay, and Bisexual Clients*. Open University Press.

Davies, D. and Neves, S. (2023) 'Gender, sex and relationship diversity therapy', in Hanley, T. and Winter, L. A. (Eds.), *The SAGE Handbook of Counselling & Psychotherapy*. London: SAGE, p. 409.

Diamond, L. M. and Alley, J. (2022) 'Rethinking minority stress: A social safety perspective on the health effects of stigma in sexually-diverse and gender-diverse populations', *Neuroscience and Biobehavioral Reviews*, 138, p. 104720. https://doi.org/10.1016/j.neubiorev.2022.104720.

Drescher, J. (2015) 'Out of DSM: Depathologizing homosexuality', *Behavioral Sciences*, 5(4), pp. 565–575. https://doi.org/10.3390/bs5040565

Drescher, J. (2020) 'From bisexuality to intersexuality', in Hertzmann, L. and Newbigin, J. (Eds.), *Sexuality and Gender Now: Moving Beyond Heteronormativity*. London: Routledge, pp. 167–209.

Foulkes, S. H. (1948) *Introduction to Group-analytic Psychotherapy*. London: Heinemann Medical Books.

Haslam, D. (2000) 'Analytical psychology', in Davies, D. and Neal, C. (Eds.), *Therapeutic Perspectives on Working with Lesbian, Gay, and Bisexual Clients*. Open University Press, pp. 5–23.

Hertzmann, L. and Newbigin, J. (2020) *Sexuality and Gender Now: Moving Beyond Heteronormativity*. London: Routledge.

Isay, R. A. (1986) 'On the analytic therapy of gay men', in Silverstein, C. (Ed.), Contemporary perspectives on psychotherapy with lesbians and gay men. Springer, pp. 139–155.

Izzard, S. (2000) 'Psychoanalytic psychotherapy', in Davies D. and Neal, C. (Eds.) *Therapeutic Perspectives on Working with Lesbian, Gay, and Bisexual Clients*. Open University Press, pp. 106–119.

Jenkins, P. and Panozzo, D. (2024) '"Ethical care in secret": Qualitative data from an international survey of exploratory therapists working with gender-questioning clients', *Journal of Sex & Marital Therapy*, 50(5), pp. 557–582. https://doi.org/10.1080/0092623x.2024.2329761

Langdridge, D. (2007) 'Gay affirmative therapy: A theoretical framework and defence', *Journal of Gay & Lesbian Psychotherapy*, 11(1–2), pp. 27–43. https://doi.org/10.1300/j236v11n01_03

Malyon, A. K. (1982) 'Biphasic aspects of homosexual identity formation', *Psychotherapy: Theory, Research & Practice*, 19(3), pp. 335–340. https://doi.org/10.1037/h0088444

Marks, D. F. (2018) 'IAPT under the microscope', *Journal of Health Psychology*, 23(9), pp. 1131–1135. https://doi.org/10.1177/1359105318781872

McDermott, E., Roen, K. and Scourfield, J. (2008) 'Avoiding shame: Young LGBT people, homophobia and self-destructive behaviours', *Culture, Health & Sexuality*, 10(8), pp. 815–829. https://doi.org/10.1080/13691050802380974

Meyer, I. H. (1995) 'Minority stress and mental health in gay men', *Journal of Health and Social Behavior*, 36(1), p. 38. https://doi.org/10.2307/2137286

Meyer, I. H. (2003) 'Prejudice, social stress, and mental health in lesbian, gay, and bisexual populations: Conceptual issues and research evidence', *Psychological Bulletin*, 129(5), pp. 674–697. https://doi.org/10.1037/0033-2909.129.5.674

Meyer, I. H. and Frost, D. M. (2012), 'Minority stress and the health of sexual minorities', in D'Augelli, A. R. and Patterson, C. J. (Eds.), *Handbook of Psychology and Sexual Orientation*. Oxford University Press, pp. 252–266.

Mollitt, P. C. (2022) 'Exploring cisgender therapists' attitudes towards, and experience of, working with trans people in the United Kingdom', *Counselling and Psychotherapy Research*, 22(4), pp. 1013–1029. https://doi.org/10.1002/capr .12559

Newbigin, J. (2020) 'Sex and the consulting room', in Hertzmann, L. and Newbigin, J. (Eds.), *Sexuality and Gender Now: Moving Beyond Heteronormativity*. London: Routledge, pp. 19–39.

Pachankis, J. E., Clark, K. A., Burton, C. L., Hughto, J. M. W., Bränström, R. and Keene, D. E. (2020) 'Sex, status, competition, and exclusion: Intraminority stress from within the gay community and gay and bisexual men's mental health', *Journal of Personality and Social Psychology*, 119(3), pp. 713–740. https://doi.org /10.1037/pspp0000282

Pachankis, J. E. and Goldfried, M. R. (2004) 'Clinical issues in working with lesbian, gay, and bisexual clients', *Psychotherapy: Theory, Research, Practice, Training*, 41(3), pp. 227–246.

Probyn, E. (2000) 'Sporting bodies: Dynamics of shame and pride', *Body & Society*, 6(1), pp. 13–28. https://doi.org/10.1177/1357034x00006001002

Rodriguez-Seijas, C., Morgan, T. A. and Zimmerman, M. (2021) 'A population-based examination of criterion-level disparities in the diagnosis of borderline personality disorder among sexual minority adults', *Assessment*, 28(4), pp. 1097–1109. https://doi.org/10.1177/1073191121991922

Rodriguez-Seijas, C., Morgan, T. A. and Zimmerman, M. (2024), 'Transgender and gender diverse patients are diagnosed with borderline personality disorder more frequently than cisgender patients regardless of personality pathology', *Transgender Health*, 9(6), pp. 554–565. https://doi.org/10.1089/trgh.2023.0062

Rohleder, P. (2020) 'Homophobia, heteronormativity, and shame', in Hertzmann, L. and Newbigin, J. (Eds.), *Sexuality and Gender Now: Moving Beyond Heteronormativity*. London: Routledge, pp. 40–56.

Ruffalo, M. L. [@MarkLRuffalo]. (2024, February 21). It is a sad truth that there now exist two types of therapists: Those who believe that psychotherapy is a critical self-examination aimed at changing something about the individual person. Those who believe psychotherapy is simply an exercise in validation. *Choose Wisely*. X. https://x.com/MarkLRuffalo/status/1760408807857856674.

Saketopoulou, A. (2023) *Sexuality Beyond Consent: Risk, Race, Traumatophilia*. New York: New York University Press.

Shedler, J. (2010) 'The efficacy of psychodynamic psychotherapy', *American Psychologist*, 65(2), pp. 98–109. https://doi.org/10.1037/a0018378

Stevenson, S. (2022) 'The impact of homophobic trauma on gay men', *Group Analysis*, 56(1), pp. 3–27. https://doi.org/10.1177/05333164221121057.

Suchet, M. (2011) 'Crossing over', in Hertzmann, L. and Newbigin, J. (Eds.), *Sexuality and Gender Now: Moving Beyond Heteronormativity*. London: Routledge, pp. 213–239.

Wadell, M., Jocelyn, C. and Stratton, K. (2020) 'Series editors' preface', in Hertzmann, L. and Newbigin, J. (Eds.), *Sexuality and Gender Now: Moving Beyond Heteronormativity*. London: Routledge, pp. xi–xiii.

Chapter 6

Staring at Shadows

Karen Pollock

Introduction

This chapter examines the therapist's multifaceted role in acknowledging and addressing the profound impact of societal norms on individual well-being. Drawing upon Plato's Allegory of the Cave, it posits that normative identities, often unconsciously adopted, can function as restrictive "chains" or obscuring "shadows", limiting individuals' awareness of their authentic selves and potential. The exploration then focuses on the person-centred approach, a cornerstone of humanistic psychology, and Carl Rogers' foundational concept of the actualising tendency – the innate human drive towards growth, fulfilment, and self-realisation. It will underscore the ethical responsibility of therapists to actively recognise and address the harm inflicted by systemic societal oppression on individuals holding non-normative identities.

What Is the Role of a Therapist?

There are as many answers to that question as stars in the sky. Many have tried to find an answer because it involves questions far older than the practice of the listening professions. Questions about our role as humans, both alone and in relationships with others, questions that are not limited to one particular gender, sex, or way of doing relationships. Questions from Plato to Hamlet, via *Buffy the Vampire Slayer* and *The Lord of the Rings,* circle around like crows in the evening sky, wheeling and turning above the trees.

> *Would he, instead, believe that the shadows he formerly knew were more real than the objects now being shown to him?*
> Plato. "The Allegory of the Cave" The Republic, Book Seven. 2007

> What is the meaning of being me?
> What is good?
> What is normal?
> What is acceptable?
> What is the point or purpose of existence?

DOI: 10.4324/9781003530848-9

And perhaps most importantly, what do we do when the answers to these questions contradict and collide?

For many centuries, before Hegel conceived his Phenomenology or Freud projected his Neurosis, these questions belonged to the realms of Philosophy and Theology. So the first attempts to answer them lie back in the depths of time we now call myth and legend.

In *The Republic*, book 8, Plato introduces one of the most famous thought experiments in the history of philosophy. Imagine people who have lived their entire lives staring at the back wall of a cave, unable to move their heads due to iron chains. Their only experience of the world is shadows cast by everything behind them. Their environment is constructed and managed to control their vision.

One of the arguments in the dialogue is that if you free one of the cave inhabitants, they would initially feel that the shadows were real. If they tried to explain the situation to those still chained, they would be met with rejection, perhaps even ridicule. As Plato explains, the freed captive might object to or become agitated at the idea of looking at the real light of the sun outside the cave.

Plato did not intend to provide a metaphor for the structural normativities which each one of us absorbs from birth in our own chains, making our own sense from the shadows cast by gender, race, class, neurotype, sexuality, disability, and a host of other intersecting, and often unnamed factors. Still, his analogy is so close to our reality that it's more than helpful. It's a reminder that dragging individuals into the light may not be the best strategy, even if we know what the light is, and that insight is neither new nor original to therapy as a profession.

The traditional adoption of the core condition of respect in therapy has been repeatedly reframed as our frames of reference have changed, but the principles remain the same. In the ground-breaking book *Pink Therapy* (Davies & Neal, 1996), which challenged normativity via a new paradigm, Dominic Davies wrote of "the core condition of respect" (p. 26). Will the cave's inhabitants respect the freed person who tells them of sunlight, rivers, trees, and streams? Or will they "know" that these are simply fictions of the imagination? Respect means "becoming a companion, not a tour guide" (p. 27) if we are not to resemble the agents Plato has Socrates imagine, dragging the prisoners from the cave towards the light. Davies may have been breaking new ground, but only by being even more fundamentally in opposition to the idea of the therapist as an expert in the client's own experience or, in Plato's analogy, the expert in what is the light.

Every iteration of The Cave asks us, "If I know they are chained and still staring at shadows, is it not my role to liberate them, speak the truth, explain the reality to help them break free?" The answer that comes back, freed from Plato's analogy and world view, is "How do you know you are not simply staring at your own shadows, unable to see your chains?" What if the light you want to direct the freed prisoner to look at is another elaborate trap within another, larger cave whose existence you are unaware of?

Suppose you have an uncomfortable emotional response to the idea that you might exist in your Platonic cave and the uncertainty it implies. In that case, I invite you to see this as an excellent opportunity. Sit with these feelings, write, think, draw, or otherwise (safely) express them. Put this book down if you need to, take a breath and feel your body, allowing all emotions to develop to trace their origins and roots before you continue. By doing so, you make space for what you feel without judgement to trace their origins and roots before you continue, for in doing so, you make space for what you feel without judgement, whilst at the same time, accepting that you cannot engage openly from a defensive or shame-filled space.

Let those feelings mature and follow them from the first roots to the spreading branches. As Rogers (1967, p. 18) says in the introduction to *On Becoming a Person*:

> *understanding is risky. If I let myself understand another person, I might be challenged by that understanding.*

Working with people in therapy has cemented for me the importance of a belief in the actualising tendency, not as a theoretical ivory tower stance but a praxis, the heart, as it were, of the approach, the foundation on which the core conditions are built. The actualising tendency is both a belief and an attitude towards others. It can present a challenge as an active choice in encountering others. In his book *The Art of Loving*, Erich Fromm (1958), a German psychoanalyst and theorist writing in the mid-twentieth century, explores the practice of love, not as a feeling but as a conscious choice to make:

> *Love isn't something natural. Rather, it requires discipline, concentration, patience, faith, and the overcoming of narcissism. It isn't a feeling, it is a practice.*

(p. 57)

The belief in the actualising tendency, like the conscious practice of love, the idea that every one of us can grow towards the light, demands trust on a level which mirrors that a child gives their parent – with the reversal here of the usual therapeutic parental projections so often discussed, that the client idealises the therapist as a parental figure. In the therapy room, we must also be like the child. The therapist has to believe in the person in therapy as agentic and actualising, much like a child feels their parent is capable of anything. We must have the child's wonder, the belief in infinite possibility, as we follow this fellow human being on their journey of discovery.

The new challenge here, as described by Mick Cooper (2019), is that, bluntly, clients "fuck up". They harm themselves and others, their actualising tendency appears to wither and die, and what are we to do then?

What Happens When the Actualising Tendency Is Killed?

For much of the history of therapy, being homosexual has been seen as a mental illness which could be treated. It is important to note that *homosexuality* was generally used as an umbrella term and included multisexual identities, other queer identities, although not typically asexual spectrum ones, and some expressions of gender diversity, although not all. In many ways, "homosexuality" was a catch-all used to mean not heteronormative, and how the degree of digression from normativity was responded to very often depended on other intersections of identity, particularly class, neurostyle, and race. Being one's best self was to be cisgender, heterosexual, and, most of all, normative, where being "normative" was determined by those with the most power and privilege at any given moment.

Sometimes, just like a dysfunctional family, the therapeutic family likes to pretend that its own intergenerational trauma does not exist. No one talks about the uncle or the grandmother whose behaviour was excused because that was "just her", and we are told, all is in the past, as if their legacy is not part of the here and now. Psychotherapy not only decided that it could treat gender, sex, and relationship diversity (GSRD) people and cure them of their differences, but it also decided it should. As the children, grandchildren and great-grandchildren of that legacy, we have to be honest about where we have come from, even if it would be easier to simply "forget" and collectively dissociate from the past. This means that abuse is free to continue, just as in a system, be it familial or societal, which denies its abusive past. Ask any neurodivergent person who has applied behavioural therapy forced on them or any trans person denied gender-affirming treatment how far we have come from the "legacy" of treating non-normative identities as illnesses to be fixed. The word legacy, with its implications of past, not present, will soon sound hollow.

Non-normative gender, sex, and relationship identities were pathologised, and it was believed, particularly with the development of behaviourist approaches to psychotherapy, that these identities could be changed – what came to be known as conversion therapy. The belief that being non-normative was a defect that needed to be fixed was so strong and pervasive that it was assumed to be a scientific fact. As queer people, we feel this in our bones; it's the definition of lived experience when the idea that we are somehow "wrong" is one so strong. In the data set, which is my own life, I still remember being different as a teenager, meaning I was broken in an unfixable way.

Whilst "homosexuality" was removed from the DSM in 1973, the ICD in 1990—a day marked each year on May 17th by IDAHOBIT (The International

Day Against Homophobia, Biphobia, Intersexphobia, and Transphobia)—not only did "disorders of sexual orientation" remain alongside a slew of new gender identity categories, but the attitudes which lay behind the beliefs persisted, both in the therapeutic and the wider world. I would argue that the pathologisation of identity does not cease simply because it no longer has a code in medical textbooks. In a separate but parallel field of neurodiversity, this has been described as the pathology paradigm. First coined by Dr Nick Walker (2016), the pathology paradigm frames a difference as lesser and needing to be fixed. One might say it is not just trying to refute that anything but the Platonic cave exists, but actively working to strengthen, or reattach the chains which keep you looking only at the shadows. Indeed, in the case of some forms of therapy and treatment, it punishes those who even dare to question if the shadows are all that exists.

Dr Walker was exploring how attitudes to autism and other forms of neurodiversity were seen as lesser due to it being a deficit or disease. Implicit in the pathology paradigm is the idea that disease must be cured, the deficit fixed, and that deviation from the norm, like a broken leg, must be straightened (pun intended).

> The pathology paradigm starts from the assumption that significant divergences from dominant sociocultural norms of cognition and embodiment represent some form of deficit, defect, or pathology. In other words, the pathology paradigm divides the spectrum of human cognitive/embodied performance into "normal" and "other than normal", with "normal" implicitly privileged as the superior and desirable state.
>
> (Walker & Raymaker, 2021, p. 6)

The pathology paradigm does not just tell other people you know what shadows they can see cast on cave walls; it tells them they are wrong if they describe something else. Imagine seeing shapes in the clouds: this one a bee, that a mountain, and over there a horse, rearing, its mane blowing wild in the wind.

> You turn to your companion and say, "Do you see that horse in the clouds?"
>
> "No", they reply, "There is no shape, you are wrong".
>
> Not different – but wrong.

Case Notes from the Cave – Seeing the Wrong Shapes in the Clouds

Persephone is close to giving up on therapy. In the last session, she tried to explain how distant she felt from other people's experiences by talking about how *Buffy the Vampire Slayer* felt when she returned from the grave in series 6 of the show. This series has always spoken to Persephone as the eponymous hero struggles to perform the parts of sister, friend, lover, and slayer expected of her, but never feels like the performance is adequate, feeling broken, and like a failure.

Persephone's therapist had listened, empathised, and asked why she found it easier to talk about a show than about herself.

A client is told they are seeing the wrong shapes, despite their neurostyle, meaning it is the best way they can express their experience authentically and meaningfully. There is empathy, perhaps even understanding, but is there respect?

Even after the mental illness of homosexuality was removed from the textbooks, the pathologisation of GSRD behaviours and/or identities continued. It continues today, with the Cass review (Cass, 2024) into Paediatric Gender Care in the UK (Horton, 2024). The report framed puberty blockers as a "bad thing" because young people who take them may continue on their gender journey in exploring gender diversity and non-cisnormative ways of being. The pathologisation was so strong that the author of the paper could not see being trans as anything but a negative outcome for the young people in question (Grijseels, 2024).

Internally held beliefs about the defect or deficit in another are not magically erased by the change in the DSM and ICD. They can be held, both consciously and unconsciously, by members of majority or minority communities. Indeed, within the LGBTQ+ communities, some believe that LGB should be separated from the T, as is evident on social media platforms. Sometimes, they express themselves in law, in banter in a bar, and it is the water we all swim in, even if we are part of those communities. This is one of the reasons that concepts such as heteronormativity and cisnormativity are as crucial in developing our understanding as terms like heterosexual and cisgender. One can be gay, queer, non-monogamous or trans, and heteronormative and/or cisnormative. Sometimes, this is simply who you are; sometimes, this is about safety, and often, it is a dance between the two that involves compromise and curtailment.

Passing, as in appearing to be as normative as you can, can be the breathing apparatus by which some people swim through the sewage. Let me be clear here, this is not a judgement, but normativity is very dependent on class, race, gender presentation, not being disabled, neurostyle, and a host of other factors. Rubin (1993) in her discussion of sex hierarchies, developed *the charmed circle,* describing the many different ways individuals could be excluded from the protections afforded to the mainstream, those deemed normative in how they engaged with sex. M.J. Barker (2018) explored *the charmed circle* in their book *The Psychology of Sex* and turned it around, looking instead at placing consent and communication at the centre. It was an attempt to ask what a non-pathologising model that placed ethical consent at the centre would look like. What would swimming in the clear waters rather than the pollution of pathologisation be like?

This polluted water of believing that non-normativity is a deficit or defect that needs to be corrected impacts all people's individual and collective life experiences. The *minority stress model,* first proposed by Meyer (1995), considered the effect of swimming in this polluted water on the mental health of gay men, and it has since become a model that has been applied to different parts of the GSRD world. It recognised that the attitudes towards GSRD people and the pathologisation of GSRD identities lead to adverse mental health outcomes. It was a vital step towards depathologisation, saying the defect is in broader society, not the GSRD individual.

Case Notes from the Cave: Seeing the Wrong Shapes in the Clouds

Orpheus has given up on therapy. They brought their fear of death and ageing after the death of a parent. They explained to their therapist, carefully chosen as GSRD, affirming how they had a relationship based on living apart together, and how it worked best for their particular intersections of kink and autism. Their therapist, blinded by their shadows, talked of polyamory, a relationship style that wasn't relevant to Orpheus, and how liberating it was. Orpheus felt like they could never have space to be themselves in therapy, as the shape of their life did not fit the queer normativities expected by their therapist.

This is not a binary split of queer therapist good, cis het bad. Imposing our own normativities, feeling safe when we do so, and taking space from our clients when it happens is something that all of us can consciously or unconsciously do. Queer paternalism is still paternalism.

What if Society Kills the Self-actualising Tendency?

Carl Rogers explicitly made this barrier to self-actualisation clear in *On Becoming a Person* (1967). According to Rogers, self-actualising tendencies can be hindered by external conditions of worth imposed by society, family, and peers. When individuals internalise these conditions, they may stray from their true selves, leading to incongruence between their self-concept and experiences.

Something he famously ignored, then learnt from as he took the risk to understand another, is captured in his two interviews with an African American client in 1977 and 1984.

In the first recorded session, Rogers seems oblivious to the client's introduction of race, his experiences as a black man in America, and how these have shaped him.

Moodley et al. (2000) write:

These "invitations" by the client to deconstruct racial/psychological iden-
tity are not taken up by the therapist.

(p. 359)

Watching with modern eyes, one of the most striking things about the first
recording is Rogers' narrative voice, as he "interprets" and speaks over the
client, the white voice given primacy over the black. We, of course, cannot
say if this is a blind spot, resistance, shame, a combination of all three, or
other unknown factors since we cannot ask Rogers himself. We can com-
pare with the 1984 recording of a different session, where the experience of
race, both outside and inside the therapy room, is both named and explored.
Growth has occurred by taking the risk of vulnerability and acknowledging
that the experiences of marginalised clients are not left in the therapist's waiting room, when instead, they are amplified and placed under the microscope.

Sometimes, we accept that shadows are being cast upon the wall, even
accepting that the shapes the person is describing are their experience.
However, the need to reassure ourselves about the reality of our own shadow
world can take over, as we *"shadows plain"* – if you will forgive a neologism.

Rogers believed the flaws came from him, not his application of the person-centred approach. His failure to address race in the therapy room did
come from his own experiences, biases and beliefs as a white American of
his gender, class, and background. However, what if those flaws and blind
spots are inherent to us all and prevent the person-centred approach from
being fully realised when working with those within society who are being
marginalised?

Notice here I say "are being", not "were". This distinction matters;
oppression is an active process, not a passive one, and is not inherent to some
identities or attitudes. For someone to be marginalised, someone else has to
be active in the process of marginalisation. For some people to be closer to
the safe centre, others have to be pushed to the side, teetering on the edge,
and for some, falling off the sides into the fathomless abyss. Oppression is
not gravity or a weak magnetic force. It does not "just" happen or mysteri-
ously manifest in society.

We cannot know what changed for Roger between 1977 and 1984, but
we can observe that change took place, a profound change that impacted
how he worked with marginalised clients. He was active, not accepting the
gravitational force of oppression but taking the risk of change.

For the majority of people reading this, you will have been brought up in a
society which has apparent hierarchies of race, gender, dis/ability, neurostyle,
religion, body type, and age, where some genders, sexualities, and relationship styles are considered more acceptable than others.

If this previous paragraph also causes a defensive or rejecting reaction, again sit with that feeling, explore what provokes it, and trace the origins and wellsprings of the response.

Living within these hierarchies, we consciously and unconsciously absorb from birth the values, the norms and the disapproval of the aberrant. As Foucault (1977) discusses in *Discipline and Punish*

> *The judges of normality are present everywhere. We are in the society of the teacher-judge, the doctor-judge, the educator-judge, the "social worker"-judge; it is on them that the universal reign of the normative is based, and each individual, wherever he may find himself, subjects to it his body, his gestures, his behaviour, his aptitudes, his achievements.*
>
> (p. 304)

We judge others and ourselves, not by comparing one another, although that happens too, but in the sense of the judge, jury, and executioner. The judge we carry within learns the laws from birth, from storybooks and t-shirts, from overheard conversations and "jokes" on TV. And it is a hanging judge, who, without active work to uncover and challenge it, will project its judgements outward and inwards, in an interplay of oppression and domination.

In his book *Empire of Normality: Neurodiversity and Capitalism,* Robert Chapman (2024) explores how normativity is imposed as a tool of capitalist control. Chapman argues that before the rise of capitalism and the Industrial Revolution, *normal* was not a desired medical norm, as communities did not have to practise machine-like efficiency. It can never be ignored that the origins of time and motion studies and their place in capitalism are with enslaved peoples in America. "*Normal*" became a tool with which one was judged, and normality was the desire projected onto all so they could enhance profits.

Like a ravenous caterpillar, corporations will gobble up those who can be deemed normal enough – as I argued earlier, "normal" is always in the gift of those with power and privilege. Pinkwashing is a term often used by LGBTQ people to describe how large corporations will cover themselves in rainbows during Pride Month to sell products, with little concern for LGBTQ issues the rest of the year. Inherent in the idea of pinkwashing is that only the normative gays are acceptable, but, after all, they are more likely to be the consumers with pink pounds burning a hole in their pocket.

When we attempt as person-centred counsellors to sit opposite the client, without understanding that all those judges of Foucault, or imperialists of normality of Chapman, also sit within us, we allow the judgements to fill the space and create something between therapist and client which poisons the actualising tendency. One of the most challenging questions for all therapists is our role if we know harm is occurring. If we expand the idea of harm here to the harm caused by being a marginalised person in a society that privileges some ways of being over others, what is our role as therapists in the face of that harm?

The idea that you may have actively oppressed or caused harm may be a challenging thought for you, particularly if you share some identities with those who more often inhabit the safe centre rather than the precarious edges of society. Perhaps you want to say that you have never personally harmed anyone or actively oppressed, even if you are white, cisgender, abled, heterosexual, monogamous, and neurotypical. This is where the metaphor of the ocean we are all swimming in may be helpful. You did not choose where you were swimming. You may oppose the dumping of sewage, the pollution of prejudice, but the water still surrounds all of us, and some are drowning.

As I write, I am very aware of my presence throughout this chapter as I swim in the same waters. Echoing the therapeutic relationship, the connection between writer and reader comprises disclosure, interconnection, transference, and projection.

I am a white, neurodivergent, autistic person of working-class origins, currently middle-class, non-binary, queer from the global north. My ancestral background includes migration from Ireland and Scotland, and the many complexities that poverty, addiction, barriers to education, and not belonging to the majority religion bring.

My process of moving from a pure person-centred approach to being anti-oppressive included recognising my position in the room, both under and over the clients I was working with. What we both bring meets, like the conjunction of two streams to make the mighty river called therapy. It also was a process that was, and is, rooted in the knowledge of harm done to me by the world, including the world of therapy. So, this chapter is not a you and I chapter but a "we" chapter. I am not the authority; I am the pilgrim seeking to understand where therapy fails us and where it can be made better.

It may seem unusual to only introduce the GSRD model almost two-thirds of the way into a chapter now. Still, those three questions are the core of the argument that the current person-centred model goes very far but not far enough when working with gender, sex, and relationship-diverse clients. The seven core components of the GSRD model are deliberately not linear; they are not equations. Instead, it is helpful to think of it as a series of water filters to clear the pollution, which is turning the water from crystal clear to murky brown.

Sometimes, we are so used to swimming in that murk that it has become how things are. We edit out the muck and dirt, or even believe it does not harm, simply what water looks like. We are, of course, entitled to make that choice. However, as therapists, we must ask a question many of us shy away from, preferring to believe the shadows are real.

What if the Therapist Kills the Actualising Tendency?

If we just learn theory, we may have academic expertise, but it does not mean we have respect. We can fall into the trap of different means that are wrong, which leads to the pathology paradigm as described by Walker. This can be a particular problem when so much of the academic literature has been produced by people who have not acknowledged their own implicit and explicit biases. The same can be the case for therapists working with GSRD communities. This is why the inclusion of fostering joy is so vital to the GSRD model. Many people can theoretically understand why being aware of barriers/structural oppression can help a therapist work better with marginalised clients. Knowing about intersectionality and the impact of multiple oppressions improves our ability to empathise and offer compassion. A grounding in contemporary sexology should challenge those normativities which are so often accepted as fact when they are just prejudice hidden in plain sight.

Joy is a feeling; it is "heart", not "head". It says not that it is "ok" to be GSRD-identified, but that it is a wonder and glorious thing. Joy overturns the pathologisation of GSRD identities and instead makes space for them to be tall trees growing in the forest, this one a birch, this one an elm, this one an oak, all different, but all celebrated parts of the whole.

If, as a therapist, we can say, "Things might have been different, but they could not have been better" (Tolkien, 2016, p. 58), and believe it with our hearts, not just our minds – then we offer something truly radical to our clients, all of them, not just a ghetto designed for those we define as different when we mean wrong. The radical overturning of the prison of normativities when we accept that we each are simply trying to make sense of shadows is revolutionary. We offer them clear water in which they can dive without fear and return to the surface with the treasures they value.

Returning to where we started, accepting difference not in a reserved or defensive way, not with shame or anger, but as a thing of joy, transforming the therapeutic relationship, and lying at the heart of GSRD therapy. It does not erase the prejudice, the harms, the abuses; instead, it makes space for both/and in a world that is so often either/or.

References

Barker, M.J. (2018) *The Psychology of Sex*. London: Routledge.

Cass, H. (2024) Independent review of gender identity services for children and young people: Final report (Cass Report). *Cass Review*. Available at: https://coilink.org/20.500.12592/95x6gzf (Accessed: 20 May 2025).

Chapman, R. (2024) *Empire of Normality: Neurodiversity and Capitalism*. London: Pluto Press.

Cooper, M. (2019) *Integrating Counselling & Psychotherapy: Directionality, Synergy and Social Change*. London: Sage.

It could be argued that 'from a radical queer perspective *(that GSRD)*, people inhabit and experience *(and perform)* the disturbance and distress that has been given to them by the world around them' (Lea, 2020, p. 16). Much of the external societal hatred, shame, and negativity becomes internalised, whereby people who identify as GSRD find themselves doing our oppressors' work and may target our distress towards ourselves and our uniqueness.

It can be helpful in clinical work with GSRD people who are experiencing self-harm and/or urges to end their life to discuss and provide psychoeducation regarding these LGBTQ+ and GSRD theories formulating self-harm and suicidality, in line with *'Understanding the specific adverse effects of oppression'* and *'Integrating core GSRD theories'* from the seven core components of GSRD therapy.

Dialectical Behaviour Therapy (DBT)

Professor Marsha Linehan (1993a, 1993b, 2015) developed DBT, a third-wave cognitive behavioural therapy, which emphasises the inclusion of mindfulness and acceptance, as well as change-focused strategies. DBT is an evidence-based treatment focusing on the 'dialectic' of change and acceptance to help a person create a life worth living. DBT is fundamentally a therapy for working with self-harm and suicidality. It was initially developed to work with people with a diagnosis of Borderline Personality Disorder (BPD) (DSM-5, APA, 2013) or Emotionally Unstable Personality Disorder (EUPD) (ICD-10, WHO, 2004) with a specific focus on reducing emotion dysregulation, self-harm and suicidal behaviours (DeCou *et al.*, 2019; Oud *et al.*, 2018, Miga *et al.*, 2019; Panos *et al.*, 2014).

> *DBT began as, and still remains, a treatment for chronic suicidal behaviour. As such, DBT has features that may be more broadly applicable to the treatment of recurrent suicidal behaviour, wherever it occurs, and not just in the context of BPD.*
>
> (Swales, 2020, p. 5).

Existing studies that have explored individuals' experiences of DBT have discussed relationships that supported change, developing self-efficacy, a shift in perspectives, DBT causing positive changes, better control of emotions and improved relationships with others (Gillespie *et al.*, 2022; Little *et al.*, 2018).

Lived Experience of Distress

On the 23rd of June 2011, Marsha Linehan shared in the *New York Times* (NYT) her own lived experience of distress and of receiving a diagnosis of BPD.

I honestly didn't realize at the time that I was dealing with myself. But I suppose it's true that I developed a therapy that provides the things I needed for so many years and never got.

(Linehan, 2011)

Educating clients about Marsha's journey and how her lived experience led her to develop DBT may be beneficial.

The Biosocial Theory in DBT

A fundamental theoretical construct in DBT is the biosocial theory developed by Linehan (1993a), which proposes that the interaction between biological vulnerabilities and an invalidating environment can create and explain the development of emotional, relational, and identity-based difficulties associated with BPD/EUPD.

Biological and Emotional Vulnerability: Some people are born with a particular temperament, whereby they have a biological vulnerability, such that they experience high sensitivity and reactivity to emotional experiences. This immediate emotional reaction and high emotional arousal 'switches off' thinking. These emotions may last for a long time with a slow return to the emotional baseline, meaning the person is primed to respond to the next emotional stimuli in the environment.

Social and the Invalidating Environment: The experience of being parented in the family situation may harm those predisposed to emotional vulnerabilities. The person's experiences and communications in the home may be viewed as unimportant, strange, or flawed in some way. The child is invalidated and possibly punished, especially when behaviour contravenes family or societal norms. Unfortunately, this repeated experience of invalidation leads the individual to mistrust their own cognitive, emotional, and relational experiences. This internalised self-invalidation means the person is constantly seeking others and the external world to validate or invalidate their personhood.

Queering the Biosocial Theory in DBT

It could be argued that a society saturated in and perpetuating historical, current, and institutional transphobia, biphobia, homophobia, and cis-heterosexist values of monogamy represents an extremely invalidating environment.

belonging to one or more minoritised groups may be sufficient alone to transact with an invalidating and oppressive environment to result in difficulties with emotion dysregulation.

(Camp, 2023a, p. 227)

In Linehan's (1993a) first description of invalidating environments, it was clear she was theorising about the invalidating impacts of abuse on the developing child, e.g. developmental trauma and childhood sexual abuse. She also viewed societal discrimination, e.g. misogyny, as representing an example of an extreme invalidating environment, leading to harm, invalidation and distress.

Utilising and understanding the component of *'Being trauma, grief and shame-informed'* within GSRD therapy is essential here. It could be speculated that GSRD people are overtly and covertly socialised into believing that aspects of themselves are invalid, unlovable, and unacceptable. It is impossible for these messages and experiences not to be digested and internalised into the psyche. Specifically, GSRD people may experience thwarted growth of their emotional, cognitive, and relational skills and capabilities, as well as a lack of sureness about themselves or identity that is free of shame. When everything around them says they are wrong, the numerous' coming outs' is a level of defiance and self-belief against an invalidating societal environment. For these reasons, we must validate and be fiercely compassionate with GSRD people at all clinical work opportunities.

Furthermore, the physical, psychological, and emotional energy expended to maintain vigilance to ensure safety in the world cannot be ignored (Diamond et al., 2022). An idea exists that GSRD people are *'hyper-vigilant,'* as opposed to *functionally vigilant* in a world that has, and may continue, to harm them. This notion must be challenged as the privileged heterosexist attack that it is to continue to enact the *'Practicing a commitment to social justice'* within the therapy room, as described within the seven core components of GSRD therapy.

When offering DBT-informed work, it will be necessary to socialise and educate people about the biosocial theory in DBT and how this links to other relevant GSRD theories. This will be especially important for helping people to formulate and understand how their difficulties developed and how they may be being maintained. For example, *'Knowing contemporary sexology'* is another core component of GSRD therapy. This will help clinicians understand sexual and sexualised behaviour within a contemporary sexology framework rather than (or alongside) a DBT-informed perspective on what the function of sexuality and sexual behaviour is for an individual. Knowing contemporary sexology alongside the principles and philosophy of DBT allows for a holistic and non-pathologising understanding of human sexuality and desire.

Comprehensive Full Programme DBT and Modes of Treatment

Within DBT, there is an attempt to focus on the behavioural difficulties and patterns experienced by people rather than a psychiatric diagnosis they have been given. In DBT, it is believed that people:

- *Experienced capability difficulties*, which mean they may have yet to have the opportunity to develop skills to live and relate to the world.
- *Experience motivational difficulties*, most likely due to an invalidating environment. They struggle to believe they can trust themselves, achieve, and create a life worth living.
- *Struggle to understand, manage, experience, and regulate emotions and affect.*

A comprehensive DBT treatment would include four treatment modalities:

1. To *enhance capabilities*, skills training is provided in a weekly educational class format for at least two hours. There are four modules taught, which are Distress Tolerance (DT: acceptance-based); Emotion Regulation (ER: change-based); Interpersonal Effectiveness (IE: change-based); Core Mindfulness (CM: acceptance-based) (Linehan, 2015).
2. To *enhance client motivation and knowledge*, people attend weekly individual DBT therapy sessions. A strong, compassionate, and validating therapy relationship is key to motivating, supporting, and collaboratively analysing behaviour patterns relating to self-harm and suicidality. This supports clients in developing solutions and practising and applying these skills in their lives.
3. To *enhance and ensure the generalisation of learning*, clients have access to telephone coaching on how to apply skills and apply them to their daily lives.
4. To *enhance therapist capabilities and motivation*, DBT therapists meet weekly for two-hour DBT consult meetings to support and develop their work with this particular client group (Swales, 2020).

A full programme DBT treatment can be offered to adults or adolescents. The original standard adult package is for a minimum of six months, though ideally would be 12 months in length (Linehan, 1993a, 2015). The more recently developed DBT for Adolescents (DBT-A) is completed over a minimum of 16 weeks, though it is usually 24 weeks, with some involvement of parents or carers in skills and generalisation (Rathus & Miller, 2015).

The authors are sharing this knowledge with the reader to ensure an understanding of what a full DBT treatment would involve. The reader needs to know that DBT-informed work, especially in the context of GSRD people, can be extremely helpful. At the same time, people who present with persistent and chronic self-harm and suicidality, coupled with significant risk, who may also have received a diagnosis of BPD or EUPD, would be better offered the evidence-based treatment of a full programme from a qualified DBT Therapist. Utilising clinical supervision to understand the clinical indicators that would suggest onward referral to a specialist is essential to maintain safe, effective, and evidence-based practice.

It is also important to note that the DBT behavioural approach to diagnosis means that all diagnostic criteria are descriptions of behaviour, i.e. emotions, cognitions, sensations and behavioural patterns, and all these behaviours are amenable to shift. Therefore, in principle, the diagnosis of BPD and/or EUPD can be removed by decreasing the overt behaviours and the experience of the internal behaviours. Thus, DBT can be seen as a clear example of an emancipatory therapeutic practice, demonstrating solidarity with *social justice* and *understanding the effects of oppression* in line with components of GSRD therapy.

Practically Applying DBT with People Who Identify as GSRD

DBT training is extensive and comprehensive, so the authors have selected some of the most relevant elements of DBT (see Linehan, 1993a, 1993b, 2015 for further details) to allow readers to supplement their routine clinical work. The authors have attempted to further Queer DBT practice in section one 'Queering DBT.' In section two, 'Using GSRD DBT Research,' the authors have utilised recent Queer focused DBT research to share and support the reader to inform their practice with these populations. It will be necessary for the reader to supplement learning from this chapter by consulting the DBT skills manuals (Linehan, 1993b, 2015) and the YouTube channel DBT-RU: DBT Skills from Experts https://www.youtube.com/dbtru.

Queering DBT

DBT Assumptions

Within DBT, there is a strong value-based approach, with value-based assumptions underpinning all clinical and therapeutic work. Therapists can easily apply this, though it requires daily practice to maintain this perspective. These assumptions can be beneficial for GSRD people who live in an extremely invalidating environment.

Assumptions about Clients

- Clients want to improve. Clients are doing the best they can, and at the same time, they need to do better, try harder, and be more motivated. Clients want to improve.
- Clients may not have caused all their problems but have to solve them anyway.
- The lives of people who want to end their lives are unbearable as they are currently being lived. Clients must learn new behaviours in all relevant contexts.
- Clients cannot fail in DBT.

Assumptions about DBT Treatment

- The most caring thing a therapist can do is help clients change in ways that bring them closer to their ultimate goals.
- Clarity, precision, and compassion are of the utmost importance in DBT.
- The therapeutic relationship is a real relationship between equals.
- Principles of behaviour are universal, affecting therapists no less than clients.
- DBT therapists can fail. DBT treatment can fail, even when therapists do not.
- DBT therapists treating this group of people need support.
- Self-harm and suicide function to solve a problem.

Reasons for Living

DBT aims to help someone create a life worth living, as it is hard to be satisfied and experience pleasure without a life that is experienced as worthy of being lived. The subjective experience of the worthiness of one's life—a life that brings happiness and joy—is a central tenet within DBT, such that therapists begin by supporting clients to develop a picture of this life and how to create it (Linehan, 2015).

For someone who feels that ending their life is the only solution to their distress, we need to begin helping them think about their reasons for living and what a life worth living may look like.

1. Possible reasons for living: people, experiences, future plans, hopes.
2. Could use the *Reasons for Living Inventory* (Linehan *et al.*, 1983). This measure is extremely heterosexist and cisgendered, though it can be useful as a foundation for you to adapt and develop for your GSRD clients.
3. What would a life worth living be like, e.g. using the DBT house exercise or tree metaphor?
4. Challenging ideas about death as a viable and/or the only solution.

> *The desire to (end one's life), however, has at its base a belief that life cannot or will not improve. Although that may be the case in some instances, it is not true in all instances. Death, however, rules out hope in all instances. We do not have any data indicating that people who are dead lead better lives.*
>
> Linehan (1993a, p. 126)

For GSRD clients, it is essential to help them understand a realistic life worth living. Whilst this should include hopes and aspirations for the future, it should also focus on removing or distancing themselves from unhelpful or harmful situations that get in the way of a life worth living. 'Fostering joy' is a key component of GSRD therapy, and understanding ways in which a

GSRD person's strengths, skills, or attributes can foster hope and queer joy is pivotal. It is also important to note that creating a life worth living in DBT for GSRD people should be conducted within *contemporary sexology* and *relationship diversity* knowledge, as suggested in a GSRD therapy approach. This would ensure that a life worth living can be expansive in its creation of living sexually and intimately to meet the joy and needs of the person rather than being constrained by heterosexism.

States of Mind

Within DBT, a Venn diagram describes three relevant 'states of mind,' which clients can experience and move between.

Emotion Mind: Emotions control thoughts, urges and behaviours; hence, emotions control our responses. Emotions have action urges, e.g. sadness makes us withdraw; shame makes us hide.

Reasonable Mind: Reason and logic control thoughts, urges and behaviours, and hence logic controls our responses. Facts without any emotions can be unhelpful relationally.

Wise Mind: This represents the intersection of the Venn diagram, whereby there is an integration of emotion mind and reasonable mind. Facts and logic are coupled with emotion and sensory information. Often described as intuitive and balanced.

Becoming aware of the state of mind people are responding to allows for a choice about their responses, with the ultimate aim being to move into a Wise Mind. A useful tool to use with GSRD clients is identifying which 'mind' your client is currently experiencing or responding to, perhaps by working together to list the various thoughts, feelings and bodily sensations your client may experience as an indicator of each mind state.

Three Core Philosophies and Techniques of DBT Treatment

Behaviourism—Change

DBT is fundamentally a behavioural therapy that focuses on change strategies, namely problem-solving techniques. DBT is interested in understanding thoughts, emotions, behaviours, and bodily sensations. DBT uses functional behaviour analysis to assess and formulate the functions of behaviour that a person engages in. Behaviours generally have four main reasons and/or functions why people engage in them (Cooper *et al.*, 2007):

i.   To gain social connection and attention with other humans.
ii. To escape something unwanted or painful.
iii. To gain access to tangibles, interests or activities in the world.
iv. To engage in sensory stimulation, soothing, and enjoyment.

Understanding behaviours as *solutions* (in other words, the function and reasons why someone engages in particular behaviours such as self-harm, by cutting or planning to end their life by ligature) helps therapists to understand what problem(s) in their life they are trying to solve. When therapists understand the functions of behaviours, then problem-solving can happen, in turn supporting the development of solutions that are less harmful and less life-threatening. These solutions may include teaching a new skill, cognitive therapy and restructuring techniques, exposure to the cue that caused the distress and/or contingency management to alter the consequences that may be maintaining the behaviour. For GSRD people, this may also include understanding queer-specific contextual or systemic influences upon behavioural strategies within a clinical formulation and subsequent therapy (see Dunlop & Lea, 2023b, for a comprehensive discussion).

Zen Practice—Acceptance

DBT is fundamentally an acceptance-based therapy, including mindfulness, radical acceptance, and validation.

The attitude that is created within DBT is that fighting against the nature of reality as it is in this moment can create increased distress and ultimately suffering. In Buddhism and DBT, there is an idea that, *pain + an unwillingness to experience pain = suffering*. This concept can be helpful to hold in mind and share with clients.

This does not mean that GSRD people must approve and agree with intersectional and structural oppression and hatred. At the same time, we may need to learn how to accept that these evils exist against us and our community at this moment. Acceptance allows us to spend our energy becoming better equipped in learning how to maintain our wellbeing in extremely invalidating environments so that we are less likely to misdirect pain and distress at our queer bodies through self-harm and suicidal behaviours. If we are able to stay alive, then we can continue to work and protest with allies to dismantle and reduce the systemic inequalities, discrimination and pain in society for GSRD people.

The three main acceptance-based techniques in DBT are:

- Mindfulness:
  i. Being mindful in everyday life.
  ii. Noticing judgements of self and others.

- Radical Acceptance:
  i. Radical means all the way, complete and total.
  ii. Radical Acceptance is *NOT* agreement, approval, kindness, resignation, passivity, or weakness. It is a brave act of defiance in the service of oneself and life.

iii. It is when you stop fighting reality. We should not allow ourselves to become bitter and resentful only because reality is not the way we want and/or need it to be.

iv. It has been suggested that in creating a life worth living, GSRD people may need to radically accept that whilst we did not create hatred, bi/homo/transphobia or cis-heterosexism, we still have to skilfully learn how to manage our responses to it, *and* with the help of community and allies, continue to strive to solve the systemic and structural difficulties that arise from this, to live and create a life worth living for our personal selves and our community.

- Validation:
    i. Finding the gold in the mud, the gold in the desert.
    ii. Validating a person or oneself in terms of the present context and situation.
    iii. Validation of clients is an antidote to the problem of self-invalidation created by the invalidating environment. It helps to begin the process of trusting and self-assuredness in themselves, their thoughts, feelings, and wants.
    iv. Radical *genuineness:* Involves the therapist as human and an equal, engaging in an authentic manner, not taking themselves too seriously or ignoring the obvious. DBT recognises and celebrates the therapist's self-revealing and self-involving disclosures, especially relevant for GSRD people (Davies, 1998; Lea *et al.*, 2010), when in the service of the client, e.g. therapists' gender diversity, sexuality, sharing skill use and examples. Dunlop *et al.* (2021) provide a framework for supporting clinicians in self-disclosure.

Dialectics - Balancing Change and Acceptance

Dialectical worldview is a synthesis or integration of opposites. As a philosophy, it is inherently queer, as it is not concerned with maintaining binaries, biological essentialism, or a single truth. The desire is to synthesise the complexity and celebrate the maintenance of multiple truths. In DBT, dialectics as a technique helps us to balance the treatment strategies of change and acceptance to create a life worth living.

Let us explore how a dialectical perspective can help us understand a person's experiences:

River loves their sibling, who is busy working two full-time jobs right now. River has been trying to reach them, which has not been possible. This really annoys River, who cares about their sibling, who is one of their favourite people, *and* them being hard to reach is something River does not like. *This is a dialectical situation.* Two seemingly opposing facts about River's feelings are both true at the same time. Using 'and' instead of 'but' is a simple and effective strategy to help your clients maintain a dialectical worldview: River cares about their sibling *and* does not like them being hard to reach.

A number of dialectics must be negotiated as part of DBT:

Constant attention to combining acceptance with change, flexibility with stability, nurturing with challenging, and a focus on capabilities with a focus on limitations and deficits is the essence of this strategy. The goal is to bring out the opposites, both in therapy and in the person's life, and to provide conditions for synthesis.

Linehan (1993a, p. 202)

Examples with clients and supporting them to:

- Try using *and*, instead of BUT.
- When black-and-white thinking appears, always search for the grey.
- Radical Acceptance. We did not create trans/bi/homophobia or cis-hetero-sexism, *and* at the same time, we have to learn how to manage the impact of this to not end our lives. So that we can stay alive and create a life worth living, finding joy, purpose, connection, and community.
- In line with one of the core components of GSRD therapy ('Demonstrating Cultural Humility and Cultural Competence') ensures that dialectical dilemmas are named and situated within culturally appropriate and culturally aligned frames of reference.

Using GSRD DBT Research

DBT Skills and Techniques

In the case of DBT-informed work, teaching skills individually, as opposed to in a group context, is appropriate and effective. It is hoped that the skills in Table 7.1 will support the reader in developing a DBT-informed approach for GSRD people who self-harm and have urges to end their life.

Current qualitative research, namely Harding, Pratt, and Lea (2025), who explored the experiences of adults who identify as Lesbian and Gay (LG) completing a DBT programme, and Camp *et al.* (2023b), who investigated GSD adolescents in DBT, both suggest that DBT is mostly acceptable and helpful for GSRD people, though further developments and research are necessary. It was positive to see findings corroborating wider GSRD research and thinking (Hudson & Bruce-Miller, 2023; McClain *et al.*, 2016), and those focused explicitly on DBT (Camp, 2023; Cohen *et al.*, 2021; Harned *et al.*, 2022; Pantalone *et al.*, 2019).

Table 7.1 Tasks and DBT Skills Relevant to Working with GSRD People

Task	DBT skills and focus area
Reduce GSRD identity distress	• Self soothe (DT) • Radical Acceptance (CM)
Reduce GSRD-related shame	• Model of Emotion (ER) • Check the Facts (ER) • Opposite Action (ER) • Self-Validation (WMP)
Develop self-confidence	• Objective Effectiveness (IE) • Self-Respect Effectiveness (IE)
Checking safety and vigilance	• Check the Facts (ER) • Pros and Cons (DT)
Worries and expecting rejection or stigma from others	• Check the Facts (ER) • Self-Validation (WMP) • Opposite Action (ER) • Radical Acceptance (CM)
Experiencing stigma from others and subsequent distress	• Check the Facts (ER) • Self-Validation (WMP) • Self Soothe (DT) • Opposite Action (ER) • Objective Effectiveness (DEARMAN; IE) • Self-Respect Effectiveness (FAST; IE) • Cope Ahead (ER) • Radical Acceptance (CM) • Distraction with Wise Mind Accepts (DT) • Improve the moment (DT) • TIPP (DT)
Coming out to others	• Pros and Cons (DT) • States of Mind (CM) • Objective Effectiveness (DEARMAN; IE)

Emotion Regulation (ER: change-based); Interpersonal Effectiveness (IE: change-based); Core Mindfulness (CM: acceptance-based); Walking the Middle Path (WMP).

A notable recommendation across numerous research projects, specifically highlighted by Harding, Pratt, and Lea (2025), was that people experienced a closer therapeutic alliance when there was a shared GSRD minority status, which was disclosed by DBT therapists. This is an area of psychotherapy that has been found and discussed numerous times within the context of LGBT affirmative therapy (Davies, 1998; Lea *et al.*, 2010). This is in line with the seven core components of GSRD therapy (Davies & Neves, 2023), meaning clinicians often share the lived experiences of growing up and living as a GSRD person with their clients, and so can more meaningfully connect to the need to be trauma, grief and shame-informed. A further important finding related to cisgender and/or heterosexual DBT therapists was additional training on the difficulties faced by GSRD people, to create DBT therapists that have an anti-homo/bi/transphobia and cis-heterosexist stance (Harding, Pratt, and Lea, 2025).

DBT's biosocial theory could more clearly incorporate GSRD theories (e.g. MST, InSoS, Social Safety) to develop a theory specific to GSRD people receiving treatment in a DBT programme. This formulation-based approach could help GSRD people understand and relate to their difficulties without being pathologised and medicalised (Dunlop & Lea, 2023b). Concerning structural health inequalities, including the InSoS framework (Dunlop & Lea, 2023a) and allowing for consideration of broader systemic variables (Dunlop, 2022) could educate and support clients and therapists to discuss and reflect on oppression and how this could have become internalised. This could be especially helpful when thinking about GSRD-specific internal and external factors implicated in self-harm and/or suicidal ideation or planning.

Table 7.2 Clinical Adaptations to Support GSRD Affirmative DBT

Clinical Adaptation to Support a GSRD Affirmative DBT	
Joy and affirming space	• GSRD visibility in the space, e.g. pride pins, lanyards, posters, etc.
	• Discussion and use of pronouns.
DBT skills manual	• Include GSRD language, relationships, and families.
	• Link biosocial theory to GSRD theories to formulate distress.
	• Case studies related to GSRD difficulties and life experiences.
DBT program	• Create group guidelines that include gender, sexuality, oppression, and respect. Include icebreakers around GSRD identity.
	• Participating in DBT skills groups with other GSRD people can create a sense of 'chosen family.'
	• A new module to discuss difficulties around identifying GSRD and specific techniques that may help.
	• Create a brave space (Arao & Clemens, 2013) based on social justice principles to learn and make mistakes about people's GSRD identity.
DBT therapists	• Additional training on the difficulties faced by GSRD people—to create DBT therapists that have an anti-bi/homo/transphobia and cis-heterosexist stance.
	• Training of DBT therapists who identify as GSRD.
	• Therapist self-disclosure of GSRD identity (when helpful).
	• Therapists create a context where people can be open.
	• Use of humour and playfulness.
	• Therapists develop cultural humility and competence with GSRD.

Participants in Harding, Pratt, and Lea (2025) study and previous research in DBT for GSRD people have expressed a desire for a more GSRD affirmative DBT, which included recommendations around the therapy environment, the DBT manual, the DBT programme and therapists (Table 7.2).

Table 7.2 recommendations from participant feedback developed from Harding, Pratt, & Lea, 2025, p.20 and previous research (Camp, 2023; Camp *et al.*, 2023; Cohen *et al.*, 2021; Skerven *et al.*, 2019, 2021; Sloan *et al.*, 2017).

Conclusion

In this chapter, we have outlined the key theoretical and practical considerations for utilising and applying DBT and its techniques with GSRD clients who self-harm and/or want to end their lives. This has included the need to understand key GSRD theories, such as Minority Stress Theory, and how this links to DBT's biosocial theory. The use of therapist self-disclosure is an area of DBT often mirrored in the work of GSRD therapists, and so capitalising on this to support the meaningful adaptation and implementation of DBT techniques and skills for GSRD clients is of benefit. Throughout the chapter, we have also highlighted ways in which the queering of DBT utilises and encompasses numerous core components of contemporary GSRD therapy. The dialectical philosophy of DBT has a perfect synergy with GSRD populations and experiences, making it an excellent treatment approach to use with GSRD clients. Integrating DBT skills and using techniques such as formulating the function of behaviours to develop solutions can also be incorporated into other therapeutic approaches when the formulation of self-harm and suicidality suggests this would be of benefit.

References

American Psychiatric Association. (2013) *Diagnostic and statistical manual of mental disorders.* 5th ed.

Arao, B., & Clemens, K. (2013). *From safe spaces to brave spaces: A new way to frame dialogue around diversity and social justice.* In Landreman, L.M. (Ed) *The Art of Effective Facilitation: Reflections from Social Justice Educators* (135–150).

Brooks, V. R. (1981) *Minority stress and lesbian women.* Lexington: Lexington Books.

Camp, J. (2023a) 'Dialectical Behaviour Therapy for sexual minority populations', in J. Semlyen & P. Rohleder (eds.), *Sexual minorities and mental health: Current perspectives and new directions.* Springer International Publishing, pp. 271–302.

Camp, J., Morris, A., Wilde, H., Smith, P., & Rimes, K. A. (2023b) 'Gender- and sexuality-minoritised adolescents in DBT: A reflexive thematic analysis of minority-specific treatment targets and experience', *The Cognitive Behaviour Therapist*, 16, p. e36. https:// doi.org/10.1017/S1754470X23000326

Cohen, J. M., Norona, J. C., Yadavia, J. E., & Borsari, B. (2021) 'Affirmative dialectical behavior therapy skills training with sexual minority veterans', *Cognitive and Behavioral Practice*, 28(1), pp. 77–91. https://doi.org/10.1016/j .cbpra.2020.05.008

Cooper, J. O., Heron, T. E., & Heward, W. L. (2007) *Applied behavior analysis*. 2nd ed. Upper Saddle River, NJ: Pearson.

Davies, D. (1998) 'The six necessary and sufficient conditions applied to working with LGBT clients', *The Person-Centered Journal*, 5(2), pp.111–120.

Davies, D., & Neves, S. (2023) 'Gender, sex and relationship diversity therapy', in T. Hanley & L. Winter (eds.), *The SAGE Handbook of Counselling and Psychotherapy*. 5th ed. London: Sage, pp. 79–85.

DeCou, C. R., Comtois, K. A., and Landes, S. J. (2019) 'Dialectical behavior therapy is effective for the treatment of suicidal behavior: A meta-analysis', *Behavior Therapy*, 50(1), pp. 60–72.

Diamond, L. M., & Alley, J. (2022) 'Rethinking minority stress: A social safety perspective on the health effects of stigma in sexually-diverse and gender-diverse populations', *Neuroscience and Biobehavioral Reviews*, 138. https://doi.org/10 .1016/j.neubiorev.2022.104720

Dunlop, B. J. (2022) *The queer mental health workbook: A creative self-help guide using CBT, CFT and DBT*. London: Jessica Kingsley Publishers.

Dunlop, B. J., & Lea, J. (2023a). 'It''s not just in my head: An intersectional, social and systems-based framework in gender and sexuality diversity', *Psychology and Psychotherapy: Theory, Research and Practice*, 96(1), pp. 1–15. https://doi.org/10 .1111/papt.12438

Dunlop, B. J., & Lea, J. (2023b) 'Clinical formulation', in J. Semlyen & P. Rohleder (eds.), *Sexual minorities and mental health: Current perspectives and new directions*. Springer International Publishing, 165–191.

Dunlop, B. J., Woods, B., Lovell, J., O'Connell, A., Rawcliffe-Foo, S., & Hinsby, K. (2021). 'Sharing Lived Experiences Framework (SLEF): A framework for mental health practitioners when making disclosure decisions', *Journal of Social Work Practice*, 36(1), pp. 25–39. https://doi.org/10.1080/02650533 .2021.1922367

Gillespie, C., Murphy, M., Kells, M., & Flynn, D. (2022) 'Individuals who report having benefitted from Dialectical Behaviour Therapy (DBT): a qualitative exploration of processes and experiences at long-term follow-up', *Borderline Personality Disorder and Emotion Dysregulation*, 9(1), pp. 1–14.

Gosling, H., Pratt, D. & Lea, J. (2022) 'Understanding self-harm urges and behaviour amongst non-binary young adults: A grounded theory study', *Journal of Gay & Lesbian Mental Health*, 27(3), pp. 340–370. https://doi.org/10.1080/19359705 .2022.2073310

Gosling, H., Pratt, D., Montgomery, H. & Lea, J. (2022) 'The relationship between minority stress factors and suicidal ideation and behaviours amongst transgender and gender non-conforming adults: A systematic review', *Journal of Affective Disorders*, 303, pp. 31–51. https://doi.org/10.1016/j.jad.2021.12.091

Harding, C., Pratt, D., & Lea, J. (2025) '"All the horrible emotions have passed, I still remained, and I was safe": A qualitative study of lesbian and gay people''s lived experience of completing a full dialectical behaviour therapy programme',

Psychology and Psychotherapy: Theory, Research and Practice, 98, pp. 1–24. https://doi.org/10.1111/papt.12555

Harding, C., Pratt, D., Wilkinson, J., & Lea, J. (2025) 'The experiences of minority stressors endured by people who identify as lesbian and gay and a member of the Global Majority within the United Kingdom: A systematic thematic synthesis', *Journal of Gay & Lesbian Mental Health*, 1–43. https://doi.org/10.1080/19359705.2024.2421546

Harned, M. S., Coyle, T. N., & Garcia, N. M (2022) 'The inclusion of ethnoracial, sexual, and gender minority groups in randomized controlled trials of dialectical behaviour therapy; a systematic review of the literature', *Clinical Psychology: Science and Practice*, 29, pp. 83–93. https://doi.org/10.1037/cps0000059

Hudson, K. D., & Bruce-Miller, V. (2023) 'Nonclinical best practices for creating LGBTQ-inclusive care environments: A scoping review of gray literature', *Journal of Gay & Lesbian Social Services*, 35(2), pp. 218–240. https://doi.org/10.1080/10538720.2022.2057380

Jackman, K., Honig, J., & Bockting, W. (2016) 'Nonsuicidal self-injury among lesbian, gay, bisexual and transgender populations: An integrative review', *Journal of clinical nursing*, 25(23–24), pp. 3438–3453. https://doi.org/10.1111/jocn.13236

Joyce, E., Pratt, D., & Lea, J. (2024) '"Where is my place?" A qualitative study of gay men's experiences of social support, relationships and community in relation to psychological wellbeing and distress', *Journal of Homosexuality*, 72(5), pp. 841–867. https://doi.org/10.1080/00918369.2024.2354408

King, M., Semlyen, J., Tai, S. S., Killaspy, H., Osborn, D., Popelyuk, D., & Nazareth, I. (2008) 'A systematic review of mental disorder, suicide, and deliberate self-harm in lesbian, gay and bisexual people', *BMC Psychiatry*, 8, 70. https://doi.org/10.1186/1471-244X-8-70

Lea, J. (2020) 'A heterosexist matrix: A critical examination of the tripartite matrix and non-heterosexual identities', *Group Analysis North*, Institute of Group Analysis, 16, pp. 14–16.

Lea, J., Jones, R., & Huws, J. C. (2010) 'Gay psychologists and gay clients: Exploring therapist disclosure of sexuality in the therapeutic closet', *Psychology of Sexualities Review*, 1, pp. 59–73.

Linehan, M. M. (1993a) *Cognitive behavioral treatment of borderline personality disorder*. New York: Guilford Press.

Linehan, M. M (1993b) *Skills training manual for treating borderline personality disorder*. New York: Guilford Press.

Linehan, M. M (2011) 'Expert on mental illness reveals her own struggle', The New York Times, June 23rd.

Linehan, M. M. (2015) *DBT skills training manual*. 2nd ed. New York: Guilford Press.

Linehan, M. M., Goodstein, J. L., Nielsen, S. L., & Chiles, J. A. (1983) *Reasons for Living Inventory (RFL)*. APA PsycTests.

Little, H., Tickle, A., & das Nair, R. (2018) 'Process and impact of Dialectical Behaviour Therapy: A systematic review of perceptions of clients with a diagnosis of borderline personality disorder', *Psychology and Psychotherapy: Theory, Research and Practice*, 91(3), pp. 278–301.

McClain, Z., Hawkins, L. A., & Yehia, B. R. (2016) 'Creating welcoming spaces for Lesbian, Gay, Bisexual, and Transgender (LGBT) patients: An evaluation of the health care environment', *Journal of Homosexuality*, 63(3), pp. 387–393. https://doi.org/10.1080/00918369.2016.1124694

Meyer, I. H. (1995) 'Minority stress and mental health in gay men', *Journal of Health and Social Behavior*, 36(1), pp. 38–56.

Meyer, I. H. (2003) 'Prejudice, social stress, and mental health in lesbian, gay, and bisexual populations: Conceptual issues and research evidence', *Psychological Bulletin*, 129(5), pp. 674–697. https://doi.org/10.1037/0033-2909.129.5.674

Meyer, I. H. (2015) 'Resilience in the study of minority stress and health of sexual and gender minorities', *Psychology of Sexual Orientation and Gender Diversity*, 2(3), pp. 209–213. https://doi.org/10.1037/sgd0000132

Miga, E. M., Neacsiu, A. D, Heard, H. L., & Dimeff, L.A. (2019) 'Dialectical Behaviour Therapy from 1991–2015: What do we know about clinical efficacy and research quality?' in M. Swales (ed.), *Oxford handbook of dialectical behaviour therapy*. Oxford: Oxford University Press, pp. 415–466.

Oud, M., Arntz, A., Hermens, M. L. M., Verhoef, R., & Kendall, T. (2018) 'Specialized psychotherapies for adults with borderline personality disorder: A systematic review and meta-analysis', *Australian and New Zealand Journal of Psychiatry*, 52(10), pp. 949–961.

Panos, P. T., Jackson, J. W., Hasan, O., & Panos, A. (2014) 'Meta-analysis and systematic review assessing the efficacy of Dialectical Behavior Therapy (DBT)', *Research on Social Work Practice*, 24(2), pp. 213–223. https://doi.org/10.1177/1049731513503047

Pantalone, D. W., Sloan, C. A., & Carmel, A. (2019) 'Dialectical behavior therapy for borderline personality disorder and suicidality among sexual and gender minority individuals', in J.E. Pachankis & S.A. Safren (eds.), *Handbook of evidence-based mental health practice with sexual and gender minorities*. Oxford: Oxford University Press, pp. 408–429.

Rathus, J. H., & Miller, A. L. (2015) *DBT skills manual for adolescents*. New York: Guilford Press.

Semlyen, J., King, M., Varney, J., & Hagger-Johnson, G. (2016) 'Sexual orientation and symptoms of common mental disorder or low wellbeing: Combined meta-analysis of 12 UK population health surveys', *BMC Psychiatry*, 16, Article 67. https://doi.org/10.1186/s12888-016-0767-z

Skerven, K., Mirabito, L., Kirkman, M., & Shaw, B. (2021) 'Dialectical behaviour therapy skills group including stigma management: a pilot with sexual and gender minority veterans', *The Cognitive Behaviour Therapist*, 14, p. e33. https://doi.org/10.1017/S1754470X21000295

Skerven, K., Whicker, D. R., & LeMaire, K. L. (2019) 'Applying dialectical behaviour therapy to structural and internalized stigma with LGBTQ+ clients', *The Cognitive Behaviour Therapist*, 12, p. e9. https://doi.org/10.1017/S1754470X18000235

Sloan, C. A., Berke, D. S., & Shipherd, J. C. (2017), 'Utilizing a dialectical framework to inform conceptualization and treatment of clinical distress in transgender individuals', *Professional Psychology: Research and Practice*, 48, pp. 301–309. https://doi.org/10.1037/pro0000146

Swales, M. (2020), 'Reducing suicidal behaviour in people with complex needs: Addressing the challenge of implementing dialectical behaviour therapy', *Suicidologi*, 24(3), pp. 4–14. https://doi.org10.5617/suicidologi.7689

Swannell, S., Martin, G., & Page, A. (2016) 'Suicidal ideation, suicide attempts and non-suicidal self-injury among lesbian, gay, bisexual and heterosexual adults: Findings from an Australian national study', *The Australian and New Zealand Journal of Psychiatry*, 50(2), pp. 145–153. https://doi.org/10.1177/0004867415615949

World Health Organization (2004) *ICD-10: international statistical classification of diseases and related health problems: tenth revision.* 2nd ed. World Health Organization.

Resources:

- DBT-RU: DBT Skills from Experts YouTube Channel https://www.youtube.com/dbtru
- Behavioral Tech Institute (previously known as The Linehan Institute) https://behavioraltech.org/
- British Isles DBT Training is the sole licensed provider of training in Dialectical Behaviour Therapy (DBT) in Great Britain and the Republic of Ireland. https://www.dbt-training.co.uk/
- The Society for DBT in the UK and Ireland. Professional DBT accreditation body. https://www.sfdbt.org/

Chapter 8

A Figure of the Affirmed Self
Gestalt and GSRD Therapy Meet

Daniel Bqk

Introduction

Gestalt therapy has always been about freedom for me. Restoration of my dignity and embodied sense of free choice were my crucial gains from years of Gestalt psychotherapy as a client. Not every experience was nourishing and healing. Trainers and therapists who skipped Paul Goodman's (Perls, Hefferline and Goodman, 1951/1994; in the Gestalt community, the book is commonly referred to as PHG) claims on therapy being informed by society, culture, and politics brought me pain, self-confusion, and temporary loss of trust in professional mental help. To the contrary, those who understood therapy as a craft co-constructed by the socio-cultural milieu supported me deeply in attempts to explore my gayness. According to Gestalt therapy, the organism cannot be understood properly without considering the environment and vice versa. For this reason, not only did meaning-making around my gayness in therapy need my attachment history or gendered and sexual recollections from the past but also an understanding of homophobia, misogyny, and patriarchy with their influences on my co-created self. Gestalt therapy delivered in the spirit of its founders (Perls, Hefferline and Goodman, 1951/1994) gave me that. This chapter merges Gestalt therapy and the core components of GSRD therapy (Davies and Neves, 2023). It will not be a difficult task. Gestalt therapy principles – by definition – allow the emergence of diverse selves and advocate for their genuineness and respectful recognition in culture and socio-political life.

Selfing at the Contact Boundary: the Gestalt Core

The Gestalt concept of the self has been revolutionary (Perls, Hefferline and Goodman, 1951/1994). When psychotherapists say or think of a self, it usually refers to a psychic entity that is an intrinsic quality of the individual only, relatively stable in time, with its changes being rather periodical than continuous. Unexpectedly, the Gestalt self is a fascinating exception among various constructs of a self in the therapy world – it may become distinct, active, and contentful during a psychotherapy session, and the same day it may almost

DOI: 10.4324/9781003530848-11

fall asleep when you do. In this quizzical approximation of the Gestalt self's nature, the taste of its peculiar presence is given. Selfing, this process of emergence of the self, is an ever-continuous action that mitigates itself only when the organism and environment do not supply enough sensory input.

Nevertheless, selfing never stops, as even the organism of a sleeping person is still able to receive and record the internal (proprioception, dreams) and external (e.g. sounds) stimuli. Moreover, it should be assumed that at least the environment provides stimuli in a never-ending fashion. The above description is valid as – according to Gestalt theory – a true locus of the self is not inside the organism, especially under the skin, but at the boundary between the organism and its environment. In Gestalt therapy, it is called the contact-boundary. The contact-boundary is Gestalt imagery of a theoretical realm where contacting occurs between the organism and environment. The self has been continually emerging from this interaction. Noteworthily, this interaction is complex and intimate. The meaning of the organism involves the environment and vice versa (Philippson, 2012). For instance, the meaning of one's sexual arousal involves the desirable other. Simultaneously, the meaning of the other's sexual attractiveness involves one's sexual arousal. For the contact-boundary phenomena are always co-created, a construct of "the organism-environment field" was introduced to emphasise the organism's and environment's inseparability (Spagnuolo Lobb, 2013). Referring to the example above, the self that is aware of its lusting – for instance, a male experiencing erection – "knows" the specificity of his lusting not only because of his penile sensations but also because there is the sexually arousing other (Is it a man? Is it a woman? Is it a trans person? Is the person wearing latex underwear? Is the person a tied up sub?). Awareness mentioned in this example is "(...) a function of the contact-boundary in the organism-environment field, involving the organism, the environment, and the negotiation/relationship between them" (Philippson, 2012, p. 139). Awareness originates from at least two sources: body sensitivity and thinking (for discussion, see Fodor, 1998). These intertwined domains of experience are being shaped by the whole organism-environment field at the moment of an encounter. For example, thoughts are "mine" – I am thinking them, but there have been more contributors than myself who have influenced the process and content of my thinking. How can we live on a daily basis with such an all-the-time-emerging self? Gestalt psychologists helped Gestalt therapists to understand this (Köhler, 1969). We are all involved in the constant figure-ground formation processes. What is important at any given moment, for example, an appetite for sex or non-sexual intimacy, becomes figural to the self and, after successful resolution, may withdraw to the ground, what makes the emergence of the next figure possible. A smooth, uninterrupted figure-ground formation is considered a sign of health (Perls, Hefferline and Goodman, 1951/1994).

Gestalt theory of the self has the fundamental implication that allows us to discern one's functioning: being capable of individual autonomy, we are always *of* the field and – above all – relationally emergent. Being *of* the field does not imply the self is merely a product of societal construction (Philippson, 2012). It means the self is emerging as a co-creation of the organism and the environment unity. I claim that the self always has growth potential independent of field conditions. How is it possible? The evolutionary history wired us for inter-human connectedness and creating relationships (Stern, 1998; Wheeler, 2011). Thus, we meet people and learn while relating. This aptitude is rooted in the body, with its nervous system, senses, and the necessity of the other's touch to survive. This potential to connect and learn is a given, always present, even under the most unfavourable field setting. This is why psychotherapy works in the first place. Furthermore, this is why human beings do not stop individuating (a never-to-be-completed process), so in this case, growing at the contact-boundary.

For example, the queerphobic field (Bąk, 2024) may result in self-hatred among homosexual men who then seek conversion practices. However, it does not preclude the possibility of one facing his own lust and emotional longing towards other men, leaving conversion attempts behind as harmful and fruitless. Not only may changes in the field conditions support such emancipation, but also coming back to the roots of our existence in the world, the body (Merleau-Ponty, 1945/2012). Senses and drives can guide the embodied being of the organism in the field on par with the setting of the field. Gay loving attachment and appetite for sex – embodied in touch, a need to share space, and pleasure of physical arousal – may battle against and win over self-loathing driven by environmental homophobia.

This chapter explores the application of the core components of GSRD therapy to the contact processes between the client and therapist in Gestalt therapy. Gestalt's theoretical framing of the self is paramount to these considerations.

The Seven Core Components of GSRD Therapy

The core components of GSRD therapy (Davies and Neves, 2023) can be divided into two interconnected but separate sets. The first batch consists of (1) practising a commitment to social justice, (2) demonstrating cultural humility and cultural competence, (3) understanding the specific adverse effects of oppression, and (4) fostering joy. This collection refers to *how* the therapist is with their client. It applies also to component no. 3, as there is a condition that precedes understanding the effects of oppression, namely recognition and acknowledgement that oppression is real. This way, a specific stance of the therapist is expressed – one of respect, carefulness, and humility when encountering differences, as well as recognition of various forms of social oppression as fundamental forces operating in the embodied relational field of the client. Together, this therapeutic attitude results in the therapist being a dignity protector who secures a therapeutic alliance with the client.

The other group of components is comprised of (5) being trauma, grief, and shame informed, (6) knowing contemporary sexology, and (7) integrating core GSRD theories. This cluster provides information about *what the therapist knows* and how GSRD-knowledgeable they are.

There is pragmatism behind this division. It helps to navigate through the chapter. These two sets of components are elaborated on separately in the context of Gestalt therapy theory and practice.

PHG Provides Theory and Therapeutic Attitude Upholding Recognition and Dignity of the Other

The careful reader would find the apparent roots of "a dignity protector" therapeutic stance in *Gestalt therapy. Excitement and Growth in the Human Personality* written by Frederick Perls, Ralph F. Hefferline, and Paul Goodman and published in 1951. It may be profoundly satisfying for Gestalt practitioners and – as a historical fact – need to be surprising at the same time. Gestalt therapy developed as a revision of Freudian psychoanalysis in the era of psychoanalysis's hegemonic domination in psychiatry and psychotherapy. While psychoanalysis emphasised the significance of the Reality Principle as a proper way of adjusting people to live in a society, Gestalt therapy suggested a rather upside-down version of how "reality" affected the human condition. The PHG offers a way of thinking about neurosis as a self-conquest. We conquer ourselves, we smash our potential – this variety of ways we could develop as human beings, using pressures that had originally been external and then turned into introjects. These introjects govern our psychic life from the inside, from the under-the-skin realm, creating an illusion of them being the true us. The constraints mentioned – parental expectations, societal moral codes and rules of proper behaviour, or current politics of identity and mental health – are Freudian reality, PHG authors said. They perceived those restrictions as oppressive towards the individual as personal growth inhibitors. The Reality Principle produced neurotics, mentally and emotionally subdued society members:

> And looked at coldly, in the terms he [Sigmund Freud] stated it, the adaptation to "reality" is precisely neurosis: it is deliberate interference with organismic-self-regulation and the turning of spontaneous discharges into symptoms. Civilization so conceived is a disease.
>
> (Perls, Hefferline and Goodman, 1951/1994, p. 300)

Perls, Hefferline, and Goodman were clear about the beneficiaries of the Reality Principle:

> Finally, with regard to the adjustment of the mature person to reality, must we not ask – one is ashamed to have to mention it – whether the

"reality" is not rather closely pictured after, and in the interests of, west-ern urban industrial society, capitalist or state-socialist?

(Perls, Hefferline and Goodman, 1951/1994, p. 303)

According to PHG, there is always a strong and immediate reaction to any energising novelty in a situation, person, or group if they revolt against the cultural and societal rules that are held as set once and for all. Some appetites must be chastened to hide that freedom is not welcome:

How does society adjust itself to attain a new equilibrium in the unequal development, to prevent the revolutionary dynamism latent in any new freedom – for any freedom would be expected to release energy and lead to a heightened struggle. The effort of society is to isolate, compartment, and draw the teeth of the "threat from below."

(Perls, Hefferline and Goodman, 1951/1994, p. 336)

When society wants to "draw your teeth," it offers ready-to-use introjects to be adopted by its bothersome members, to starve them of spontaneity and organismic vividness that could endanger society's rules of the settled order. The self-hurting consequences of introjection are precisely described in PHG:

Neurotically the introjector comes to terms with his own frustrated appe-tite by reversing its affect before he can recognize it. This reversal is accom-plished simply by the inhibiting itself. What one wants is felt as immature, disgusting, etc. Or conversely, if it is an impulse to reject something that is inhibited (an opposition to forced feeding), he persuades himself that the unwanted is good for him, is what he indeed wants, etc. But he bites it off without tasting or chewing it.

(Perls, Hefferline and Goodman, 1951/1994, p. 453)

The above quotations do not refer directly to GSRD issues. However, such a reference can be pursued contemporarily. The GSRD realm in the Westernised world teems with socio-cultural messages on gender, sex, and relationships, which – if introjected – confuse behaviours, feelings, identities, and the lives of GSRD individuals, for example: "there are only two gen-ders," "boys do not cry," "trans identities are none of the true ones," "true transness is binary," "homosexuality is a sin, perverted and unnatural," "bisexuality is a fake," "asexuality is just disturbance of sexual drive," "sex-ual acts should always be about love, beauty, and cleanliness," "there is no other form of a mature relationship, but a dyad in love," "only traumatised/ sick people are into kink," etc. Undoubtedly, such acts of introjection are a form of violence directed at the self. The socio-cultural order of gender and sexuality is readily weaponised by institutions and ways of conduct typical of a given culture or country, and in this form is used by individuals as a tool of self-conquest. It might have been visible as persecution of homosexuality by psychiatry and psychoanalysis in the 20th century. Even today, there are gay men (usually) looking for healing, meant as "getting rid of homosexuality out of them," who introjected self-harming messages from their therapists, counsellors, priests, and religious or spiritual communities that their gayness is against nature or God. In such a situation, the wholeness of the person is lost. What is crucial about the gendered and sexual core of the individual, for example, a non-binary identification or homosexuality, must be annihilated or repressed by them. As a result, neither does the self see itself fully nor does the environment acknowledge the person's entirety. There will be a call to hide the unfinished business of, for instance, one's homosexual desire, exercised by both parties – the individual and society represented by, among others, mental health professionals. In this manner, emotional attunement to one's gender or sexual diversity is refused by definition. Not only in the clinical setting, this refusal disenables restoration of dignity (Jacobs, 2009) by the GSRD people who introjected self-harming messages. These apparently "defective" or "incomplete" humans become deprived of dignity. They do not consider themselves of value, and societal approval for them is painfully conditional.

Not only does PHG introduce a construct of self-conquest and describe its tools and dynamics, but it also equips the therapist and client with an understanding of how to oppose external factors that inhibit personal growth:

> Above all, we must remember that where the contestants are natural drives – aggressions, special gifts, sexual practices that in fact give pleasure, etc. – they cannot be reduced, but their manifestations only deliberately suppressed, bullied or shamed out. When all the contestants are in awareness and in contact, a man may make his own hard decisions; he is not a patient. The hope is that in such a case a difficult drive will spontaneously find its measure in a new configuration, by creative adjustment and convalescent organismic self-regulation.
>
> (Perls, Hefferline and Goodman, 1951/1994, p. 358)

Perls, Hefferline, and Goodman highlight the significance of awareness and contact. It is a therapist's role to facilitate the client's selfing at the client/environment boundary (with the therapist being an important, sometimes crucial, part of the environment) in a way that favours awareness and contacting on the client's side. How would such awareness and contact look?

This is a fictitious clinical vignette of Nick, a 37-year-old cis-man presenting with unwanted homosexuality, who started Gestalt therapy eight months ago in a regular, weekly setting. The therapist is a 45-year-old cis-man identifying himself as gay. He is known in the local gay community as "a safe person to go to," and Nick knew that while scheduling his first session. This is Nick's second therapy attempt. It was 12 years ago when Nick decided to seek help at a conversion facility that operated in his hometown and offered to-be-successful so-called therapy "to uncover his true self of a heterosexual man" (as he was informed). The self-hatred he was experiencing at that time made him desperate to try conversion. After two months, he came to be disappointed with no change in his sexual urges – as he used to label his romantic and sexual longings towards men – and blamed himself for having sex with one of the facility clients. This time he says that he does not expect sexual orientation to change, but he just wants "to sort out his sexuality, finally." Today, Nick brings to therapy a story that, on the face of it, sounds typical of him. Nick uses a gay dating app to hook up with men a few times a week. Usually, they have sex. "No kissing, no hugging, never bottoming, I am always a top, meeting only once or twice – no further engagements," this way Nick has described his sexual experiences to the therapist until today. Nick's embodied homophobia has been a strong driver of objectifying sexual partners as "pussy" or "gayarse." When a sexual encounter was over, he used to despise himself and his partner.

Nevertheless, it occurs that yesterday evening was different. Nick enters the room and sits down in front of his therapist with apparent signs of embodied confusion. He greets the therapist but looks down. He sits but turns his head so as not to look at the therapist. For the therapist in this in-betweenness with Nick, shame emerges almost palpably. Out of his own awareness, the therapist asks, "What happened?" Nick replies: "My date yesterday was bizarre," still without a look at the therapist, his voice slightly shakes. The therapist asks Nick to tell him what happened with an additional request for speaking from the here-and-now perspective as if the encounter is taking place at the moment of speaking. Nick recapitulates as if in a present moment with Richie, his date: "Up to a certain point, nothing is new or surprising. Almost no touching each other. He is giving me a blow job, then taking it up the ass. That is it! I am still lying on the bed but ready to go home. And then this asshole is turning his body towards me and starting to spoon! Then he is biting my neck slightly and kissing it in the end." Nick stops talking, which is a definite stop, as he is petrified. There are signs of shame and confusion on his face. His head is lolled, and his eyeballs move skittishly. The therapist reminds him of breathing, which Nick accepts with nodding. Then the therapist asks Nick: "What do you feel in your body while saying it?" Nick replies: "My body is wooden and cold right now, but my neck. The neck where Richie touched me with his teeth and lips is warm. My body is dead, but the neck. I like this warmth and I hate Richie's teeth and lips." The therapist asks: "How are you not allowing yourself to like the bite and kiss?" Nick replies momentarily: "It is not me who forbids it! I should not like it! It is insane! I should not want to see Richie again! I am not this kind of a homo, am I?!" He bursts into tears. Nick sobs for a few minutes. The therapist's awareness becomes a part of the situation-of the relational field from which Nick's suffering emerges. The therapist attunes to Nick's despair, feeling sad and tearful himself. Nick's "should-nots" bring thoughts about modifying contact through introjecting. When crying saturates itself, the therapist asks Nick about his current moment. Nick says: "I have this too vivid imagery of Richie in my head, his gentle face, his hands, his hard cock. I can almost hear his sighs when I am inside him." The therapist says: "You wanted to see him, you said." Nick replies in a way that the therapist associates with relentlessness: "No, I should not!" "Why not?" the therapist further explores. "Homosexuality is unnatural and sick!," Nick almost screams. The therapist says: "Who told you this?" Nick comes back at the therapist reproachfully: "My school peers, the parish priest, my mother, and previous therapist, everybody!" The therapist with compassion: "It seems you have believed them, right?" Nick cries again. After a while, when dialogue is possible again, the therapist says: "In my professional opinion, you and Richie are both fine, young, healthy men." Nick sits with his head hung low, not even glancing at the therapist. The therapist runs a check: "Nick, have you heard what I said?" The client replies: "Yes, I have." The therapist: "How do you feel having heard my words about you and Richie being all fine?" Nick retorts: "I hate you!" and after a while "Plus, I would like you to hold my hand for a moment." The therapist calmly: "What would this mean to you, if I held your hand?" Nick replies: "That I am homosexual, have I even said that!?, and not repulsive to you. That you can touch my hand without nausea." Nick's embodiment changes. His eyes become tearful without crying. His chest moves smoothly, inhaling and exhaling. Nick's contacting modified by introjecting is further investigated till the end of the session.

During the session, Nick became aware – in Gestalt terms – of his psycho-sexual longing towards men. Not only was he conscious of his same-sex sexual drive – which he obviously knew before the session, but he was also contacting his senses and emotions. At the contact-boundary with the therapist, Nick could hear himself shouting with despair, feel the wetness of his tears running down his cheeks, "see" and "hear" Richie in the sudden imaginative recollections of the crucial evening, scream the harming messages on homosexuality and perceive associated body vibrations. Moreover, he could experience the emotionally attuned presence of the therapist. Peter Philippson (2012) hits the mark, reminding therapists that working through harmful introjects should involve the embodied domain of drives and senses at the contact boundary instead of verbal interventions being an offer to replace an old introject with a new one. Nonetheless, in the clinical vignette above, the therapist openly affirmed homosexuality as a normative sexual identity. In turn, this verbal intervention invited the embodied response in the client. I claim that with GSRD clients affirming non-heteronormative identities is not to convince them they are mentally healthy (it would be suggestive of a new introject). It is to convey contemporary knowledge of psychology and sexology instead of prejudiced messages on gender and sexuality. GSRD identities have been pathologised for so long that counter-balancing this violence by clear GSRD-affirmative statements from mental health professionals needs to be considered ethical and atonement towards the GSRD population.

Nick's session brought a psychic novelty to him: Nick's hope that his homosexual embodied self might be received by the other gently and with acceptance. This faith was expressed in the client's wish to hold his hand as proof of his homosexual body being acceptable. From the Gestalt theoretical perspective, Nick started aggressing his environment. In Gestalt therapy, "to aggress" means to existentially choose between alienation and assimilation (Philippson, 2012; Spagnuolo Lobb, 2013). This decision-making of what is me and what is not can operate fully in the state of awareness. Nick's decision to risk a new perception of his own body was an act of aggressing a homophobic environment. According to Paul Goodman (Perls, Hefferline and Goodman, 1951/1994), Nick made an important step in quitting being a patient.

The GSRD-Knowledgeable Gestalt Therapist

The editorial limits do not allow for the address of all aspects of the core components of GSRD therapy. My choice is to present how Gestalt therapy is a ground supportive of contemporary sexology and how the Gestalt theory of shame effectively assists therapy with GSRD clients.

Selfing, this emergent activity *at* and *of* the contact-boundary, is just happening. One cannot pause or stop it. Gestalt roots in Husserlian phe-nomenology (Husserl, 1936/1970) invite Gestalt therapists to think of the contact as intentional, then always directed towards or being about the object. Awareness is a vector (Philippson, 2001), which means that selfing is a process of never-ending change that has intention then also direction. However, as objects occur, disappear, or change, so may the intentionality of contacting. As a result, selfing is subject to alterations of its directedness. Gendering and sexuality emergence are aspects of selfing. This notion brings important theoretical and practical consequences. It means that our gendered and sexual being-ness is continually undergoing change or metamorphosis. We never stay the same. Labels such as "gay," "bisexual," "non-binary," or "straight" may have validity to the external socio-cultural world and grant "the owner" the sense of identity changelessness at a given time. However, this declared fixity is illusionary. We know the labels frequently change with time. Moreover, at a given moment, the same label may translate into differ-ent qualities for different people. From the Gestalt theory perspective, this is obvious and expected. Directedness of the present moment means there was *before* and will be *after*. Our gendering and sexually emergent selves have their own biographies. These biographies are always co-shaped by the fields of experience the organism has encountered over its lifetime. This relationally and field-informed approach contributes significantly to contemporary sexology. Difficulties like, for example, one's uncertainty about gender or sexual identity ("Am I non-binary? How can I know it?"), body dysphoria in trans clients ("I hate my vagina!"), anatomical constraints ("I need to leave him as I cannot bottom" in a case of anodyspareunia), or relationship clashes around kink ("Do I have to do this?!" in a case of wife's disgust towards the husband's spanking kink) would only benefit from applying the Gestalt perspective. For instance, in the last case, disgust comes from the couple's in-between. The wife reports it but disgust has been emerging as a field phenomenon. A question is how do both parts add to disgust occurrence? How is disgust associated with the wife's and husband's current selfing? How is the husband's wish to be spanked a part of the broader field (the one expanding beyond the couple) right now?

Readers interested in GSRD and Gestalt therapy sexological intersections may reach for the latest anthology *Queering Gestalt Therapy* (Alman, Gillespie and Kolmannskog, 2023). Gestalt methodology was also implemented to explore more general issues, for example sexual difficulties as understood in medical narratives of ICD-10 (Amendt-Lyon, 2013), intimacy (Klepner, 2014), erotic vs. sexual (O'Shea, 2020), sexuality and its place in psychotherapy (Philippson, 2022), desire and the love-lust dilemma (Resnick, 2012), and HIV and culture (Warburton and Kuykendall, 2005).

The understanding of shame, an affect abundantly present in GSRD populations, has been thoroughly developed in Gestalt theory. The field-informed and constructivist model (Wheeler, 2008) has been the most referenced theoretical perspective on shame in the Gestalt community. It assumes that shame stems from a break in connectedness in a social field, which equates to: "the unacceptability of the personal self of needs and characteristics and desires in the social field where the integrative self-process is trying to take place" (Wheeler, 2008, p. 48). In this model, rescue comes as field supports that are considered facilitators of re-establishing connectedness between the individual and their environment. For example, the model explains how the sense of being accepted as a GSRD person in a GSRD therapy group reduces shame associated with non-heteronormative identity. Interestingly, Philippson (2012) argues with the above model, focusing on the exchange between the "shamer" and "shamed." He defines shame as a retroflection of the disgust reflex. According to Philippson (2012), shame arises when the individual inhibits a natural reflex to refuse what is psychologically indigestible and harmful, simultaneously taking it as a part of their own self. In such a situation, therapeutic interventions aim to restore the client's ability to stay with disgust and reject what is damaging to the self. In terms of GSRD therapy, this concept seems to clarify, for instance, the occurrence of clinical consequences of minority stress and microaggressions in the form of internalised homo-, bi- and transphobia.

Summary

Bringing the chapter to a conclusion, I think of joy, one of the core components of GSRD therapy. In line with Gestalt therapy principles, joy is a co-created relational phenomenon in and of the field. The emergence of joy is anchored in the client and therapist together. The therapist may or may not be a co-facilitator of joy. Gestalt practitioners have all the needed theoretical tools at hand to support GSRD clients in becoming joyful in the context of their GSRD identities, whether it means romantic relationships, sex, friendships, parenthood, getting older, or adopting a new GSRD identity. Gestalt theory embraces GSRD identities and practices by definition. Human diversity revealing itself as a variety of GSRD identifications is an obvious consequence of selfing at the contact-boundary. Nonetheless, GSRD-affirmative theory needs a GSRD-affirmative therapist. It would require supplementary work in addition to Gestalt therapy training, including personal therapy with a GSRD-knowledgeable therapist to explore one's gendering and sexuality, anti-discrimination training, and a specialist course in GSRD-informed mental health.

References

Alman, A., Gillespie, J. and Kolmannskog, V. (2023) *Queering Gestalt therapy: an anthology on gender, sex & relationship diversity in psychotherapy*. Abingdon: Routledge.

Amendt-Lyon, N. (2013) 'Relational sexual issues: love and lust in context', in Francesetti, G., Gecele, M. and Roubal J. (eds.) *Gestalt therapy in clinical practice: from psychopathology to the aesthetics of contact*. Milan: Instituto di Gestalt HCC Italy srl, pp. 571–588.

Bąk, D. (2024) 'When home becomes a threat: Polish experience of homo-, bi-, and transphobia', in Chrząstowski S. and Vetere A. (eds.) *Safety, danger, and protection in the family and community: a systemic and attachment-informed approach*. Abingdon: Routledge, pp. 36–47.

Davies, D. and Neves, S. (2023) 'Gender, sex, and relationship diversity therapy', in Hanley, T. and Winter, L.A. (eds.), *The SAGE handbook of counselling and psychotherapy*. 5th edn. London: SAGE, pp. 409–414.

Fodor, I. (1998) 'Awareness and meaning-making: the dance of experience', *Gestalt Review*, 2(1), pp. 50–71.

Husserl, E. (1936/1970) *Crisis of European sciences and transcendental phenomenology: an introduction to phenomenological philosophy*. Evanston, IL: Northwestern University Press.

Jacobs, L. (2009) 'Relationality: foundational assumptions', in Ullman, D. and Wheeler, G. (eds.) *Co-creating the field: intention and practice in the age of complexity*. Santa Cruz, CA and Orleans, MA: GestaltPress, pp. 41–66.

Klepner, P. (2014) 'Exploring intimacy – a Gestalt therapy approach', in Bloom, D. and O'Neill B. (eds.) *The New York Institute for Gestalt therapy in the 21st century: an anthology of published writings since 2000.* Peregian Beach: Ravenwood Press, pp. 353–375.

Köhler, W. (1969) *The task of Gestalt psychology.* Princeton, NJ: Princeton University Press.

Merleau-Ponty, M. (1945/2012) *Phenomenology of perception.* Abingdon: Routledge.

O'Shea, L. (2020) 'Erotic ground: always and already there', in Clemmens, M.C. (ed.) *Embodied relational Gestalt: theory and applications.* Santa Cruz, CA and Eastham, MA: GestaltPress, pp. 123–168.

Perls, F., Hefferline, R.F. and Goodman, P. (1951/1994) *Gestalt therapy: excitement and growth in the human personality.* London: Souvenir Press.

Philippson, P. (2001) *Self in relation.* Gouldsboro, ME: The Gestalt Journal Press, Inc.

Philippson, P. (2012) *Gestalt therapy: roots and branches – collected papers.* London: Karnac Books Ltd.

Philippson, P. (2022) *The 'active principle' in Gestalt therapy and other essays.* Manchester: Manchester Gestalt Centre.

Resnick, S. (2012) *The heart of desire: keys to the pleasures of love.* Hoboken, NJ: John Wiley & Sons, Inc.

Spagnuolo Lobb, M. (2013) 'Fundamentals and development of Gestalt therapy in the contemporary context', in Francesetti, G., Gecele, M. and Roubal J. (eds.) *Gestalt therapy in clinical practice: from psychopathology to the aesthetics of contact.* Milan: Instituto di Gestalt HCC Italy srl, pp. 22–52.

Stern, D.N. (1998) *Interpersonal world of the infant: a view from psychoanalysis and development psychology.* London: Karnac Books Ltd.

Warburton, G. and Kuykendall, J. (2005) 'HIV and culture', in Levine Bar-Yoseph, T. (ed.) *The bridge: dialogues across cultures.* Metairie, LA: The Gestalt Institute and Relationship Center of New Orleans, pp. 87–101.

Wheeler, G. (2008) 'Self and shame: a new paradigm for psychotherapy', in Lee, R.G. and Wheeler, G. (eds.) *The voice of shame: silence and connection in psychotherapy.* Santa Cruz, CA and Orleans, MA: GestaltPress, pp. 23–58.

Wheeler, G. (2011) 'Who are we? Narrative, evolution, & development: our stories and ourselves', in Lee, R.G. and Harris, N. (eds.) *Relational child, relational brain: development and therapy in childhood and adolescence.* Santa Cruz, CA and Orleans, MA: GestaltPress, pp. 5–52.

Chapter 9

Internal Family Systems (IFS) to Support GSRD People Dealing with Body Image Difficulties

Alessio Rizzo

Introduction

This chapter explores how Internal Family Systems (IFS) therapy can support members of the GSRD community facing problems related to their body image.

The IFS model allows therapists to take a non-pathologising approach to body image issues and supports clients to move from extreme behaviours and thoughts related to body image to a more harmonious and balanced relationship with their body. An IFS model of working with GSRD people is proposed by taking into consideration the parts, and their burdens about body image, involved in sexuality, gender identity and expression, and adherence to societal, cultural and legacy norms.

Case examples and research findings are provided to address three subgroups of the GSRD community: sexual minority men, lesbian women, and transgender individuals. This highlights the importance of adapting existing theories, used to explain body image issues in the broader population, which might not apply in the same way to all GSRD people. More research is needed to gather a fuller understanding of how different subgroups within the GSRD community experience body image issues, and also on how to use IFS with body image issues and GSRD clients.

Brief Overview of Internal Family Systems (IFS) Therapy: Core Principles and Concepts of IFS

Internal Family Systems (IFS) therapy was developed in the 1980s by Dr Richard Schwartz. He originally trained in family therapy and noticed that his clients spontaneously described having conflicting parts within themselves. He observed that these parts held their own beliefs, emotions, and desires and organised within the internal world, forming a system, like a family.

In the psychotherapeutic field, the concept of subpersonalities (Jung, 1969) offers a useful starting point for describing the parts within IFS.

DOI: 10.4324/9781003530848-12

At the root of IFS is what Schwartz calls the multiplicity of mind, which posits that the normal functioning of our mind involves a multiplicity of thoughts, emotions, physical sensations, and impulses occurring simultaneously. Unlike the monomind paradigm, which considers that there is one unique state of being at one time, the multiplicity of mind allows us to reframe all aspects of human experience as the presence and interaction of parts within our mind.

Schwartz (2021) discovered various features of the inner world or internal system. His most significant discovery was that the inner world is not just inhabited by parts, which form a network of relationships, but also by something he named the Self (Schwartz, 2021). The Self is not a part and represents the essence of an individual, remaining intact despite the degree of trauma a person experiences.

Schwartz experimented with asking parts inhabiting the internal world to give space to his clients' core essence. To his surprise, once parts stepped back, all clients entered an expansive, relaxed, and compassionate state of consciousness. Everybody has a Self, which is characterised by the so-called 8 C's (Schwartz and Sweezy, 2020): curiosity, compassion, calm, confidence, connectedness, courage, clarity, and creativity.

When our system undergoes traumatic events, the natural harmony of our inner world is broken, and parts organise internally amongst themselves to protect the system from being hurt again. In this process, the affected parts lose connection with the Self and, instead, deal with the trauma's injury in the best ways they can. As a result, some parts carry the pain of the traumatic events and move to the edges of the person's consciousness as if they were exiled. Other parts prevent similar traumas from happening again, and others help the system quickly move away from painful inner states whenever they occur.

By disconnecting from the Self, parts remain stuck in the time and place of the injury, carrying various burdens in the form of emotions, somatic experiences, and beliefs associated with the traumatic events. As long as parts keep interacting with each other and not with the Self, little change occurs, and they keep carrying their burdens.

The Paradigm Shift of IFS: A Non-pathologising Approach That Brings Compassionate Curiosity to the Inner World

Often, people hesitate to engage with IFS because they hold the belief that having parts inside means living with a dissociative disorder. Furthermore, it is challenging for people who have held negative beliefs about themselves their entire lives and are convinced that they are broken to their core to embrace the idea that we all have a Self.

Dr Schwartz's motto has been that there are "no bad parts" (2023), which is the title of his most recent book. His message is that not only do we have a Self that exudes beautiful qualities, but our parts, even when they engage in behaviours that seem inadequate (like self-harming, bingeing, self-hate, substance abuse, aggressive, and hurtful behaviours, etc.), do it because they have taken an extreme protective role in the system and believe there is no other choice.

Given the above, we can see that IFS has queered the mind and traditional psychotherapy by questioning and redefining who we are at our core and how our inner world works. Considering that no parts are inherently bad not only makes IFS a non-pathologising model but also reinforces the necessity for therapists to remain curious and compassionate towards all parts (and people), regardless of how bad their behaviours might seem.

IFS fosters a continuous inner search for determining one's own identity and lifestyle from within. The overall goals of IFS therapy, along with a description of parts and the Self, can be found on the IFS Institute's website. IFS therapy's goals of achieving inner balance and harmony, supporting the Self to become the leader of the system and facilitating parts in releasing their burdens, i.e. being "Self-led" (Schwartz and Sweezy, 2020), help people deconstruct all the false ideas and identities they have accrued due to trauma, including oppression.

The latest developments of IFS (for example, Floyd, 2024) are shedding light on the many types of burdens that people carry, including ancestral and cultural burdens. From an IFS perspective, burdens in the form of oppression and prejudice against GSRD people exist within the internal system because they have been absorbed from culture, society, families, institutions, and any form of media that carries such burdens.

Through compassionate inquiry within their inner world, as parts begin to unburden and relinquish extreme and unhealthy protective roles, people can discover all aspects of their identities, including those that had to be exiled due to oppression.

The centrality of the Self in IFS therapy implies that IFS therapists aim to connect to their clients from their Self rather than their parts. Hence, IFS therapists are constantly encouraged and reminded to become familiar with their parts and their burdens, ensuring that these burdens do not impede the therapeutic work.

At the same time, while every IFS professional strives to bring compassion and curiosity to their client's inner system, offering acceptance to the landscape of sexual and gender identities is not easily done if the therapist is not aware, themselves, of the complexities related to sexuality and gender diversities. It is, therefore, important for IFS professionals working with GSRD clients to have an awareness not only of how their system organises around sexuality and gender, but also to be humble enough to investigate with curiosity and respect the system of their clients.

Using IFS When Body Image Issues Affect Different GSRD Populations: Sexual Minority Men, Lesbian Women, and Transgender Individuals

A study by Diemer *et al.* (2018) showed that societal expectations and heteronormative standards significantly affect body image amongst GSRD individuals, and the connection between poor body image and mental health issues such as anxiety, depression, and self-esteem are other well-documented outcomes (McClain & Peebles, 2016).

Convertino *et al.* (2021) have shown that, by integrating sociocultural and minority stress theories, it is possible to better explain how subcategories of the GSRD community are affected differently by body image issues. In particular, they highlight how community involvement, which generally has a positive impact on mental health for minority groups, does not always have a positive effect on body image issues for all GSRD people. There are, therefore, differences amongst the GSRD sub-communities, confirmed by Muzi *et al.* (2023), who state the importance of considering the nuances specific to GSRD individuals.

Merino *et al.* (2024), having analysed and compared articles on the impact of social media and physical measurement on body image published in the past 20 years, define body image as "an individual's perception, feelings, and emotions around their physical appearance". Merino *et al.* (2024 p 3) provide a list of three sociocultural theories: objectification theory (Fredrickson and Roberts, 1997), social comparison theory applied to body image (Krayer *et al.*, 2008), and Self-Discrepancy theory (Higgins, 1987) that can be used to understand the phenomenon of body image dissatisfaction. These theories are not specific to the GSRD population, but they can be integrated with minority stress theories when supporting GSRD clients.

It is to be noticed that research, despite the growing number of studies focusing on GSRD people, has not come to a conclusive understanding of the impact of sexual and gender differences on body image issues (Kalash *et al.*, 2023; Muzi *et al.*, 2023). Many studies show that sexual minority men are more likely to experience body dissatisfaction than heterosexual cisgender men (He *et al.*, 2020). Any other differences in body image difficulties based on sexual and gender diversity have not been backed by consistent results amongst studies.

In what follows, we are going to have a closer look at three populations within the GSRD community, for which we have several studies: sexual minority men, lesbian women, and transgender people.

Sexual Minority Men

Soulliard *et al.* (2023), who define sexual minority as "men who identify as gay, bisexual, or queer; other men who have sex with men" (p. 1), state that a combination of minority stress theories and intra-minority stress is needed to explain better how sexual minority men are affected more than their heterosexual counterparts on the following aspects of body image (p. 1):

- Greater body and weight dissatisfaction.
- Increased drive for both muscularity and thinness.
- Social comparison of their bodies.

Soulliard *et al.* (2023) show evidence that interactions within the community of sexual minority men increase the possibility of experiencing body dissatisfaction. They therefore introduced the "gay-community-stress theory" to indicate that, for sexual minority men, the pressure coming from within the community adds to the already present minority stress, like heterosexism. This is in line with research on intra-community stressors experienced by gay men (Hammack *et al.*, 2021) around body image in addition to the ones listed above. For instance, it is widely common for sexual minority men to experience body stigma in the form of discriminatory comments on mobile apps, like "no fats, no fems" (Chow, 2021). Often, gay men are asked to indicate a subgroup (usually called a tribe) that they belong to based on body features that create expectations in terms of sex roles (bear, twink, clean-cut, etc.). Stigma and prejudice can also stem from one's ethnicity, sexual preference, and gender expression, with sexual minority men who are gender non-conforming and assuming the bottom position during anal intercourse being perceived as less attractive (Ravenhill and de Visser, 2017).

Other findings highlight the importance of intersectionality in relation to body image. Black GSRD individuals, for example, experience unique stressors that influence their body image differently from their white counterparts (Mereish *et al.*, 2022).

> Jay (he/him) is a 22-year-old mixed-race (Chinese and English) cisgender gay man living in London. He grew up in the UK, away from a big city, and moved to London during his university years. Despite completing his studies and having a good job, he has not had a satisfactory dating and/or sexual life in London. He seeks therapy to boost his confidence, and when the therapist asks how he has tried to tackle this problem, Jay reveals that his efforts have focused on changing his body and appearance because he believes it to be the problem.

Using IFS, the therapist remains curious about the parts of Jay that have taken on the role of acting on the body to achieve more confidence. Probably these parts are protectors who have learnt that society, and the gay scene in particular, rewards people who behave and appear in a certain way. For these parts, confidence comes from external validation, which they seek in various ways, such as concealing some of their body features on dating apps by choosing photos that do not reveal their Asian heritage and using the gym and specific food supplements to increase their muscle mass.

From an IFS perspective, confidence is an innate quality of the Self, which is therefore available to Jay's system regardless of his body shape. The therapist invites Jay to reflect on how successful he has been in finding satisfactory romantic and/or sexual partners and if he could consider doing something different about the problem. Jay reluctantly admits that the gym routines are challenging to maintain and that, despite all his efforts, he feels less satisfied with his body than he did before. The therapist then invites the parts of Jay who hold the image of what his body should look like to come forward.

Jay discovers that these parts want to change his body because, otherwise, people categorise him as a "bottom Asian", when, in effect, he is versatile when it comes to anal sex preferences. Jay's system is angered and grieved by how often people treat him because of these assumptions. The therapist invites Jay's Self to meet those parts affected by such complex emotions. Such parts, once in connection with the Self, manage to share the impact of all the times in which Jay had been discriminated against because of his body image.

The therapist helps Jay's parts identify how, as a result of these unhealed wounds of rejection, they had been burdened by the belief that the only way to be accepted is to change his appearance. Thanks to his cultural competence in the field, the therapist supports Jay in realising that his system is experiencing not only personal burdens due to the episodes of rejection he went through, but also cultural burdens and, in particular, burdens that are specific to the Western gay community.

These beliefs are released from the system by recognising that the system does not need these burdens and by the compassionate inner connection between parts holding such burdens and the Self. Gradually, parts that fear further rejection can develop an inner relationship with the Self, which, over time, can become an inner source of validation and acceptance. Consequently, Jay's system becomes less affected by other people's opinions and projections on him, and it becomes easier for Jay to interact with people he is attracted to. As parts leave their extreme protective role of worrying and checking the body, Jay finds confidence in feeling good, from the inside out, about the way his body is.

While Jay's inner work has not solved the sad issues related to the existing discrimination in the gay scene, he has managed to heal his wounds and create a connection to his Self.

Lesbian Women

As stated earlier, research has not found sufficient evidence to suggest that there are differences between lesbian and heterosexual women regarding body dissatisfaction (Owens *et al.*, 2003). Some studies, though, have shed light on differences between heterosexual and lesbian women when it comes to how social norms are internalised, with lesbian women being less focused on physical attractiveness (Siever, 1994), and less prone to see themselves as overweight or have a negative body image due to their body size (French *et al.*, 1996). However, despite these differences and the tendency of lesbian women to embrace feminist ideals that encourage more tolerance towards body image (Rothblum, 1994), Owens *et al.* (2003) argue that lesbian women end up being affected by sociocultural expectations as much as heterosexual women, as research data suggests. This can be explained from an IFS perspective by examining how the person has integrated feminist ideals into their system.

Let us consider the example of Linda (she/her), a 30-year-old cisgender English white-skinned lesbian woman. Linda is the middle child of three sisters who attended girls' schools for most of their education. Linda started dating women at 18 and came out to her family when she was 17. She is now in a relationship and has recurring dissatisfaction with her body shape since she gained some weight in the last year of her life.

Due to her upbringing, Linda is likely to have experienced significant pressure from her family and broader society, as she is constantly compared to her sisters. Many people often complimented her for being slimmer than her sisters, and she received various comments at school, where her body was frequently compared to that of her peers. Linda is unlikely to carry many personal burdens related to her body. Still, surely her parts have understood that they will be judged based on their bodies, either positively or negatively. Therefore, parts started to monitor how others judged her body at home, school, and other social circles.

After coming out, Linda embraced feminist ideas that rejected the objectification of women's bodies. At times, her memories of all the comments she had received about her body through the years make a part of her feel angry. In IFS, parts that assume a protective role to prevent something from happening again are called managers (Schwartz and Sweezy, 2020). A manager, part of Linda, decides she will no longer allow these comments to come her way and bother her. To achieve this, Linda takes distance from people who continue to share their opinions about her body, and also pushes away her anger because she does not want to feel it or show it. When Linda looks at herself in the mirror, she finds that a part of her judges her body harshly.

From an IFS perspective, Linda's system is an example of how managers can embrace new ideals and values and impose them on the system as if there were new rules in the internal world. The hope is that these new ideals and values will prevent certain unpleasant things from happening again.

Unfortunately, the imposition of new rules, despite giving Linda a sense of strength and belonging, does not guarantee that the old beliefs and burdens about body image no longer influence the system. Some parts continue to remain unchanged inside the system, forming the following painful dynamic:

- A part judges the body harshly despite the new rules imposed by the manager's part. The manager has simply imposed new ideals, but some still hold old beliefs and habits. Whenever the manager's part reduces the level of control, old patterns emerge.
- It is also likely that another part still exists that holds the pain of all the times Linda's body was the target of various comments. This part will feel pain again when the same judgement is expressed internally, potentially resulting in feelings of shame.

Working with IFS, Linda would learn to identify and connect with all these parts and introduce the Self to connect with them all. Through this connection, old beliefs and wounds about body image can be released, and the parts that hold internal judgement might no longer have a reason to do so. As the pain around body image leaves the system and parts change their behaviours about the topic, all parts can embrace feminist ideals without needing to be forcefully imposed on the system by a manager part.

Transgender Individuals

Tabaac *et al.* (2018) carried out the first study that demonstrated how discrimination experienced in society is linked to poor body image satisfaction in transgender people. This confirms results from previous studies showing that transgender people experience more body dissatisfaction than cisgender men and women (Vocks *et al.*, 2009).

Another study by Meneguzzo *et al.* (2024) confirmed that body objectification and body weight dissatisfaction influenced transgender people in ways that cause higher levels of body dissatisfaction than in other populations.

These recent studies point to the need for a way of treating body image dissatisfaction for transgender people by considering the complexities specific to them, and IFS can embrace such complexities by inviting people to become familiar with their burdens, and with the current and past circumstances and situations that have generated them.

Let us consider Andrea (she/her). Andrea is 43 years old, White and British; she was assigned male at birth and, during therapy, embraced her transgender identity and decided to start gender-affirming hormone therapy. The main presenting issue is her face, which she dislikes profoundly.

Before identifying the parts at play in her dislike of her face, the therapist takes a step back and wonders how the issue of looks relates to external factors, such as society and culture, and internal factors linked to identity.

Inviting Andrea to look inside her system with an open mind, an aspect of the Self, made it possible to connect with the parts that played a role in her deep dislike of her face. This led to the discovery of various forms of inner judgement, falling into two similar but distinct categories.

- My face is ugly.
- This face is not mine.

These two categories require different therapeutic approaches in IFS. The first one ("my face is ugly") is similar to what we discussed in earlier examples. It can be treated as a burden that Andrea's system has taken on by being subject to cultural and social norms linked to beauty standards, which can be released.

The second category ("this face is not mine") represents an aspect of what is generally called body dysphoria. From an IFS perspective, the therapist needs to approach the feeling that "the face is not mine", not as the result of interference and trauma, but as an element of the transgender identity.

"This face is not mine" is not a burden to be released, but a painful experience that the system has carried for a long time and needs to be honoured and treated with compassion. The burdens here are linked to the sense of helplessness and isolation that resulted in carrying that experience in a world that discriminates against non-cisgender people.

An IFS Model to Work with GSRD Systems

As we have seen in the earlier examples, personal, cultural, and legacy burdens enable the individual to understand how their internal system has been shaped by the social landscape in which they grew up, lived, and continue to live. When it comes to the GSRD community, beliefs and expectations regarding gender roles that are projected onto toddlers from conception can give birth to burdens that the system carries in ways that are pre-verbal. For example, if a mother has parts of her system that have issues with the sex of the newborn baby, this could potentially plant the seed of the burden "I am unlovable" in that newborn baby.

Growing up, how "boys" and "girls" behave, walk, interact and look after their appearance are heavily codified by culture, social media, peers and adults. Shaming, bullying and discrimination flourish as soon as anybody's body and behaviour do not fit into the sexual and gender norms of society. For GSRD people, already dealing with the challenges linked to gender and sexual differences that make it difficult to grow up feeling healthy, confident and secure (Anderson, 2025), body image issues contribute to an already precarious situation.

Anderson (2025) explains that, when working with GSRD clients, he identifies parts of the system that carry the wounds (exiles) linked to sexual or gender differences, and four types of parts that are in charge of protecting such wounds. These are:

1. Parts connected to sexuality.
2. Parts connected to gender.

3. Parts associated with culture and society.
4. Parts associated with family legacy.

A cisgender heterosexual person might not have as many wounds associated with sexuality and gender as a GSRD person and, therefore, might not need to have highly protective parts connected to these areas. A body image issue in this case could be primarily helped by addressing cultural and legacy problems. For a GSRD person, the same body image issue could potentially affect all four dimensions, thus causing a much more substantial impact on the system. Figure 9.1 (adapted from Anderson, 2025) illustrates how a GSRD system is impacted by issues surrounding gender and sexuality.

While the diagram might sometimes oversimplify the internal landscape of a GSRD person, it is helpful to notice how we can find issues related to identity vertically and issues related to the influence of culture and family horizontally. By looking at the two directions individually, we can understand

GSRD System Mapping

Identity

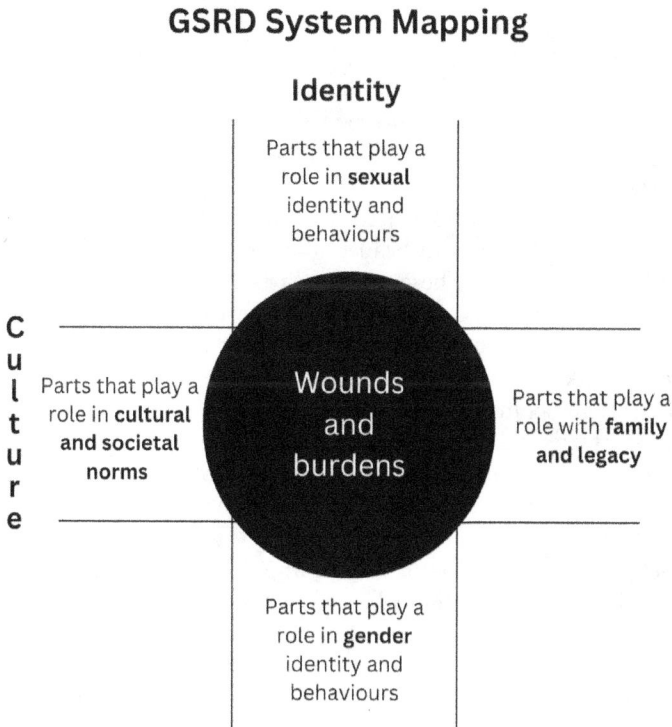

Parts that play a role in **sexual** identity and behaviours

Culture

Parts that play a role in **cultural and societal** norms

Wounds and burdens

Parts that play a role with **family and legacy**

Parts that play a role in **gender** identity and behaviours

Figure 9.1 GSRD system mapping

the nuances of how body image issues affect GSRD people in ways that are different from the rest of the population.

Let us begin with the vertical direction by temporarily ignoring the impact of external factors on society and the family, bearing in mind that we can never fully disentangle the external from the internal world.

Body image issues, when considered as an aspect of gender, take on the form of body dysphoria when an individual has parts that identify as a gender (or no gender) that do not correspond to the biology of the physical body. The burdens carried by these parts revolve around identity issues like "This is not my body".

When it comes to sexuality, one person may experience themselves as attractive, sexually empowered, and confident when their body has a specific image. This might, or might not, have to do with societal norms, and parts might want to modify the body to align with one particular sexual identity. For example, someone might want to cross-dress for a sexual encounter (with no necessary implications on gender identity). If we go back to the example of Jay discussed earlier, there might be a need to adjust and modify body image to adhere to the expected gender expression of a gay man who has a particular sexual preference. Parts learn that, to feel attractive and sexual and find the right partner, the body and the entire demeanour of a person need to fit into specific standards. Burdens in this area revolve around "I cannot be sexual in this body", or "If I do not move/dress/talk/walk/speak a certain way, my sexual preferences will not be believed".

If we now consider the horizontal dimension (culture), a new set of burdens can be added about the "shoulds" of body image inherited by the external system. The parts associated with society and culture are those who quickly learn about the current beauty standards propagated by peers, community, and social media. These are the parts that invest energy in shaping body image to cope with and gain acceptance from the communities they want to belong to. Dieting, exercising, food control, fashion choices, posture adjustments, makeup, and surgery are all strategies these parts can employ due to societal and cultural beauty standards.

If such strategies and body image modifications align with the system's gender and sexual identity, then the actions of these parts might comfort the entire system. In the presence of agreement within parts, we can consider this behaviour Self-led.

If societal standards impose a way of appearing not in line with the system's inner identities, then the behaviour is not Self-led and leads to inner struggles. For example, a gay genderfluid person assigned male at birth might have parts who want to appear hyper-masculine to have success on dating apps. Even if this strategy is successful, the parts holding a genderfluid identity might need to be constantly put aside and have no expression, which can lead to internal struggles.

The same body image feature could be problematic on identity and cultural levels. For example, certain features like the shape of the nose might attract comments from the family since birth, like "all the women in the family have that ugly big nose", while it also bothers parts that hold the belief that "women should have a small nose".

Finally, parts associated with family and legacy commonly show up as guilt and shame. Homophobic and transphobic messages are part of the commonly used language in many countries around the world. These parts quickly learn how wrong it is not to be heterosexual or cisgender and employ strategies to hide gender and sexual identities from oneself and the family. A typical example of this is when a baby wears colours or clothes of the "wrong gender", and gets told off and/or shamed by their carers/peers/or educators.

An IFS therapist, knowing that societal standards of body image have existed since birth, might use that knowledge to ask specific questions that are not included in the standard IFS protocols. For example, if a part negatively judges the body, the therapist can suggest questions like the following.

- When did this part start holding this judgement?
- Did the part learn it from anyone, like family, friends, or communities?
- What does the part achieve by holding on to this negative judgement?
- What does the part do to change the body?
- Are there other parts that would like the body to be and look different to what it is because it does not feel like it is "my" body?

In what follows, we will explore how the two main IFS protocols can be applied to address body image concerns.

Introduction of Specific IFS Techniques for Addressing Body Image Concerns

As discussed earlier, body image issues can be caused by parts that adopt certain extreme behaviours to cope with the wounding inside the system. With IFS, we can start by observing all the behaviours, feelings, emotions, and impulses associated with body image issues. From these observations, by guiding the client through a technique called "in-sight" (Schwartz and Sweezy, 2020), we can understand the parts involved in the body image issues and what is causing them to act in those specific ways.

We may be able to use the map provided earlier, or we may need to adapt it to the individual's specific system, for example, by adding space for experiences related to disabilities (whether visible or not). It is not necessary to have an accurate map of the system from the beginning. Still, the professional needs to have in mind all the elements of the map that can contribute to body image issues, as well as the particular spectrum of needs and circumstances of GSRD people, so that differences that are not within the direct experience of the therapist are not minimised or overlooked.

At this point, it is necessary to describe how IFS conceptualises the body. A recent development of IFS in the neurodivergent field (Christiansen and Martinez-Dettamanti, 2023) considers that parts are comparable to the "software" of our system that, to function, needs the "hardware", which is the body and all its components, including the brain.

With IFS therapy, we can investigate how parts (software) are coping with the body (hardware) provided. In the case of gender dysphoria, we can consider parts wanting to function in ways that are not compatible with the body provided. In the case of body dysmorphia, we can think of parts as pieces of software that constantly check, analyse, and evaluate the shape of the body in a way that leads to a distorted appraisal of the body image.

Regardless of the complexity of the presenting issue, IFS uses two main protocols to deal with parts: one called "the 6 F's" used to create a relationship between a protector part and the Self, and the "healing steps" (Schwartz and Sweezy, 2020) used to help a part connect to the Self and release burdens. The name "6 F's" comes from the fact that it is composed of six steps that happen to either start or contain the letter "F" in the English language; these are:

1. Find
2. Focus
3. Flesh out
4. Feel towards
5. BeFriend
6. Fears.

These steps allow the IFS therapist to help a part in consideration (technically called the target part) to enter into contact with the Self of the client, and, once the connection between Self and part is strong enough, establish an inner conversation that can reveal the following (for example linked to calorie counting)

- What the part is trying to achieve through its behaviour - "when I count calories, I feel more in control and calm".
- What fears there are in case the part stopped doing it - "I need to control my weight at all costs; if I stop counting calories, I will eat with no end, and I will get fatter".
- What is keeping the part in that extreme role - "If I get fat, people will leave me and I will have no friends and no sexual life".

Usually, the last step (Fears) reveals the existence of another part holding pain and being protected by the part being interviewed. In the example above, the fear that people will leave the person hints at the fact that there is at least another part holding wounding related to abandonment. The IFS therapist might, therefore, ask the client to check if there is, indeed, a part inside the system that is feeling the pain of being abandoned by people.

Generally, this opens a path to help the part holding the wound of being left alone. This is when IFS uses the "the healing steps" protocol, facilitating a healing connection between that part and the client's self. It is at this point that the wounded part reveals issues related to gender and sexuality, as well as any other complex and traumatic experiences, which can be witnessed through the compassionate presence of the Self.

Traumatic memories can be safely revisited and healed thanks to the presence of the client's Self inside the system and the guidance of the therapist's Self from outside the system. Burdens acquired due to traumatic events, including all the negative beliefs acquired about oneself and the world as a result of the trauma, can be discharged safely.

One of the healing steps offers the opportunity to "do over" in the internal world and correct wrongdoings that parts were subjected to. An example of a do-over could be that a part, after having the Self witness the bullying and discrimination that were happening due to body differences, race, and sexual diversity, asks the Self to be there during the episodes of bullying and tell the bullies to leave.

The healing steps and the subsequent unburdening of parts heal those deep wounds that have resulted in dysfunctional behaviour related to body image. IFS then proceeds to reconnect the client's Self with those parts dealing with body image issues to update them that some wounds have been healed. Parts, unless there is further wounding or other reasons yet to be discovered, naturally and happily abandon their extreme roles involved in body image issues.

Conclusion

In this chapter, we have explored issues related to body image through an IFS lens, including specific aspects of GSRD experiences linked to gender and sexuality, as well as other minority stresses coming from legacy, family or cultural circumstances that have wounded and burdened the system.

. We have also seen how IFS is a non-pathologising trauma-informed approach that is in line with the principles of GSRD therapy and requires, nevertheless, professionals to acquire GSRD-specific knowledge to support their clients. The examples provided of a gay man, a lesbian woman and a transgender person aimed at providing current findings from literature on body image issues experienced by GSRD people.

We have seen how, with IFS, it is possible to distinguish between aspects of body image issues related to gender identity ("This is not my body"), and matters concerning legacy and culture ("This is how my body should and should not look like").

IFS techniques allow us to identify the parts involved in body image issues and hear, directly from them, the inner causes that lead these parts to have extreme behaviours that, in the more acute cases, manifest in eating disorders and body dysmorphia. Without using pathologising language, IFS brings us back to the healing power of connecting the Self to those parts and follows the protocols to heal the wounds fuelling body image issues.

I am currently the only GSRD voice within the current discourse about how IFS can support body image issues for the GSRD community, and further development is needed to adapt and refine the existing IFS protocols when working with GSRD people. There are currently some training programmes organised in North America that GSRD trainers and staff provide to GSRD people. Alolkoy (2024) recently published a memoir of their IFS journey to unburden their system from various gender-related burdens. Further research is also needed to better understand the typical internal structure and landscape of different subgroups of GSRD clients.

The healing and unburdening IFS protocols offer the entire community an excellent opportunity to move on from past wounds and reduce the impact of current stressors linked to body image. Due to its friendly language and favourable media coverage, IFS spread quickly around the globe, with members of the public seeking IFS therapy before the official IFS training is available in all languages. This chapter encourages GSRD professionals to seek IFS training to initiate a discourse and research on how IFS can best serve and provide healing to the GSRD community.

References

Alolkoy, K. (2024) *Gender unburdening: Using internal family systems to heal from gender socialization*. Two Hawks Press.

Anderson (2025, November) 'Embodying IFS with sexual orientation: Trauma healing as a path to the integrated self', in Riermersma, J. (ed.) *IFS integration: A comprehensive guide to applying internal family systems across modalities, populations, and clinical presentations*. PESI Publishing & Bridge City Books.

Chow, J. (2021) 'No fats, no fems, no problems? Working out and the gay muscled body', *Sexualities*, 25. https://doi.org/10.1177/13634607211018331

Christiansen, C. and Martinez-Dettamanti, M. (2023) 'Embodying IFS with neurodivergent clients: A neuro-inclusive approach for therapists', in Riemersma, J. (ed.) *Altogether us: Integrating the IFS model with key modalities, communities, and trends*. Pivotal Press, p. xx.

Convertino, A.D., Helm, J.L., Pennesi, J.L., Gonzales, M. IV and Blashill, A.J. (2021) 'Integrating minority stress theory and the tripartite influence model: A model of eating disordered behavior in sexual minority young adults', *Appetite*, 163, p. 105204. https://doi.org/10.1016/j.appet.2021.105204.

Diemer, E.W., White Hughto, J.M., Gordon, A.R., Guss, C., Austin, S.B. and Reisner, S.L. (2018) 'Beyond the binary: Differences in eating disorder prevalence by gender identity in a transgender sample', *Transgender Health*, 3(1), pp. 17–23. https://doi.org/10.1089/trgh.2017.0043.

Floyd, T. (2024) *Listening when parts speak: A practical guide to healing with internal family systems therapy and ance*stor wisdom. Hay House.

Fredrickson, B.L. and Roberts, T.-A. (1997) 'Objectification theory: Toward understanding women's lived experiences and mental health *risks'*, *Psychology of Women Quarterly*, 21(2), pp. 173–206. https://doi.org/10.1111/j.1471-6402.1997.tb00108.x

French, S.A., Story, M., Remafedi, G., Resnick, M.D. and Blum, R.W. (1996) 'Sexual orientation and prevalence of body dissatisfaction and eating disordered behavi*ors: A population-based study of adole*scents', *International Journal of Eating Disorders*, 19(2), pp. 119–126. https://doi.org/10.1002/(SICI)1098-108X(199603)19:2 .

Hammack, P.L., Grecco, B., Wilson, B.D.M. and Meyer, I.H. (2021) '"White, tall, top, masculine, muscular": Narratives of intracommunity stigma in young sexual minority men"s experi*ence on mobile apps'*, *Archives of Sexual Behavior*, 51(5), pp. 2413–2428. https://doi.org/10.1007/s10508-021-02144-z .

He, J., Sun, S., Zickgraf, H.F., Lin, Z. and Fan, X. (2020) 'Meta-analysis of gender *differenc*es in body appreciation', *Body Image*, 33, pp. 90–100. Available at: https://doi.org/10.1016/j.bodyim.2020.02.011 (Accessed: 20 May 2025).

Higgins, E.T. (1987) 'Self-discrepancy: A theory relating self *and affect'*, *Psychological Review*, 94(3), pp. 319–340. doi://doi.org/10.1037/0033-295x.94.3.319.

Jung, C.G. (1969) 'Archetypes and the collective unconscious', in Adler, G. and Hull, R.F.C. (eds.) *The collected works of C.G. Jung*, Vol. 9, Pt. 1. Princeton University Press, p. xx.

Kalash, N., Harb, H., Zeeni, N., El Khoury, M. and Mattar, L. (2023) 'Determinants of body image disturbance and disordered eating behaviors among self-identified LGBTQ individuals', *Journal of Eating Disorders*, 11(1), p. 87. https://doi.org/10.1186/s40337-023-00810-2 .

Krayer, A., Ingledew, D.K. and Iphofen, R. (2008) 'Social comparison and body image in adolescence: A grounded theory approach', *Health Education Research*, 23(5), pp. 892–903. https://doi.org/10.1093/her/cym076.

McClain, Z. and Peebles, R. (2016) 'Body image and eating disorders among lesbian, gay, bisexual, and transgender youth', *Pediatric Clinics of North America*, 63(6), pp. 1079–1090. https://doi.org/10.1016/j.pcl.2016.07.008.

Meneguzzo, P., Zuccaretti, D., Tenconi, E. and Favaro, A. (2024) 'Transgender body image: Weight dissatisfaction, objectification & identity—Complex interplay explored via matched group', *International Journal of Clinical and Health Psychology*, 24(1), p. 100441. https://doi.org/10.1016/j.ijchp.2024.100441.

Mereish, E.H., Parra, L.A., Watson, R.J. and Fish, J.N. (2022) 'Subtle and intersectional minority stress and depressive symptoms among sexual and gender minority adolescents of color: Media*ting* role of self-esteem and sense of mastery', *Prevention Science*, 23(1), pp. 142–153. https://doi.org/10.1007/s11121-021-01294-9.

Merino, M., Tornero-Aguilera, J.F., Rubio-Zarapuz, A., Villanueva-Tobaldo, C.V., Martín-Rodríguez, A. and Clemente-Suárez, V.J. (2024) 'Body perceptions and psychological well-being: A review of the impact of social media and physical measurements on self-esteem and mental health with a focus o*n body image* satisfaction and its relationship with cultural and gender factors', *Healthcare*, 12(14), 1396. https://doi.org/10.3390/healthcare12141396.

Muzi, L., Nardelli, N., Naticchioni, G., Mazzeschi, C., Baiocco, R. and Lingiardi, V. (2023) 'Body uneasiness and dissatisfaction among *lesbian, gay, bisexual, and heterosexual persons*', *Sexuality Research & Social Policy*. https://doi.org/10.1007/s13178-023-00805-3.

Owens, L.K., Hughes, T.L. and Owens-Nicholson, D. (2003) 'The effects of sexual orientation on body image and attitudes about eating and weight', *Journal of Lesbian Studies*, 7(1), pp. 15–33. https://doi.org/10.1300/J155v07n01_02.

Ravenhill, J.P. and de Visser, R.O. (2017) 'Perceptions of gay men's masculinity are associated with their sexual self-label, voice quality and physique', *Psychology & Sexuality*, 8(3), pp. 208–222. https://doi.org/10.1080/19419899.2017.1343746 .

Rothblum, E.D. (1994) 'Lesbians and physical appearance: Which model applies?', in Greene, B. and Herek, G.M. (eds.) *Lesbian and gay psychology: Theory, research, and clinical applications*. Sage Publications, pp. 84–97.

Schwartz, R. (2021) *Introduction to the internal family systems model*. 2nd edn. Trailheads Publications.

Schwartz, R. (2023) *No bad parts: Healing trauma & restoring wholeness with the internal family systems model*. Vermilion.

Schwartz, R.C. and Sweezy, M. (2020) *Internal family systems therapy*. 2nd edn. Guilford Publications.

Siever, M.D. (1994) 'Sexual orientation and gender as factors in socioculturally acquired vulnerability to body dissatisfaction and eating disorders', *Journal of Consulting and Clinical Psychology*, 62(2), pp. 252–260. https://doi.org/10.1037/0022-006x.62.2.252.

Soulliard, Z.A., Lattanner, M.R. and Pachankis, J.E. (2023) 'Pressure from within: Gay-community stress and body dissatisfaction among sexual-minority men', *Clinical Psychological Science*, 12(4), pp. 607–624. https://doi.org/10.1177/21677026231186789.

Tabaac, A., Perrin, P.B. and Benotsch, E.G. (2018) 'Discrimination, mental health, and body image among transgender and gender-non-binary individuals: Constructing a multiple mediational path model', *Journal of Gay & Lesbian Social Services*, 30(1), pp. 1–16. https://doi.org/10.1080/10538720.2017.1408514.

Vocks, S., Stahn, C., Loenser, K. and Legenbauer, T. (2009) 'Eating and body image disturbances in male-to-female and female-to-male transsexuals', *Archives of Sexual Behavior*, 38(3), pp. 364–377. https://doi.org/10.1007/s10508-008-9424-z.

Chapter 10

Biopsychosocial – and Mysterious! A Queer Jungian Perspective on the Meaning of GSRD

George Taxidis

Introduction

This chapter explores possible meanings of gender, sex, and relationship diversity (GSRD) and its intersection with areas such as religion, spirituality, the divine, the irrational, the transcendental, the mystical, and a sense of awe towards the universe. I will share some thoughts about how these areas are relevant to the GSRD experience and, therefore, to psychotherapy with GSRD clients.

Firstly, although in my view, exploring the origins of GSRD is not, by definition, queer-phobic, the fantasy that we can fully account for the reasons behind any GSR phenomenon is the result of a rationalistic epistemology that dismisses inexplicable and mysterious phenomena, resulting in a therapy that is eternally on a mission to uncover the unconscious roots of the patient's GSR. I will argue that Jungian psychology offers a welcome antidote to this approach by deepening "born this way" narratives, rather than rejecting them outright.

Contrary to rationalistic epistemology, which risks turning our queerness into a pedestrian, soulless experience, GSRD psychotherapy with a Jungian inflexion pays attention to what brings joy and is open to the possibility that some GSR experiences can be felt as spiritual experiences.

If a therapist who has no religious faith or spiritual leanings is to work with a client who does, they need to have a view of their client's spirituality that doesn't deride and dismiss it – isn't this the position that we would hope a cis-het therapist might hold when working with GSRD? Through discussing some strategies GSRD people of faith use to reconcile their religion or spirituality with their GSR, I am hoping that therapists who are not religious or spiritual may be better equipped to sit with these clients.

I am writing this chapter as someone who was an atheist until about fifteen years ago. I held my atheism so firmly that when I was taught Petrŭska Clarkson's (2003) five relationship therapy integration model, I would light-heartedly tell my peers that to me, it was a four-relationship model: the fifth relationship, the transpersonal one, was *obviously* nonsense. This chapter is,

DOI: 10.4324/9781003530848-13

therefore, also a letter to my younger self, who had to be an atheist to survive the homophobia and conservatism of the Christian Orthodox context in which I grew up, but later came to resonate with the inscription on Jung's front door: *"Vocatus atque non vocatus, Deus aderit"* – which translates to "whether summoned or not, God [I'd say "the gods"] will be present".

On Aetiology

In an interview, writer and performance artist Alok Vaid-Menon discussed exploring questions around the origin of their gender, including the experience of their father's absence, growing up around women, and being allowed to wear girls' clothes. This made them ask questions about what was organic and what was imposed.

> And then I realised that that's a false binary and a misleading framework. Because I don't think it's possible to separate the "me" from the "us". And I think that that's both tragic and incredibly beautiful; that we are deeply enmeshed in culture and everything around us … And so, when I started to experiment with my femininity, I removed any idea of purity [and] authenticity, and I instead subscribed to joy. Meaning, does this give me joy? … A beard, a full face of make-up, lipstick, and a mini skirt. That's just where I feel the most me.
>
> (Alok Vaid-Menon, in Masters, 2022)

Asking questions about the causes of non-normative GSR is, understandably, contentious. However, what often matters more than the content of these questions is who is asking them and their aims. As Adam Philips put it, "it is always a question of tone … We should not ask, for example, is the author right, but is he bitter? […] Not, what does she believe, but what does she dread?" (1996, p. 31).

Perhaps GSRD people ask the kinds of questions Alok was asking themself because our experiences are so often pathologised. Some might even say that the only possible reason for asking these questions is internalised shame, and their only possible aim is to convert everyone to cis-het mono-normativity. In my experience, anyone can benefit from being curious about their GSR, and having had to defend ourselves from accusations of pathology, we are better placed to contribute to these discussions. Moreover, these discussions can potentially lead to increased enjoyment of one's body, body modifications, desires and kinks, gender expression, relationship configurations, and a deepening of such experiences rather than converting them to cis-het mono-normativity.

It is widely agreed that many biopsychosocial factors interact with each other and contribute to one's GSR (Denman, 2004). Unsatisfying and pathologising views are often simplistically focused on one aspect of the biopsychosocial matrix that we are all affected by. For example, theories of "rapid onset gender dysphoria" (discredited, for instance, by Literski, 2021; Kesslen, 2022) make the mistake of privileging the social factor; that is, they attribute the seemingly large numbers of young trans people to influences from peers. Similarly, so-called feminists and others explain away the existence of trans men as a symptom of the patriarchy – interestingly, they don't interpret the lower numbers of trans women who approach gender clinics as a symptom of misogyny and transmisogyny. Researchers from positive sciences who have incessantly tried to find the "gay gene" have privileged the biological factor, and perhaps, the "born this way" slogan also often implies a biological basis for non-normative GSR.

The therapeutic tradition I have been most influenced by, depth psychology (a term sometimes used to refer to psychoanalysis and Jungian psychology jointly), has been notorious for disproportionately privileging the impact of individual psychology (overbearing mothers, absent fathers, unconscious wishes of either parent, among others) at the expense of societal factors. For decades, the obsession in psychoanalysis with trying to account for the causes behind GSRD subjectivity has had harmful results (Lewes, 1988; Hansbury, 2017).

However, some voices in depth psychology critique this, such as those of Saketopoulou and Pellegrini (2024). The authors republish in their book an earlier paper by French psychoanalyst Jean Laplanche, initially written in 2003, where he acknowledges that gender expressions are "neither purely biological, nor purely psychological, nor purely sociological, but a *curious mixture of the three*" (cited in Saketopoulou & Pellegrini, 2024, p. 112, my emphasis).

An expression of the inadequacy of single-factor explanations, as I see it, is evident in the question of a student of Pellegrini's who, memorably for their teacher, remarked "I get it, I get it … Heterosexuality and homosexuality are socially constructed and recent historical inventions. Fine. But what I want to know is what made *me* a lesbian" (Saketopoulou & Pellegrini, 2024, pp. xviii–xix, authors' emphasis).

The authors offer a new perspective, building on previous work by Saketopoulou (2020, 2023), who coined the terms traumatophilia and traumatophobia. A traumatophobic stance can only view the (usually non-normative) GSR that is contributed to by earlier experiences of trauma as not real, and it fantasises returning to an idealised pre-traumatic state (and therefore normative development). Instead, the authors argue that *everyone's* GSR is the result of trauma and invite clinicians to take an active (traumatophilic) interest in what individuals creatively do with their traumatic experiences, whilst not denying the often devastating effects of trauma.

I understand this in practice to mean that, for example, a therapist would be open to the possibility that Alok's father's absence may have been traumatic, and it may have contributed to their closer relationship to their "femininity".

Equally, a monogamous cis-het boy may have been traumatised by his exclusion from the relationship between his parents (what psychoanalysis calls the Oedipus complex), and his "solution" to this trauma was that he pledged to be just like daddy (a cis man), find a woman just like mummy (be heterosexual), and be with her exclusively, forever (thereby warding off the pain of exclusion). Talking about the childhood trauma of absence or exclusion does not have to lead to the masculinisation of Alok (thankfully), just like it doesn't usually lead the cis-het and monogamous man of my example to consider consensual non-monogamy as another solution to his Oedipal trauma.

As Saketopoulou and Pellegrini remind us, even Freud admitted that when one believes that they have fully uncovered the early life events that caused someone's homosexuality, for example, a closer and more honest look reveals "that there might have been another result, and that we might have been just as well able to understand and explain the latter" (cited in Saketopoulou & Pellegrini, 2024, p. xxvi). It's an awkward admission that phenomena, including those of the GSR kind, cannot be simply "reverse engineered" because, as Laplanche says in the quote above, they are a curious mixture of many factors that cannot be isolated and undone.

"Born This way": Biological or Spiritual?

Saketopoulou and Pellegrini reject "born this way" narratives, even though they recognise that they can "feel genuinely true to the subject" (2024, p. 19). They acknowledge that the aim of such narratives is often to fight for equal rights – if we are born this way, we are not sick; therefore, we should be accepted as we are. The authors go on to say that "the dominant cultural trope of inborn sexuality/gender strengthens the narrative that many queer subjects weave about the felt true-ness of their own gender/desires – and then recite to researchers, doctors, analysts" (2024, p. 19). I doubt that this interpretation will always be helpful.

Indeed, there are obvious risks to adopting the "born this way" narrative when it implies a concrete view of identity, which views it as fixed and unchangeable. However, there are also dangers (which Saketopoulou and Pellegrini also point out) to adopting a view of GSR as straightforwardly acquired, namely that they can be converted to normative ones. Equally, a simply biological "born this way" narrative can encourage fantasies of identifying the queer gene and eliminating it. But "born this way" doesn't need to be biologically essentialist. For many individuals, it has a spiritual or religious meaning, and Jungian thought provides a helpful lens through which to understand this.

It is well known that Jung and Freud's professional relationship (and bromance!) ended because, among other reasons, Jung valued the spiritual or religious dimension of the psyche, whereas Freud mostly saw religion as pathological. My Jungian slant is therefore expressed in my use of the word "mysterious" in the title of this chapter, instead of Laplanche's "curious". Furthermore, knowing Vaid-Menon's other work, their suggestion that it's impossible to separate the "I" from the "us" refers not only to the interpersonal and societal levels but nods towards the idea and experience of interconnectedness between living beings, which is found in most spiritual traditions. Paraphrasing Vaid-Menon, I would propose that this interconnectedness is both tragic and magic – tragic, in that we can't escape this world that shapes us and often wounds us, and magic in that we are connected to this world in ways that we cannot always understand with reason alone.

Jung questioned the narrative that Enlightenment rationalist notions of cause and effect represented the peak of epistemological development and proposed that, in addition to causes, phenomena (including, for example, dreams, fantasies, and symptoms) also had a purpose (Papadopoulos, 2006). The less controversial version of this is that a symptom, say, depression, may have a cause (such as an earlier trauma). Still, it may also have a purpose (perhaps to draw attention to the individual that their life isn't satisfying). The word purpose, however, also evokes a metaphysical framework, a version of which would be the idea of "God's plan" for me.

GSRD individuals relate to this in different ways. One example is in the show "September Mornings" ("Manhãs de Setembro") with trans character Cassandra, played by trans actor and singer Liniker. When Cassandra's friend suggests that God brought someone into her life for a reason, she says, "Darling, God wanted me to be a man, and look how that went!" (Marcone & Pinheiro, 2021). At the other end of the spectrum, Muslim drag performer Glamrou asserts that their shows reinforce their "faith that Allah's plan was for me to twirl onstage in a skirt" (Al-Kadhi, 2020, p. 10).

A related irrational idea is that of queer ancestors. When Heyam describes "the many people who disrupted gender" as "ancestors" (2022, p. 163), or when I see photos from parties at Hirschfeld's Institute of Sexual Science and I see the revellers as my ancestors, we are not, of course, referring to a *biological* lineage. I would say that I am speaking of a lineage of a transpersonal nature. Jung's epistemology is helpful here, as it is less concerned with whether such an idea is literally true. From the beginning of his career, when he studied Helene Preiswerk's communication with spirits during séances, he "was not interested in whether the spirits existed or not but... in the psychological meaning and implications" (Papadopoulos, 2006, p. 18) of these séances. Similarly, I would argue that a more respectful approach to spirituality, meaningful coincidences, and "born this way" narratives is to work with their psychological truth and their meaning to the individual.

Joy: Defensive or Divine?

Depth psychology has typically been suspicious of understandings of GSR expressions, especially non-normative ones, simply in terms of what brings joy. In numerous discussions or seminars I have taught, senior colleagues and trainees sometimes define our tradition as asking questions about the deeper meanings of phenomena. Less thought is often given to phenomena that do *not* attract these questions. For instance, I have anecdotally heard several accounts of individuals in analysis who remarked that the only time their analyst showed much emotion was in response to the patient having children. *That* joy is seldom questioned, dissected, or dismissed as resulting from indoctrination or trauma.

Part of the suspicion towards the emphasis on joy is that it is interpreted as a kind of intellectual and emotional cowardice, a resignation from the complex but purportedly essential task of achieving complete insight into the (usually traumatic) roots of (usually non-normative) GSR. Joy can therefore be defensive and superficial in this paradigm. Various terms can be used to describe this defensiveness. Bion, for instance, spoke of a resistance to knowledge, which he symbolised with -K (Symington & Symington, 1996) which is the opposite of what Klein (1930) called the epistemophilic instinct – the desire to know, the first instance of which is the infant's curiosity about the caregiver and their body, which is then directed towards the self and the world at large. Joy can also be interpreted in Kleinian thinking as a manic, triumphant defence (Segal, 1988), and some Jungians may interpret it as a denial of the shadow – "the thing [one] has no wish to be" (Jung, 1954, p. 262). Therefore, we may be resorting to a defensive experience of joy because we avoid our psyche's unpleasant parts.

All these ideas can generally be helpful in therapeutic practice. I don't doubt that joy *can* be defensive or lack depth, or that it can be experienced by individuals who have little or no engagement with or curiosity about its depth. However, it is not uncommon for clinicians to use the depth psychological terms mentioned above when faced with phenomena they are not familiar with or something that personally challenges them (Hansbury, 2017; Saketopoulou, 2022; Taxidis, 2024).

The Jungian emphasis on the cross-cultural figure of the wounded healer (Merchant, 2012) contributes to cultivating humility as it "makes of the [therapist] the patient's [sibling] rather than [their] master" (Guggenbühl-Craig, 1979, p. 97). The implication is that psychotherapists can help not because we are healthy and the patient sick, but because we are (hopefully!) better acquainted with our wounds and have more more experience in grappling with them. I intentionally avoid terms such as "processing" or "addressing" trauma, because they can reinforce a narrative of a finite task, which, in my view, allows some clinicians to believe that their self-knowledge is such that they seldom have to doubt themselves – the most dangerous kind of clinician.

Jung's view of the unconscious was that it is infinite. This, alongside the awareness of the therapist's woundedness, invites us to adopt a position of humility that is necessary when encountering the other. This includes being open to the possibility of misinterpreting the client's joy and that the therapist may be defending against knowledge, joy, and acknowledgement of their shadow.

A queer Jungian approach allows for the possibility of joy in GSR experience to have spiritual value. I have elsewhere written about the potential of specific first GSR experiences to make individuals feel that they are in the presence of something profound and divine (Taxidis, 2024). In that paper, I also connected with Jung's assertion that "spirituality and sexuality are not your qualities, not things you possess and encompass. Rather, they possess and encompass you, since they are... manifestations of the Gods" (2012, p. 529).

GSRD in Religion and Spirituality

Many GSRD people have been brutally hurt in religious contexts, so we have every right to be mistrustful of organised religion, and many in our communities are entirely unreceptive to any notion of spirituality. A UK report found that of those who were offered conversion therapy, more than half were offered it in a faith organisation or group (Gov UK, 2021). Many leave their religious communities because of discrimination and rejection. Unsurprisingly, on average, there is less prevalence of religious faith among GSRD individuals (*Most LGBT people are not religious – Census*, 4 April 2023). GSRD people of faith invariably report that many around them believe that their GSR and their faith are completely incompatible (e.g. Ladin, 2019; Hunt, 2020).

In recent years, however, many GSRD people are redefining, or discovering, previous configurations of spirituality, faith, and GSR. Faith groups have an increased presence at some pride marches, and there have been more GSRD-inclusive churches, synagogues and mosques in some locations, as well as a range of support spaces for GSRD people of faith, such as Imaan, a Muslim LGBTQ+ group in the UK. Smaller events such as Queer Pagan Camp in the UK have evolved into the larger Queer Spirit festival, attended by hundreds of queer souls in recent years. Trans mystic and artist Jonah Welch designed billboards that read "trans people are sacred", which became a popular slogan on social media. They were also the first words uttered by Joan in the remarkable play "I, Joan" at the Shakespeare Globe Theatre in 2022, which, controversially, presented Joan of Arc as a non-binary visionary and mystic who used they/them pronouns.

This tendency is difficult to understand for many religious and non-religious people alike, especially when the notion that religion is incompatible with progress or liberation is taken for granted – a dominant narrative, especially in Western, white-majority countries. An essential step in understanding these phenomena is to recognise the different functions of religion. Jungian author Jason Smith offers a valuable model to do this, adapted from Joseph Campbell's model of understanding myth.

The first function is psychological and ethical, and relates to values about leading a good life and gender roles. A second, related function is the sociological one, which regulates the individual's life in their societal context. The third is the cosmological function – a narrative on the universe's origins. Finally, most religions have a mystical function, which Campbell described as "eliciting and supporting a sense of awe before the mystery of reality" (cited in Smith, 2020, p. 89).

To suggest that all these functions are indispensable to each other is, I would argue, the most simplistic view of religion, held by both conservative religious people and liberal atheists – the former use this to exclude GSRD people, the latter to suggest that religion and spirituality are *intrinsically* regressive. It is not only legitimate but also necessary to critique the political function of religion from a social justice perspective. Claims that various injustices are part of God's plan, or that the spiritual person's aim is only equanimity and never protest, have provided significant support for the societal status quo for many centuries.

But it is also true, for example, that whilst the Bible contains passages that justify slavery, parts of it that refer to freedom, equality or resistance had to be redacted to prevent enslaved people from rebelling against their owners (Mills, 2009). In addition, there is a long tradition of liberation theology, particularly in Latin America (Boff, 1987), and more recently queer theology (Althaus-Reid, 2000). Using concepts by Italian revolutionary Marxist Antonio Gramsci, Hill argues that religion can be hegemonic in some contexts and counter-hegemonic in others (2010, p. 63).

It's impossible to make sense of these contradictions if one is wedded to the idea that religion is a monolith or that every word in the scriptures is the word of God. Although not usually associated with notions of social justice, Jung offers a framework to understand this, especially in his distinction between an archetype and an archetypal image. Knox explains that Jung spoke about archetypes in four distinct ways, one of which is that they are "organizing mental frameworks of an abstract nature... with no symbolic or representational content" (2003, p. 23). This model enables us to look at religious scriptures as human-made (archetypal images) that are only the current, social-context-dependent representation of something unknown, and even unknowable (archetype). God, as a white, bearded older man, would be an archetypal image in this model, which could, in another context, be a Goddess, a non-binary deity, multiple deities, the universe, Tao, etc.

This approach is essential for spiritual GSRD people, enabling multiple interpretations of spiritual ideas and religious doctrines. This is probably what Pàdraig Ó Tuama means when he says that he found it liberating to read the Bible as poetry (2020, p. 16) and this is the area that Joy Ladin explores when she says that she "felt that being transgender brought me closer to God because I, like God, was invisible and incomprehensible to those around me" (2019, p. 13). More than another interpretation of religious doctrine, some

GSRD people of faith, like liberation theologians, claim that compassion and social justice are at the heart of their faith, so that Amrou Al-Kadhi can say that they "had only ever pictured Allah as a fascistic punisher who built the world on strict, rigid lines – but the more I discovered about Islam, the less this seemed to be the case" (2020, p. 7).

A tolerance of diversity of interpretations of scriptures and theologies often aligns with an emphasis on individual spiritual experience (the fourth function in the Campbell/Smith model), which also represents a common ground with Jungian psychology, so much of which is based on individual active imaginations by Jung, recorded in *The Red Book* (2012) and not published until almost a century later. It is not a coincidence that Jung discovers that "you can hardly say of your soul what sex it is" (2012, p. 227) and that there are many examples of gender and sexual variance in mystical traditions such as Gnosticism, Sufism, Kabbalah, Tantra and indigenous spiritual traditions.

GSRD people have held spiritual and healing roles in many pre-colonial and non-monotheistic contexts. For example, part of the initiation of shamans, who were both healers and spiritual leaders, was going beyond ordinary gender roles (Merchant, 2012). Other well-known examples include Two-Spirit people in North America and hijras in South Asia (Heyam, 2022). Gloria Anzaldúa even asserts that those who experience oppression and marginalisation – women, queer people, people of colour – have what she calls *la facultad,* a capacity to see beyond ordinary ways of seeing, whereby "we can see through things, view events in depth, a piercing that reaches the underworld (the realm of the soul)" (1987, p. 39).

Understandably, such experiences raise an essential question: when and why do we view them as psychotic? Some have seen Jung's experiences in *The Red Book as* psychotic, and he was aware of this potential, as is evident from one of his active imaginations, in which he encounters a doctor who diagnoses him with "religious madness" (2012, p. 337). Jung, however, was also one of the first psychiatrists who felt that, even though such experiences can be profoundly disturbing, they can have meaning. Similarly, Al-Kadhi (2020) describes a narrative of spiritual emergence from a psychotic breakdown during which they concretely believed that they were a prophet, only to eventually suggest light-heartedly that perhaps they are a prophet of sorts, precisely because Allah threw them into their breakdown to gain a better understanding of their queerness and Islam.

Conclusion

Jung believed that whatever we are powerfully drawn to, from political beliefs to football teams, and from pop stars to an obsession with driving cars, "compels the same belief or fear, submission or devotion which a God would demand from [humans]" (1958, p. 86). Jungian psychology offers the opportunity to look at powerful experiences which sometimes defy rational understanding "like an Olympus full of deities", that is, with a sense of awe and respect – whether that's a top surgery, a sense of euphoria when you catch yourself in the mirror wearing lipstick, a meaningful or enjoyable hookup, a BDSM session, that euphoric feeling after a trans rights protest, or your love for all your lovers and theirs.

Acknowledgement

I am grateful to Greek queer musician Runes for allowing me to listen to their song, «Μέσα πλήττω» ("Indoors I'm Bored"), before its release, whilst I was writing this chapter. Their voice, trained in Byzantine psalmody, and the queer-affirming lyrics could serve as the soundtrack to this chapter.

References

Al-Kadhi, A. (2020) 'The queer prophet', in Hunt, R. (ed.) *The book of queer prophets: 24 writers on sexuality and religion.* London: HarperCollins UK.

Althaus-Reid, M. (2000) *Indecent theology: Theological perversions in sex, gender and politics.* London: Routledge.

Anzaldúa, G. (1987) *Borderlands, La frontera – The new mestiza.* San Francisco: Aunt Lute Books.

Boff, L. (1987) *Introducing liberation theology.* Tunbridge Wells: Orbis Books.

Clarkson, P. (2003) *The therapeutic relationship.* London: Whurr.

Denman, C. (2004). *Sexuality: A biopsychosocial approach.* Basingstoke: Palgrave.

Gov.UK. (2021, October 29) 'The prevalence of conversion therapy in the UK'. Available at: https://www.gov.uk/government/publications/the-prevalence-of-conversion-therapy-in-the-uk/the-prevalence-of-conversion-therapy-in-the-uk (Accessed: 29 August 2024).

Guggenbühl-Craig, A. (1979) *Power in the helping professions.* Dallas: Spring Publications.

Hansbury, G. (2017) 'Unthinkable anxieties: Reading transphobic countertransferences in a century of psychoanalytic writing', *TSQ : Transgender Studies Quarterly,* 4(3–4), pp. 384–404.

Heyam, K. (2022) *Before we were trans: A new history of gender.* London: Seal Press.

Hill, S. (2010) *The no-nonsense guide to religion.* Oxford: New Internationalist.

Hunt, R. (2020) 'Introduction', in Hunt, R. (ed.), *The book of queer prophets: 24 writers on sexuality and religion.* London: HarperCollins UK.

Jung, C. G. (1954) 'The psychology of the transference', in Read, H., Fordham, M., Adler, G., & McGuire, W. (eds.), *Collected works Vol XVI, the practice of psychotherapy.* Princeton: Princeton University Press.

Jung, C. G. (1958) 'Psychology and religion' (R. F. C. Hull, Trans.), in Read, H., Fordham, M., Adler, G., & McGuire, W. (eds.), *Collected works Vol XI, psychology and religion: East and West.* Princeton: Princeton University Press.

Jung, C. G. (2012) *The red book — Liber novus: A reader's edition* (S. Shamdasani, Ed.). New York: W. Norton & Co.

Kesslen, B. (2022). How the idea of a "transgender contagion" went viral—and caused untold harm. *MIT Technology Review.* Available at: https://www

.technologyreview.com/2022/08/18/1057135/transgender-contagion-gender
-dysphoria/ (Accessed: 26 August 2024).

Klein, M. (1930) 'The importance of symbol-formation in the development of the
ego', *International Journal of Psychoanalysis*, 11, pp. 24–39.

Knox, J. (2003) *Archetype, attachment, analysis: Jungian psychology and the
emergent mind*. London: Taylor & Francis.

Ladin, J. (2019) *The soul of the stranger: Reading God and Torah from a transgender
perspective*. Waltham: Brandeis University Press.

Lewes, K. (1988) *The psychoanalytic theory of male homosexuality*. New York:
Simon & Schuster.

Literski, N. S. (2021) 'Defacing Dionysus: The fabrication of an anti-transgender
myth', *Psychological Perspectives*, 64(3), pp. 360–368.

Marcone, A. (Writer), & Pinheiro, L. (Director). (2021) 'Take care of your own
problems (Season 1, Episode 2) [TV series episode]', in A. Barata Ribeiro & B.
Berlinck (Producers), *September mornings*. O2 Filmes; Amazon Studios.

Masters, J. (Host). (2022, June 21) 'Alok Vaid-Menon: Trans people have always
existed [Audio podcast episode]', in *LGBTQ&A*. Available at: https://podcasters
.spotify.com/pod/show/jeffrey-masters/episodes/Alok-Vaid-Menon-Trans-People
-Have-Always-Existed-e1kji1d (Accessed: 23 May 2025).

Merchant, J. (2012) *Shamans and analysts: New insights on the wounded healer*.
London: Routledge.

Mills, D. C. (2009) *Unholy: The slaves Bible*. Los Angeles: Ghetto Kids Enterprises.

Most LGBT people are non-religious – Census. (4 April 2023) 'Humanists UK'.
Available at: https://humanists.uk/2023/04/04/most-lgbt-people-are-non-religious
-census-2021/ (Accessed: 04 September 2024)

Ó Tuama, P. (2020) 'Let my people', in Hunt, R. (ed.), *The book of queer prophets:
24 writers on sexuality and religion*. London: HarperCollins UK.

Papadopoulos, R. K. (2006) *The handbook of Jungian psychology: Theory, practice
and applications*. London: Routledge.

Philips, A. (1996) *Monogamy*. London: Faber & Faber.

Saketopoulou, A. (2020) 'Risking sexuality beyond consent: overwhelm and
traumatisms that incite', *Psychoanalytic Quarterly*, 89(4), pp. 771–811.

Saketopoulou, A. (2022) 'On trying to pass off transphobia as psychoanalysis and
cruelty as "clinical logic"', *Psychoanalytic Quarterly*, 91(1), pp. 177–190. https://
doi.org/10.1080/00332828.2022.2056378.

Saketopoulou, A. (2023) *Sexuality beyond consent*. New York: NYU Press.

Saketopoulou, A., & Pellegrini, A. (2024) *Gender without identity*. New York: The
Unconscious in Translation.

Segal, H. (1988) *Introduction to the work of Melanie Klein*. London: Karnac &
Institute of Psycho-Analysis.

Smith, J. E. (2020) *Religious but not religious: Living a symbolic life*. Asheville:
Chiron Publications.

Symington, J., & Symington, N. (1996) *The clinical thinking of Wilfred Bion*.
London: Routledge.

Taxidis, G. (2024) 'Living your animal: Listening to wild gender and sexuality',
Psychological Perspectives, 67(4), pp. 378–393. https://doi.org/10.1080/00332925
.2024.2442280

Chapter 11

Mentalising Internalised Stigma

Wilson Gallego Hoyos

Introduction

Mentalising is an imaginative capacity that allows individuals to make sense of their behaviour and that of others. By engaging in mentalising, individuals can understand the underlying thought processes, emotions, and intentions that drive behaviour and thus gain insight into the complex workings of the human mind.

It has been suggested that the ability to mentalise is a common factor relevant across various therapeutic modalities and effective treatments. Improving this ability can yield benefits for all forms of therapy and all types of interactions. Therefore, enhancing mentalising skills should be considered a worthwhile pursuit for individuals in the field of mental health who wish to improve the efficacy of their therapeutic interactions (Bateman and Fonagy, 2016, 2018; Sharp and Bevington, 2022).

On the other hand, gender, sex, and relationship diversity (GSRD) therapy (Davies and Neves, 2023) is a growing approach that questions, among others, society's binary thinking and its impact on people. Davies and Neves remind us that "cisgenderism, heteronormativity, mononormativity and body-negative, sexual shaming cultures, religious persecution, ableism and racism" can significantly affect a person's development and sense of self, leading to adverse outcomes in mental health, "internalised oppression and negative core beliefs" (2023, p. 411).

One such outcome is what has been called internalised homophobia/stigma,[1] the "LGB individual's direction of societal antihomosexual attitudes toward the self" (Newcomb and Mustanski, 2010, p. 1020).

In this chapter, I will present some considerations about internalised stigma and its clinical approach from the developmental perspective offered by mentalising research and clinical practice led by Peter Fonagy, Anthony Bateman and their collaborators.

DOI: 10.4324/9781003530848-14

Mentalising

The importance of mentalising in mental health was suggested by the London Parent-Child Project research (Fonagy *et al.*, 1991). The study supported the idea that the bond between infants and their mothers is the leading platform for intimate discussions and emotional learning. The findings suggested that the quality of this bond predicts the child's understanding of emotions at ages five, six, and eleven (Steele and Steele, 2011). This means that a caregiver's ability to empathise with their children and recognise them as individuals with their own emotions and thoughts will support the child's understanding of themselves and others, thus influencing their mental health positively.

These findings led Fonagy and colleagues to propose a developmental model based on children's growing awareness and understanding of their mental and social world, achieved through mental maturation. Furthermore, this conceptualisation of psychological development allowed a redefinition of the core challenges in people diagnosed with borderline personality disorder (BPD), using the new language of mentalising.

The establishment of a mentalisation-based therapy (MBT) is grounded on the idea that resilience cannot thrive in a mind that cancels mentalising; therefore, the inhibition or impairment of such capacity is related to psychopathology and suffering (Fonagy *et al.*, 2017a, 2017b).

The Development of Mentalising

Mentalising develops when the infant's caregiver interacts with them, attributing intentions and needs to their actions. This interaction, mediated by language, helps the infant build models of the caregivers and themselves, attributing beliefs, wishes, needs, ideas, and feelings to observed behaviour, which determines their behaviour (Fonagy *et al.*, 2002). When a parent picks up her[2] crying baby and responds to his distress by wondering if he is hungry, as it has been a couple of hours since she last fed him, the caregiver imagines a motivation for the baby's cry. She might add, "You are upset as I am taking this long to give you the bottle", considering possible emotional states in the baby's distress. This process is what is called mentalising.

Fonagy *et al.* (2002) propose that children undergo several developmental tasks before they understand that people have their own minds. Each task helps the child understand two aspects of experience: what is happening inside themselves and in their social world. These tasks occur in three developmental stages: psychic equivalence, teleological mode, and pretend mode[3].

These modes are modified and integrated into mentalising when the child is about four or five years old. However, later in life, when under stress or arousal, we all tend to function predominantly in one of these modes or the other. Nonetheless, once the stress is gone or is successfully regulated, we can find different ways to cope and regain the capacity to mentalise. This kind of event challenges the mentalising capacity as it requires balancing its internal and external components and expressing it appropriately according to the context.

Mentalising happens more often when there is a background of secure attachment, as the child feels understood by the people around him and can rely on the relationships formed with them. This situation fosters an open-mindedness to learning about his environment and himself. At the same time, it can be thwarted when the child's intentions are constantly misunderstood, neglected or punished.

Mentalising is a capacity developed in attachment relationships. Internalised stigma denotes taking something from the outside and putting it within the self; I propose it can start early on in the relationships with early caregivers who introduce culture to the child and is then enhanced by the perceived response a person has concerning gender non-conforming behaviours, thoughts and feelings (irrespective of gender identity or object choice).

Development and Internalised Stigma

How mentalising unfolds depends on biological and social elements, as the baby inherits the social environment in which he is born. Mainly, mentalising develops within attachment relationships "through the experience of one's complex emotions contingently and markedly 'mirrored' by attachment figures" (Desatnik et al., 2023, p. 3).

As Grosse Weismann and Southgate remind us, "Despite having a schema of their own body from the first months of life and a rudimentary sense of agency […] infants are not believed to develop an explicit concept of themselves as subject of their own first-person experience and actions before the middle of their second year of life when infants start recognizing themselves in the mirror" (2021, p. 58). Around this time in toddlerhood, the child starts developing better verbal and social skills, having a concept of and referring to themselves as "I" or "me". It is also the stage of development where some social emotions such as shame, pride, or embarrassment (Sharp and Bevington, 2022, p. 41) start to be present. With a growing awareness of a sense of self, there are more intentional interactions and further complex responses to others' reactions within the child's environment.

The Alien Self

The alien self can be defined as the result of the consistent deviation of parental affect-mirroring of a child's mental state (Fonagy et al., 2002, p.11). Constant, insensitive, and misattuned failures by the child's environment will create complex, unrepresented experiences in developing the psychological sense of self. This is similar to Winnicott's idea that rather than finding themselves in the caregiver's mind, the child sees the caregiver with their negative mental state: "it is not contingent with the self-state: it does not match it in quality, intensity, timing, or tone. This discontinuity within the self is the 'alien self'" (Bateman and Fonagy, 2016, p. 20).

Vignette, Alberto

Alberto, a 32-year-old gay man from Latin America, remembers that his grandmother used to sit him on her lap when he was about eight years old and read to him some passages of the Bible where the possibility of sexual contact between men was considered an abomination. Alberto did not understand what "laying with mankind" or "abomination" meant, but he knew it was bad by the look on his grandmother's face.

When a caregiver struggles to accept a child's expression of a gender nonconforming activity, the child perceives the judgement and rejection of such action and may inhibit it, even without recognising what is wrong with what he is doing. Eventually, the child's consideration about it could align with the caregivers', appropriating their reaction and being judgemental of those actions in others. As an adult, Alberto pondered whether his grandmother reacted to his giving occasional "musical shows" to her and his mother, but rather than mirror his self-state, he was met with the seriousness of the Bible passages.

As the child's intentions were likely playful or a way to experience an aspect of themselves that important people modelled in their lives, if the reaction of their social environment was negative or punishing, they learn that there is something wrong and unacceptable in their actions or within themselves. This can be a shameful experience where the child's expression is not wanted. "The infant is forced to internalize the representation of the object's state of mind as a core part of himself. But in such cases, the internalized other remains alien and unconnected to the structures of the constitutional self" (Fonagy *et al.*, 2002, p.11).

The child may deal with this through externalisation, but the effects when there is a stronger and more cohesive sense of self could vary greatly. "The alien self is mostly pernicious when later experiences of trauma in the family or the peer group force the child to dissociate from pain by using the alien self to identify with the aggressor" (Fonagy *et al.*, 2002, p.12). Some people internalise this unmirrored experience as shame or guilt that becomes a split part of the self. That is why it is easier for some to see that disowned part of themselves in others (as in some homophobic aggressions), as looking within the self can be painful; the alien self contains the image of the aggressor and the affect generated by their actions. It is a survival strategy.

When Alberto started school, his peers bullied him. They called him names and said he was more of a woman than a man. He was puzzled by this and realised that in order not to be picked on, he needed to behave differently. Although he thought about talking to his parents, they had also commented about his behaviour, and he thought he would be punished rather than helped.

From this perspective, the alien self is born initially as a coping strategy to adapt to the child's context. In the end, we are social creatures and find rejection painful. Later in development, the defensive use of the alien self can give way to emotional pain as it disrupts the emergence of an authentic self and creates, instead, a self-critical and punishing other within, an aspect often found in internalised stigma, "the person resolves an internal incoherence, normally covered over by a capacity to create an illusion of coherence through mentalizing, by ridding oneself of its source—the alien self—on to someone in the external world" (Bateman and Fonagy, 2016, p. 21).

Connections with GSRD Research

These ideas from the mentalising literature can be observed in the body of research advanced by other researchers from different traditions, such as Meyer (2003) or Rosario and Schrimshaw (2012). Meyer's concept of minority stress is based on his research into the mental health of lesbian, gay, and bisexual populations in the US.

Meyer states that when a person internalises negative societal attitudes, this can result in decreased self-regard and demoralisation. In contrast, perceived stigma, which encompasses the expectations of rejection and discrimination owing to one's minority status, can lead to hypervigilance towards experiences of prejudice and discrimination. This idea rests on the assumption that the person knows about their status as a minority. "However, a broad definition of minority, gay-related, or sexual minority stress refers to experiencing society's stigmatization for being or being perceived to be a sexual minority [...] Therefore, sexual minority stress may be experienced in childhood, before any self-awareness of a minority status" (Rosario *et al.*, 2022, pp. 534–535). As markers of proximal stress, such as identity concealment, are absent in the absence of a coherent and formed identity, the idea of minority stress only applies in its generic sense of the adverse effects that stress poses in a person's life. This can happen when people around the developing child infer, consciously or unconsciously, gender non-conforming characteristics (GNC) or attitudes. Such was the attitude of Alberto's grandmother and his peers at school.

Rosario reminds us that some studies have found that parents who perceive their children as GNC tend to be less accepting of such characteristics and respond negatively to them (Rosario *et al.*, 2022, p. 536). These reactions occur before the child is aware of being a sexual minority. The parents' and other caregivers' rejection and lack of appropriate mirroring help instil a sense of "wrongness" within the child. As it becomes consistent, it allows the creation of an alien self in the shape of internalised stigma. The carers may try to "correct" what they perceive as inadequate, thwarting the spontaneous flourishing of a sense of self and instilling a socially normative one instead.

How the child reacts to this depends on who else is available in their environment. Suppose the child does not have other people who mirror their mental state adequately. In that case, they might withdraw from contact with his parents, possibly making him more vulnerable to experiencing abuse by others.

A social network of people perceived as similar fosters a sense of belonging. It reduces the chances of internalising symptoms (Andrews *et al.*, 2021, p.112). It helps form a social identity and a "sense of distinctiveness among members of any identity group" (Rosario and Schrimshaw, 2012, p. 89).

However, young people who identify as LGB often face an incongruity between societal norms and their own cultural needs and experiences. This can create a challenging and complex situation for those individuals to navigate (Newcomb and Mustanski, 2010, p. 1020). The long-lasting consequences will continue to affect them throughout their lifespan in myriad ways. For instance, Totenhagen, Randall and Lloyd found that people with higher levels of internalised homophobia also experienced relationship problems linked to increased depressive experiences triggered by internalised homophobia (2018, p. 400). Also, Newcomb and Mustanski (2010, p.1027) considered that internalised homophobia is related to depressive symptomatology as there is a negative appreciation of oneself, whilst the constant hypervigilance associated with the perceived stigma and minority stress is correlated with anxiety.

Alberto had a couple of girlfriends during adolescence and his early 20s, but after finishing university, he realised he preferred being involved with other men. He formed friendships with like-minded people and finally felt he could belong somewhere. However, after dating a few men, he started getting frustrated as he felt paralysed when attempting to become sexual with his partners.

Traumatic responses like flight, fight, or freeze are activated in the presence of a perceived threat to the psychological self of a GNC person. However, they have survival value, and when affecting the fluid state of a person's life, it becomes a problem. People with such histories come to therapy because they have difficulty figuring themselves out or due to relationship problems (not so different from non-GSRD clients). At other times, they come due to other situations, and eventually, the topic of internalised stigma and that of the alien self appears in the session.

Clinical Considerations

The experience of being held in mind by another, specifically, the experience of having one's mental states represented by another person, is a crucial component in restoring a sense of agency and control and, ultimately, a sense of selfhood (Luyten *et al.*, 2021, pp. 666–667). This is especially so for people who have experienced trauma.

The significance of this process cannot be overstated, as it represents a powerful tool in the hands of those who seek to assist individuals in recovering from traumatic experiences and consequent internalised stigma. By emphasising the importance of being held in mind by others, we can provide a pathway to personal growth for those who, coping with emotional turmoil derived from invalidation and rejection of their expressions, resort to creating an alien self.

Therapists must remain vigilant to subjective experiences that may indicate a discontinuity in a person's self-structure related to their GSRD identity. This may manifest as an individual having a sense of a belief, wish, or feeling that does not align with their identity and how they have presented to the therapy so far.

As there could be externalisation of such aspects of their experience, the clinician must monitor their reactions to this topic and their experience of the patient. The therapist can find herself suddenly disliking her patient, accepting his hostility towards himself as natural and expected. If the clinician is herself GSRD, there could be collusion with the alien self by adopting it and feeling inadequate herself. The capacity to think and be curious gets obscured, and non-mentalising modes set in. This could be a good moment for self-reflection, personally or in supervision, as "[t]he Mentalizing Stance asks for humility, intellectual curiosity, and the willingness to learn" (Sharp and Bevington, 2022, p. xv), which are coincidentally also key to Davies and Neal's seven core components of GSRD Therapy.

There is also a thin line when the client works with a GSRD therapist. Internalised stigma can "undermine the therapeutic alliance's impact as the client projects that sense of being 'worth less' onto the therapist" (Sharon, 2023, pp. 250–251). Bringing the topic and recognising its existence provides a good start to consider the implications of living in a neglectful and rejecting environment. If the therapist is perceived as cis-heterosexual, she could also be regarded as privileged. Bringing the topic to the fore reflects the therapist's humble stance and her interest in knowing, not assuming, what is in the client's mind.

The crucible of the clinical encounter "aims to reverse or mitigate the impact of these adversities and help move clients towards more secure forms of thinking and relating" (Holmes and Slade, 2018, p. 17). The first step is always establishing a safe relationship where the client is willing to explore his mind, finds ways to regulate his emotional responses, or uses the clinical relationship for co-regulation. The therapist needs to validate the client's experiences and recognise the impact of minority stress, shame and the establishment of the alien self as a survival strategy.

Alberto was initially uncomfortable when talking about his sexual difficulties. However, when compiling his background information, he was increasingly conscious of the messages he received when he was growing up about gay people, even before he realised he was interested in men. He had a fantasy that his sexual issues were a payback for hurting other people, like his grandmother, who wanted him to be heterosexual and not an abomination, or the girls he dated at university, as he thought he just used them.

When the client can talk about the impact all this had on his life and how he used the alien self as a survival strategy, he might be ready to make meaning of his need to protect significant figures by adopting a compliant self that would avoid rejection or punishment. At this point, even the therapeutic relationship can be questioned as part of reevaluating his learned ways of relating. Sensitivity, acceptance, and non-retaliation from the therapist would be pivotal.

As the work continued, Alberto started to see that presenting himself as others expected him to be was damaging his sense of self. He was confused, resentful, and angry at trying to be a "good boy", but lost his authentic self. He was wary of our work, as recognising those emotions jeopardised his disposition towards his family. I recognised his ambivalence and encouraged him to take the perspective of his family's values and actions and the damaging impact of society on his psychosexual development.

Finally, with the exploration and meaning-making, some changes are usually evidenced in the client's narrative about his everyday activities or relational interactions. The movement from dysregulation to regulation in the clinical encounter can be generalised to the situations outside therapy. As the client expresses himself more openly and with an increased sense of safety, he also feels an increased sense of agency and a more nuanced perspective towards the self and others. At this point, the client will be "prepared to revise outmoded attachment patterns and assumptions" (Holmes and Slade, 2018, pp. 19–20).

During the last months of our work together, Alberto considered coming out to his family. This time, he wanted to make his family participate in his intimate relational life, and he acknowledged that some of them may not react well. He spoke about the life he wanted for himself and how he was working towards that. He met a man who was open to communication and was willing to take their sexual life slowly. Despite it not being perfect, Alberto was more optimistic about being the version of himself that he wanted.

The embodiment of such experiences should also be explored. As Judith Butler (1997) pointed out, "One only need consider how the history of having been called an injurious name is embodied, how the words enter the limbs, craft the gesture, bend spine" (p. 159). Being able to move from the pre-mentalising modes and allowing the negative experience to be recognised, marked, and mirrored will help the spontaneous gesture and unintegrated part of the self to be reconsidered and reappraised in the company of another who is willing to accompany the patient in the contemplation of their pain and their journey through integration.

Conclusion

This chapter presented a view of internalised stigma/homophobia from a mentalising perspective. This reflection does not intend to be "a universal" about how people respond to environments that invalidate their GSRD nascent or established status. Neither does it try to give a "how-to" approach to deal with it clinically. Instead, in the best mentalising spirit, it considers the importance of trust in others as a requisite for knowledge about oneself and growth. These others are sometimes called parents, family, peers, friends, or therapists.

As mentalising refers to an imaginative capacity, it is pivotal to any clinical endeavour to understand "how we got to our unique representations of reality, how those representations differ from the representations others have formed, and how our differing representations may be impacting upon our own feelings and actions, and upon those around us" (Sharp and Bevington, 2022, p. 104). Under this light, I think the impact of internalised stigma in the shape of shame and an alien self needs to be re-examined, understood, and deconstructed so that the person can grow and experience a coherent sense of self.

The experience of seeing oneself in another appears to gradually tame our sense of shame by creating symbolic representations that help regulate rather than exacerbate emotional reactions from chastising experiences due to what Winnicott would refer to as a *"spontaneous gesture"* (Rodman and Winnicott, 1999).

In the clinical encounter, in the words of Holmes and Slade, "relational safety is the precondition for co-regulation and meaning-making" (2018, p. 50), eventually leading to self-regulation and mentalising.

Notes

1 Although I am conscious of the ongoing debate concerning this concept, I intend to use it generically as defined here. I also prefer the term "internalised stigma" as it encompasses a process across GSRD issues.
2 As a way to reduce confusion, I have opted to use she/her to refer to the carer/ therapist and he/his to refer to the baby/client.
3 I will not elaborate on these in this chapter; however, I recommend the reader review the book by Sharp and Bevington (2022) for a clear and concise overview.

References

Andrews, J. L., Ahmed, S. P. and Blakemore, S. J. (2021) 'Navigating the social environment in adolescence: The role of social brain development', *Biological Psychiatry*, 89(2), pp. 109–118. doi: 10.1016/j.biopsych.2020.09.012.
Bateman, A. and Fonagy, P. (2016) *Mentalization-based treatment for personality disorders: A practical guide.* Oxford, UK: Oxford University Press.

Bateman, A. and Fonagy, P. (2018) 'Mentalizing as a common factor in psychotherapy', in Dewan, M. J., Steenbarger, B. N. and Greenberg, R. P. (eds.) *The art and science of brief psychotherapies: A practitioner's guide*. New York: American Psychiatric Pub, pp. 29–38.

Butler, J. (1997) *Excitable speech*. New York, NY: Routledge.

Davies, D. and Neves, S. (2023) 'Gender, sex and relationship diversity therapy', in Hanley, T. and Winter, L.A. (eds.) *The SAGE handbook of counselling and psychotherapy*. London: Sage, pp. 409–415.

Desatnik, A., Bird, A., Shmueli, A., Venger, I. and Fonagy, P. (2023) 'The mindful trajectory: Developmental changes in mentalizing throughout adolescence and young adulthood', *PLoS One*, 18(6), e0286500. doi: 10.1371/journal.pone .0286500

Fonagy, P., Gergely, G., Jurist, E. and Target, M. (2002) *Affect regulation, mentalization and the development of the self*. New York: Other Press.

Fonagy, P., Luyten, P., Allison, E. and Campbell, C. (2017a) 'What we have changed our minds about: Part 1. Borderline personality disorder as a limitation of resilience', *Borderline Personality Disorder and Emotion Dysregulation*, 4, pp. 1–11.

Fonagy, P., Luyten, P., Allison, E. and Campbell, C. (2017b) 'What we have changed our minds about: Part 2. Borderline personality disorder, epistemic trust and the developmental significance of social communication', *Borderline Personality Disorder and Emotion Dysregulation*, 4(1), p. 9.

Fonagy, P., Steele, M., Steele, H., Moran, G. S. and Higgitt, A. C. (1991) 'The capacity for understanding mental states: The reflective self in parent and child and its significance for security of attachment', *Infant Mental Health Journal*, 12(3), pp. 201–218.

Grosse Wiesmann, C. and Southgate, V. (2021) 'Early theory of mind development: Are infants inherently altercentric?', in Frith, C. D. and Frith, U. (eds.) *The neural basis of mentalizing*. Cham: Springer International Publishing, pp. 49–66.

Holmes, J. and Slade, A. (2018) *Attachment in therapeutic practice*. London: SAGE.

Luyten, P., De Meulemeester, C. and Fonagy, P. (2021) 'The self–other distinction in psychopathology: Recent developments from a mentalizing perspective', in Frith, C. D. and Frith, U. (eds.) *The neural basis of mentalizing*. Cham: Springer International Publishing, pp. 659–680.

Meyer, I. H. (2003) 'Prejudice, social stress, and mental health in lesbian, gay, and bisexual populations: conceptual issues and research evidence', *Psychological Bulletin*, 129(5), pp. 674–697. https://doi.org/10.1037/0033-2909.129.5.674

Newcomb, M. E. and Mustanski, B. (2010) 'Internalized homophobia and internalizing mental health problems: A meta-analytic review', *Clinical Psychology Review*, 30(8), pp. 1019–1029.

Rodman, F. and Winnicott, D. W. (1999) *The spontaneous gesture: Selected letters of DW Winnicott*. London: Karnac Books.

Rosario, M., Espinosa, A., Kittle, K. and Russell, S. T. (2022) 'Childhood experiences and mental health of sexual minority adults: Examining three models', *Journal of Sex Research*, 59(7), pp. 834–847.

Rosario, M. and Schrimshaw, E. W. (2012) 'The sexual identity development and health of lesbian, gay, and bisexual adolescents: An ecological perspective', in

Patterson, C. J. and D'Augelli A. R. (eds.) *Handbook of psychology and sexual orientation*. Oxford University Press, pp. 87–101.

Sharon, E. (2023) '"Blurred facilitation stand"–the hidden factor when working with LGBTQ: Diagnosis and addressing an unspoken effect of internalized homophobia', *European Journal of Psychotherapy & Counselling*, 25(3), pp. 247–262. https://doi.org/10.1080/13642537.2023.2240821.

Sharp, C. and Bevington, D. (2022) *Mentalizing in psychotherapy: A guide for practitioners*. London: Guilford Press.

Steele, M. and Steele, H. (2011) 'On the origins of reflective functioning', in Busch, F. N. (ed.) *Mentalization: Theoretical considerations, research findings, and clinical implications*. London: Taylor & Francis, pp. 133–158.

Totenhagen, C. J., Randall, A. K. and Lloyd, K. (2018) 'Stress and relationship functioning in same-sex couples: The vulnerabilities of internalized homophobia and outness', *Family Relations*, 67(3), pp. 399–413.

Chapter 12

Mirror Ball Encounters – Group Therapy with GSRD Communities

Niki D and Tim Foskett

We would like to introduce this chapter with a poignant quote commonly attributed to Maya Angelou: *"If you are always trying to be normal, you will never know how amazing you are."*

Humans are social creatures. Across the span of our lives, we are embedded in and reliant upon social groups and networks to differing degrees. These networks have particular significance in the early and psychologically formative years of our lives.

For people growing up with gender or sexuality experiences that are unconventional, this dependency is often fraught. What we feel, need, want or desire is often at odds with the norms and expectations of the groups we depend on.

The consequences of revealing these often transgressive aspects of ourselves to our social groups can include experiences of being unwelcome, criticised, humiliated, rejected, bullied, abandoned, physically attacked or even murdered.

As a result, the vast majority of GSRD people learn to hide parts of themselves from the caregivers, family or community on whom they depend. The intensity of this hiding varies from the more subtle forms of adjusting how we express ourselves and adopting behaviours that help us pass as (more) normative, through escalating vigilance, monitoring, masking and code-switching, to a full-scale internal psychological assault on the parts of ourselves that we understand might threaten our very existence if they were to be expressed.

Most trans and queer people have not enjoyed the validating and attuned relationships that humans need to function well and to thrive, within an affirming and mirroring social context. To put it another way, the mirror balls of our fabulous queer selves have seldom been recognised, kept safe, polished, celebrated and brightly lit from several angles, by the loving groups and networks we inhabit. In reality, they have often become tarnished, dulled or broken if they are revealed or we have felt compelled to keep them tightly wrapped up in a dark and secret place and never exposed to the light.

That's no life for a mirror ball. (*Thanks to Amanda Middleton for inspiring the image of the mirror ball as a queer symbol in discourse about therapy*: Middleton 2022).

DOI: 10.4324/9781003530848-15

We appreciate that not all queer and trans people will relate to the metaphor of being a mirror ball. We recognise that GSRD people come in an infinite number of different shapes, sizes, expressions and metaphorical flavours. Indeed, there are potentially as many different queer metaphors as there are different queer people.

Therapeutic groups for trans and queer people have a long history of offering a space for the gentle or radical emergence of our queer selves.

Through the mutual sharing of our journeys, the knocks and mistreatments, the exiling and hiding, the missing pieces, and the pain, deprivations and losses that social prejudice has wrought. Other systems of oppression such as those pertaining to race, social class, neurodivergence, disability, health status and age will also affect our personal mirror ball in multiple ways.

GSRD group therapy can be a rebalancing and transformative experience in the presence of others who mirror back to us parts of who we are. Who affirm what they see and relate to, including how we differ and vary within the greater family of queerness, and who recognise and understand our experience. The normative cultural silence surrounding queerness, transness and relationship diversity means that at some point in their lives, many trans, polyamorous and queer people experience isolation believing that they are "the only one." The power of being with others in a therapeutic group, which doesn't just tolerate the hidden parts of ourselves being shared but positively invites us to do so, and celebrates when we do, cannot be overstated.

Group therapy offers feedback, mirroring and light from multiple sources and multiple angles – a much wider range than is available in individual therapy – thereby illuminating and reflecting back our lives in infinite ways.

In this context, we can learn to let our mirror balls shine and multiply the light between us. We can attend to and even celebrate the broken parts, queer shapes, and vibrant shades of our mirror balls – in glorious technicolour.

GSRD Group Therapy Factors

Below, we discuss various ideas about what makes GSRD therapeutic groups effective. We invite you, whilst reading, to recall your own queer group experiences or other group experiences that reflect an aspect of your identity. In what ways have these experiences been healing and growthful for you? What hopes and fears were stirred up? In what ways did you feel included or excluded? Did you feel seen and heard or become invisible and silenced?

Yalom's Therapeutic Factors and Queer Developments

In 1976, Irvin Yalom published his vast textbook *The Theory and Practice of Group Psychotherapy* – now in its 6th Edition with Molyn Leszcz (Yalom & Leszcz, 2021). Yalom articulates a rationale for core factors contributing to effective group psychotherapy, backed up by research and practice. Much of what Yalom proposes has been endorsed by others and a broad consensus has formed between academics and practitioners around twelve key group factors.

For many of our readers, it is probably self-evident how these factors might benefit GSRD clients and groups. They impact differently depending on whether the group is exclusively or predominantly GSRD in comparison to when a GSRD person is in a minority or possibly the only member of a group that is otherwise culturally normative.

In the following section, we introduce a queer perspective on each of the therapeutic factors proposed by Yalom, in the Tables numbered 12.1 to 12.12.

Each table provides the Name and the Definition of a therapeutic factor, a note on the Relevance of the factor to GSRD group therapy, a group Example and an authentic Quote from a GSRD group taken from our feedback forms or end-of-term group exercises. The final column notes the GSRD Therapy Core Components relevant to the group factor. The definitions are drawn from the American Group Psychotherapy Association Practice Guidelines (AGPA 2007).

The group examples we include are from diverse groups and are anonymised or invented. We include specific reference to race, social class and other intersectional identity factors when there is a direct relevance to the GSRD situation being described.

Table 12.1 Universality: Members Recognise that other Members Share Similar Feelings, Thoughts and Problems

GSRD Relevance	GSRD Group Therapy Example	Quote	GSRD Therapy Core Components
The conspiracy of silence about trans and queer lives in normative culture means many GSRD people have been exposed to a highly distorted version of events about human lives and relationships. Meeting other queer people in a therapy group is often revelatory and deeply affirming as more accurate and diverse queer narratives of life emerge from the lived experiences of the members.	Sara is a lesbian, cis woman raised in a culture and country where homophobic laws could result in state-sanctioned murder. The group was her first experience of being welcomed and understood, where her experiences of "otherness" were shared. At the end of a group term, Sara cut her hair short, which she had long dreamed about, and came out to her sisters and close friends. She told the group their support allowed her to take this step.	*"I feel a sense of belonging in a queer space. There is a community of other diverse people who get what it is like to be queer, whether that is sexually or gender-wise or poly. I don't have to explain who I am or why I don't fit into the box society thinks I should be in."*	1 Integrating core GSRD theories 2 Knowing contemporary sexology 3 Trauma, grief and shame informed 4 Understanding the adverse effects of oppression

Table 12.2 Cohesion: Feelings of Trust, Belonging, and Togetherness Experienced by the Group Members

GSRD Relevance	GSRD Group Therapy Example	Quote	GSRD Therapy Core Components
Exclusion, rejection and *not* belonging in groups are core to most GSRD people's life experience. The powerful experience of authentic cohesion that can happen in a group therapy setting can be life-affirming, even life-changing, for GSRD group members.	Melo, a black, cis, pansexual man in a culturally and ethnically mixed therapy group, experienced much-needed recognition from another black bisexual group member. To have multiple aspects of his intersectional identity and experience reflected back to him left him feeling truly seen and understood in a group context for the first time.	"I feel less alone as I listen to other people sharing similar experiences, and this is different from individual therapy where you don't have that sharing of experiences, that reciprocity."	1 Fostering joy 2 Trauma, grief and shame informed 3 Understanding the adverse effects of oppression 4 Demonstrating cultural humility and cultural competence 5 Practising a commitment to social justice

Table 12.3 Catharsis: Members Release Strong Feelings about Past or Present Experiences

GSRD Relevance	GSRD Group Therapy Example	Quote	GSRD Therapy Core Components
To be witnessed during emotionally vulnerable moments in a supportive group can be releasing, healing and growthful. Queer, polyam and trans shame, fear and loneliness exist in the shadows, so bringing them into the light of a GSRD group can be a liberating experience.	Chui, a kinky, queer, cis woman, is a survivor of childhood and adult sexual abuse from straight cis men. The group's acceptance and encouragement made a significant impact on her trauma recovery, as she shared her feelings about moving from an oppressive relationship with a man on the swingers scene to forming a poly relationship with two women and de-escalating her previous relationship.	"I felt safe enough in the group to express my sadness, my frustrations, doubts and hopes during my relationship transition to polyamory. There is no way I could have been so open in a 'normal' therapy group. Here, I didn't fear your judgments as I already knew that you understood so much of my experience from how you all shared yours."	1 Fostering joy 2 Knowing contemporary sexology 3 Trauma, grief and shame informed 4 Understanding the adverse effects of oppression 5 Demonstrating cultural humility and cultural competence

Table 12.4 Self-Understanding: Members Gain Insight into Psychological Motivation, Underlying Behaviour and Emotional Reactions

GSRD Relevance	GSRD Group Therapy Example	Quote	GSRD Therapy Core Components
Understanding ourselves is a central aspect of a therapeutic endeavour. GSRD groups offer a safer space to understand our motivations, behaviours, resilience and patterns of relating to others–away from the inhibiting and prejudiced glare of normative culture. This process includes support to *discover* our unique GSRD self, to *differentiate* from other members of the group at times and *develop* in authentic ways.	Sissy is a queer, polyamorous cis woman struggling with pressure to hide her multiple relationships and her sex work from family, lovers and friends. She used the group as a space to lay out all the different aspects of her identity, and the dilemmas she faced. With the group's support, she was able to understand where her psychological and relational patterns originated, and ultimately find her own way forward to build a life that better met her authentic needs	*"The group helped me in ways I never expected. To meet other queer polyamorous people in a therapy group and a group therapist who actually knew what all of this meant, was so helpful to me in working out what actually makes me tick, and how I want to relate to others going forward. Although many of us are poly, we all do it in slightly different ways. Support for that diversity was crucial."*	1 Fostering joy 2 Integrating Core GSRD theories 3 Knowing contemporary sexology 4 Trauma, grief and shame informed 5 Understanding the adverse effects of oppression

Table 12.5 Imparting Information: Education or Advice Provided by the Therapist or Group Members

GSRD Relevance	GSRD Group Therapy Example	Quote	GSRD Therapy Core Components
In normative cultures, helpful and positive information about GSRD identities is scarce. The practical guidance and resource sharing in group therapy can provide a social lifeline, critical medical or sexual health knowledge, help with coming out, living a queer, open/polyamorous or trans life, hate crime support and relationship guidance.	Jamal, a gay, cis man in his 50s, feels like he's late to the gay party, having only acted on his sexual feelings recently. The group provides information about gay life in tea breaks as well as within sessions. It also reminds him of all the life experiences he brings with him into gay life, which he had previously negated.	*"No one ever tells you how to navigate the gay scene as a person of colour when you first come out, how to use the apps, how to look after your sexual health. We have discussed all these points in my group and more. It's been the queer sex education I never had."*	1 Integrating core GSRD theories 2 Knowing contemporary sexology 3 Trauma, grief and shame informed 4 Understanding the adverse effects of oppression

Table 12.6 Imitative Experience/Identification: Members Expand their Knowledge and Skills by Observing Group Members' Self-Exploration, Reflection, and Interpersonal Processing

GSRD Relevance	GSRD Group Therapy Example	Quote	GSRD Therapy Core Components
A therapeutic environment allows group members to try out new versions of themselves and be inspired by how others live and relate. Many GSRD people are deprived of such poignant self-exploration due to social alienation, and a lack of mirroring in the normative community.	Kae and Justin seemed an unlikely pairing in the queer therapy group. Kae, a non-binary person, struggles to assert themselves in many situations. Justin, a trans man, came to the group saying he had difficulties controlling his temper and had been accused of dominating in intimate relationships. Over time in the group, Kae found that they could absorb some of Justin's feisty-ness, first in group interactions and later in experiences outside of the group. Justin felt he could "relax his guard" in the group and was deeply affected by Kae's "softer" approach to people and life. The group was a safe enough place for him to try on that way of being. He found he liked it.	*"There is relatable stuff that other people bring up. It is motivating to hear similarities in other people's struggles or experiences and interesting to see how other people process issues and have different ways of responding."*	1 Integrating Core GSRD theories 2 Knowing contemporary sexology 3 Trauma, grief and shame informed 4 Understanding the adverse effects of oppression 5 Demonstrating cultural humility and cultural competence 6 Practising a commitment to social justice

Table 12.7 Development of Socialising Techniques: The Group Provides Members with an Environment that Fosters Adaptive and Effective Communication

GSRD Relevance	GSRD Group Therapy Example	Quote	GSRD Therapy Core Components
A consequence of minority stress is psychological alienation, which can leave some GSRD people shut down and their communication in social settings strained. A supportive trans and/or queer group offers modelling from other members as well as the opportunity for free-flowing and open conversations where censorship is not required to maintain safety. The valuable experience of joyful contact and skills of listening, attunement and empathy are also cultivated.	Jaz had learned to survive in their family of origin and local community as a non-binary person by being extremely nice to everyone. This was their primary socialising strategy. They used group therapy to experiment with inhibiting their knee-jerk "niceness" and expanding their range of social interactions to include authenticity, challenge, and sharing a different perspective, including an exchange over several weeks that was often tense and heated on how they defined themselves in their queerness.	"Group therapy members help me 'see' things differently, which is so valuable. Also, to take the risk of meeting group members outside of the group at queer, poly spaces, meant I had support in those spaces AND was able to talk it all through afterwards."	1 Fostering joy 2 Integrating core GSRD theories 3 Trauma, grief and shame informed 4 Understanding the adverse effects of oppression 5 Demonstrating cultural humility and cultural competence

Table 12.8 Interpersonal Learning: Members Gain Personal Insight into their Interpersonal Impact through Feedback Provided by other Members

GSRD Relevance	GSRD Group Therapy Example	Quote	GSRD Therapy Core Components
The feedback that many GSRD people are exposed to in normative culture is often prejudiced and hostile. The type of affirming feedback that GSRD therapeutic groups engender allows members to feel seen in their strengths and vulnerabilities. Queer feedback can land in a different way when defences are lowered in the safety of a GSRD group.	Dida is a butch lesbian in her 50s, older by a decade than the other group members. Her "armour" to cope in a homophobic world had left her divorced from her tender and vulnerable sides. A young gay woman in the group found a way of communicating to Dida how she saw her strength but also saw her care, allowing Dida to let her guard down and become increasingly open in the group.	*"As awkward as those group exercises were, I really enjoyed meeting your gaze and the fact that you saw past all the bullshit, the barriers that I construct for everyone else. Thank you for listening, and thank you for giving me such valuable and challenging feedback."*	1 Integrating Core GSRD theories 2 Knowing contemporary sexology 3 Trauma, grief and shame informed 4 Understanding the adverse effects of oppression 5 Demonstrating cultural humility and cultural competence

Table 12.9 Corrective Recapitulation of Primary Family ExperienceOpportunity to Reenact Critical Family Dynamics with Group Members in a Corrective Manner

GSRD Relevance	GSRD Group Therapy Example	Quote	GSRD Therapy Core Components
Family dynamics are typically our first experience of group interactions. Already complex enough, but for most GSRD group members, family prejudice or ignorance and the resulting alienation they often experience causes deep ruptures in family group experiences. A GSRD therapy group can allow members a space to process family wounds, and imagine new ways to experience affirming and joyful configurations of queer 'family'.	Lee, a bisexual, cis woman was exposed to emotional neglect from her parents and biphobic bullying from her older brother in the family home. A recent autism diagnosis allowed her to accept her difficulty with eye contact and to manage relational dynamics in her own way. She tentatively shared how the times she was particularly quiet in a group session, she was feeling invisible, which could result in her having suicidal thoughts after the group. The group responded with care and respect. In subsequent sessions, if she were quiet, someone would check in with her until a point when she was joining in regularly with the group conversation.	*"There is such value in a queer group where you have five other people not shaming you for something but just accepting and encouraging you. That group acceptance is so healing."*	1 Fostering joy 2 Integrating Core GSRD theories 3 Trauma, grief and shame informed 4 Understanding the adverse effects of oppression 5 Demonstrating cultural humility and cultural competence 6 Practising a commitment to social justice

Table 12.10 Altruism: Members Gain a Boost in Self-Concept by Extending Help to other Group Members

GSRD Relevance	GSRD Group Therapy Example	Quote	GSRD Therapy Core Components
The unity that can come from GSRD group therapy invites reciprocity in collective connection as members receive and offer support. Members sharing their GSRD journeys can provide solace, resources and encouragement to others both directly and indirectly.	Troy, a trans masc member, delights in his chest following top surgery after years of struggle with dysphoria. He readily lifted his t-shirt to show his chest in a group session as an offering for two non-binary AFAB people who wanted gender-affirming surgery but carried lots of fears about it and were isolated in their lives.	"I love how much you both grew in front of us. I felt that we 'saw' each other and that felt good. I hope the next steps of your journeys include happiness, laughter, joy and love."	1 Fostering joy 2 Trauma, grief and shame informed 3 Understanding the adverse effects of oppression 4 Demonstrating cultural humility and cultural competence 5 Practising a commitment to social justice

Table 12.11 Existential Factors: Members Accept Responsibility for Life Decisions, Face their Personal Agency and Aspects of Existence that are Unchangeable

GSRD Relevance	GSRD Group Therapy Example	Quote	GSRD Therapy Core Components
Existential factors like intersubjectivity, meaninglessness and embodiment are particularly relevant for GSRD folk, who are tasked with finding their place amongst others, creating meaning for their lives, and building a positive experience of being in their bodies. All this is against a backdrop of social hostility in normative cultures.	Leo, a straight, trans man, made the most of a group where the majority of members were trans-masc presenting. He expressed and processed his experiences of trans embodiment and the meaning and values he gave to his masculinity. His growing confidence in the group led him to challenge transphobia in his workplace as he took risks to come out and be seen as a proud trans man rather than living in stealth for fear of being exposed to transphobia.	"I have truly appreciated your trans alliance within the group and welcomed listening to your eloquent interpretation of trans experiences. Your understanding of the shitstorm we go through regularly has helped me digest and process some of the madness out there. You and the others helped me be truly vulnerable in the group as I accepted what I could change and what I couldn't."	1 Integrating Core GSRD theories 2 Knowing contemporary sexology 3 Trauma, grief and shame informed 4 Understanding the adverse effects of oppression 5 Practising a commitment to social justice

Table 12.12 Instillation of Hope: Members Feelings of Optimism for their Own and others Development are Enhanced

GSRD Relevance	GSRD Group Therapy Example	Quote	GSRD Therapy Core Components
Something profound can be rebalanced in a GSRD group. A life-affirming element gained or regained is often hope. Hope for oneself as queer/trans/poly/kinky in the world. Hearing and witnessing other people overcoming personal struggles of structural prejudice, family rejection, and community alienation can offer optimism for a vibrant and connected life without having to hide oneself.	Alix, a trans femme, non-binary member, carried deep shame about their genitals that had prevented them from seeking intimate relationships. In a GSRD group they witnessed a trans woman's transition as she claimed her changing body and brought to the group her successes and trials of surgery, dating and sex parties. The significance of this for Alix led to them adopting gender-affirming language for their genitals and going on dates with other pansexual people.	*"You have such a wonderful, unique trans energy that shines in our group, as I'm sure it does in your world. I can only thank you on repeat for listening and truly seeing me for who I am. I feel so much closer to being at ease being trans since being in the group because of you and the others."*	1 Fostering joy 2 Trauma, grief and shame informed 3 Understanding the adverse effects of oppression 4 Demonstrating cultural humility and cultural competence 5 Practising a commitment to social justice

Queering Group Psychotherapy

Having added a GSRD perspective to Yalom's model of group therapy, we want to address specific factors that have arisen in our work with GSRD therapy groups and why the "queering" of group therapy holds relevance.

By queering group therapy, we mean radically re-examining the fundamental assumptions behind different therapeutic models and questioning whether these practices truly serve the marginalised communities we focus on. Or whether they perpetuate the same oppressions that GSRD people have faced for millennia.

In this chapter, queering means *centring* and *prioritising* GSRD people who have often been invisible, pathologised or a tokenistic after-thought in the development of psychotherapeutic perspectives in general, including models of group therapy. It offers a voice to those silenced in society and the opportunity of much-needed reflections from others previously isolated and alone. It means legitimising those who are de-legitimised by oppressive systems of social exclusion. It means celebrating aspects of queer, trans and relationally diverse life and identity that are otherwise rarely raised up as valuable and valued.

Queering group psychotherapy can also include deconstructing the "power over" positions taken by therapists holding a so-called expert position and imagining new models that are more democratic, horizontal, and explicitly anti-oppressive in their formulation and development.

For this to happen, the group therapist needs to be GSRD aware and have some GSRD lived experience to bring personal insight and recognition alongside their groupwork knowledge. This includes being well-versed in some of the affirmative language used by different GSRD communities, such as polyamorous terms, asexual spectrum awareness, sex worker inclusivity, gender diversity and neurodivergent knowledge.

Queering group therapy invites us to be curious and critical. How many of the sacred cows of the group psychotherapy discourse might need to be reconsidered, adapted, or even thrown out when working in a queer context?

These questions also require us to critique ourselves, questioning the group therapist's role. In this way, we believe that the group therapist is not *above* or *outside* the group, but *part of* the group with a specific task of helping the group to notice, clarify and give meaning to the relational challenges and potentialities of the group members and the group as a whole.

Group therapy is always a multidimensional endeavour. It occurs *in* the group, *with* the group and can therefore be understood to be therapy *by* the group. It can be a humbling for the group therapist to realise that the most important interventions are often from other group members.

This perspective means that we are included in the conversations that flow around us in group sessions and can share, when relevant, our own GSRD experience, alongside holding and supporting the group in ways that maintain its therapeutic context and prevent it from becoming a support group or social space (though these informal aspects can also be a part of therapy groups). We question language that supports the "power over" position inherent in titles like group leader. Niki moves between using the terms "group host" and "group therapist" to reflect her flexible "power with" role. At times, she takes the role of a group therapist when a direction is required, or meta comments about the group might help the group process; other times she is solely the group host, providing the environment, the tea and a quiet holding of the group. Tim uses the terms group therapist and group leader and believes ethical practice involves a constant consideration of – and dialogue about – the power relations within and between group members, including himself.

Working together on this chapter we realise there is a book to be written about this vast topic. In the space that remains, we touch on a few key themes relevant to GSRD group therapy, including shame, therapist self-disclosure, working with intersectional identities and creating an anti-oppressive culture in groupwork.

GSRD Shame

Robert Downes (2022) in *Queering Psychotherapy* writes poignantly, "To really work with shame means we get to reveal to ourselves in the company of another/others the wretchedness inside, the devastation, the unmet need, the desire, the shapes we take in the face of hatred, the destructive aspects of ourselves that we often struggle to contain that we turn against ourselves." (p.53)

GSRD group therapy offers companions to those with the courage to reveal uncomfortable aspects of themselves or their life experiences. We have seen the transformative effect when the group meets someone's shame-filled sharing with compassion and understanding. People offer back their experiences of resonance to what is shared and invite context and community to counterbalance the individual group members' sense of isolation and rejection.

GSRD Groupwork with Intersectional Identities

We cannot do justice to this critical topic in a few paragraphs, but here are some pointers that have emerged from our work with GSRD groups.

As previously discussed in this handbook, *understanding the specific adverse effects of oppression* and *demonstrating cultural humility and cultural competence* are part of the guiding principles of GSRD therapy.

It is helpful to consider the following questions to increase the intersectional reach of your group or service and the steps you can take to create a group within an anti-oppressive paradigm:

Where will the group take place? The venue will convey specific values about the group and will likely attract and put off certain demographics. Will it be online or in-person? A community space will have a different impact to a corporate office in the city, as will a venue that is or isn't mobility accessible.

Who will facilitate the group? The identities of the facilitator(s) will impact who wants to join. In our experience, people from marginalised groups are more likely to join groups facilitated by people who share aspects of their identity and experience.

Who is the group for, and what will the group's focus be? Is the group theme relevant to just one niche within the GSRD communities or purposefully broad? Anti-oppressive practice means responding to marginalised people and working with them to construct a group culture that is responsive to their needs.

Who will pay for the group? The economics of a therapy group will significantly affect who joins it. A group based in a community setting and paid for by a funding organisation will have a different draw than one set up in private practice. Will concession or sliding scale rates be available?

How will the group be publicised? The job of publicity is to reach relevant GSRD communities. The values you project through your publicity will affect who approaches you.

Will there be a selection process and pre-group preparation process? How will you ensure that unconscious bias and other forms of discrimination are not enacted and human diversity is welcomed and recognised in the process? How will you ensure a balanced and diverse group is assembled? What is the process of pre-group preparation that you will go through with each potential member?

Group Composition. Yalom and Leszcz (2005) argue that group composition benefits from some heterogeneity (a mix of differences) and some homogeneity (some similarities – for example in identity or group focus). A group that is too diverse may find it hard to cohere. A group that is too similar may become stale, or overly safe and therefore unproductive.

It is essential, wherever possible, to have more than one person with a given intersectional identity in a mixed group. Mirroring is a significant aspect of group effectiveness. If mirrors are absent or minimal in a GSRD group, this aspect of group psychotherapy will be limited.

You may not be able to offer a GSRD group as diverse as you would like. For example, you may have to choose between offering a person with racialised experience a space in an otherwise white group or not offering them a space at all. Or a member of an initially single-gender group may come out as non-binary or trans within the lifetime of the group, and you can't immediately offer them a mirroring experience.

Where this cannot be avoided, we recommend dialogue with the person concerned as part of the pre-group preparation. Asking them how they feel about this shares the power and choice. In our experience, some prospective clients are still keen to join a group as long as there is some mirroring of other aspects of their identity. Others, of course, will rule themselves out of a group that does not reflect critical aspects of their identity or experiences, judging that this experience could be counterproductive for them at this point in their journey.

Creating an anti-oppressive group culture. It's a given in GSRD therapy group that oppression in all its myriad forms is recognised, named and explored as part of the culture of the group. The therapist will significantly influence the group's culture as the "architect" of the group. How the therapist addresses issues of oppression in the pre-group preparation, the material clients bring, the interactions between group members and the broader social context within which the group takes place will affect the climate in the group and the likelihood of clients bringing up those themes and feeling safe to address them. One example is how pronouns are addressed. For example, periodically inviting all group members and co-therapists to share their pronouns is a powerful intervention. Any mistakes with pronouns are best addressed in the group as a whole, so the focus does not stay solely with the person being misgendered or the person who made the mistake. It can lead to important conversations about the ways group members feel when they are "seen" in ways that invalidate them or how "policed" or fragile members might feel in group contexts.

A therapy group is a place for difficult conversations. As Eugene Ellis (2021) observes in his book *The Race Conversations*, our nervous systems become aroused when themes of race come up in an interaction or group. This also applies to other issues about which people have strong feelings. Tolerating this arousal, exploring it and learning how to talk about emotive topics with others is grist for the mill of a therapy group.

It is a key responsibility of the group therapist to remain closely attuned to a group member who may be marginalised in some way so that they are not left alone with this experience. The therapist should attend to the group field and watch for what an isolated individual may need from them or other group members. This will include addressing any empathic failures, scapegoating, aggressions (micro/macro) or ruptures that the individual or the group are not naming. There is a pace and balance to find here, for if the therapist steps in prematurely or overly frequently, the group and individual members could be disempowered.

Finally, we want to address neurodiversity in groups. As the voices of neurodiverse people have become louder and more assured in our groups in recent years, it is clear that neurodivergent people are likely to make up a significant proportion, and often a majority, of any GSRD group. Insisting on groups norm of quiet voices, direct eye contact and still-bodied listening, for example, is oppressive to people who need to move or use a fidget gadget. We have found that groups can integrate different needs (including knitting for members needing to keep hands engaged). And the process of doing so validates many neurodivergent people who often have a long history of masking and of feeling isolated in groups and networks to which they belong.

Working well with intersectionality and creating an anti-oppressive culture in a group is no small task and requires more awareness than any therapist will have at any given time (even on a good day!). It's good practice for the therapist to periodically invite feedback and critique from the group and to model receiving, responding to, taking accountability for and repairing ruptures when they happen in the group process. An appropriate and well-placed apology from a group leader who has "missed" a group member in some critical way can be one of the most powerful interventions we will ever make.

Working within GSRD Communities and Therapist Self-Disclosure

For many GSRD people, there will be overlapping connections in smaller queer communities, especially those who are part of particular subcultures within the broader queer world, such as queer people of colour, trans, kinky, sex workers and/or polyamorous people. Consequently, group therapy endeavours within the queer community need to adapt to this reality. This might include having an intake procedure for new members joining an existing group to check there isn't a pre-existing relationship with group members that could compromise the therapy.

In small social networks, contact outside the group will happen occasionally. Over decades of practice, we have found that there is typically benefit in this interaction, particularly for queer and trans people who may form friendships of depth within a therapeutic space. Of course, care must be taken to manage boundaries and safety, and not every group therapy setting could adopt this approach. In our groups, the agreement is to bring back to the group any significant events that happen between members outside the group.

Given the reality of being part of these smaller communities, practitioners must consider the ethical management of multiple roles/dual relationships which inevitably occur. Dominic Davies (2023) writes an informative chapter "living and working within our communities" in *Relationally Queer*. We are aligned with his belief that; "Boundary violations are harmful to the therapeutic relationship, whereas boundary crossings are not and indeed can be beneficial" (2023: 210). Davies promotes GSRD therapists using a Professional Boundary Statement to prepare clients for boundary overlap and to offer guidance on how to navigate complex crossover that can result whilst protecting the therapeutic relationship.

As GSRD therapists, we share relevant aspects of our GSRD identity and experiences with group members and within our marketing material. The questions to reflect on before self-disclosure include: *Who is this disclosure for? How will it benefit the group or individual group members? How will I feel about my clients knowing this about me?*

We will typically enquire how the group receives something personal we share and have an awareness that therapist self-disclosure is not solely in the information given but in the manner and behaviours of the therapist, their physical environment, their appearance, their values expressed and their silences too.

Conclusion

Clearly, the project of queering group psychotherapy are complex, but who would suggest psychotherapy should or could be simple? An ethical approach requires a commitment to reflexive practice, ongoing peer conversations and accountability, inviting feedback and critique from group members, updating our knowledge with CPD and acknowledging our shared humanness in all its flawed and wonderful ways.

We hope you have found some value in this whistle-stop tour of GSRD Group Therapy. We imagine we have raised as many questions as we have offered answers.

If you are running groups or planning to do so one day, this chapter provides some guidance, concepts, and insights into what might be needed in a therapy group that genuinely serves the needs of people from GSRD populations.

We hope the mirror ball encounters in your groups are joyful, vibrant, rainbow-coloured, and emanate light in all directions!

References

AGPA (2007) *Practice guidelines for group psychotherapy*. Published by the American Group Psychotherapy Association, Science to Service Task Force.

Davies, D. (2023) 'Living and working within our communities', in Neves, S. & Davies, D. (eds.) *Relationally queer. A pink therapy guide for practitioners.* Abingdon, Routledge.

Downes, R. (2022) 'Queer Shame: Notes on becoming an all-embracing mind', in Czyzselska, J.C. (ed.) *Queering psychotherapy*. London, Karnac Books, pp. 43–64.

Ellis, E. (2021) *The race conversation: An essential guide to creating life-changing dialogue.* London, Karnac Books.

Middleton, A. (2022) 'Adventures in time, gender and therapeutic practice. Embracing a queer systemic way of working with gender expansive families', *Murmurations: Journal of Transformative Systemic Practice,* 5(2), pp. 28–44. https://doi.org/10.28963/5.2.4

Yalom, I. (1976) *Theory and practice of group therapy.* New York, Basic Books.

Yalom, I. and Leszcz, M. (2005) *Theory and practice of group psychotherapy revised.* 5th edition. Cambridge, Basic Books.

Yalom, I. and Leszcz, M. (2021) *Theory and practice of group psychotherapy revised.* 6th edition. New York, Basic Books.

Chapter 13

Decolonising the Vision of Wellbeing in Emotional Psychosexual and Relational Health for GSRD Clients

Rima Hawkins

Introduction

GSRD clients generally identify through their intersectionalities of gender (e.g. cisgender, transgender, agender, genderqueer, non-binary, etc.), sexuality (e.g. heterosexual, gay, lesbian, asexual, bisexual, pansexual, etc.), erotic (vanilla, kinky, fetish, etc.) and relationship diversity (e.g. monogamous, monogamish, polyamorous, polygamous) (Davies and Neal, 1996, 2000). In addition to these complex intersectionalities, other dimensions and factors will influence their lives and narratives. These are political, social and cultural influences and experiences. A person's values, integrity, self-esteem, and beliefs are based on the information around them during their developmental years and as adults. It is most important for therapists to meet their clients with complete curiosity about their experiences. If therapists identify as GSRD, it is also crucial to be curious about what is evoked in the therapist, especially if there are profound and explicit similarities with the client. This chapter will discuss GSRD people's emotional well-being beyond traditional Western therapy.

Seeing a Client Through Sameness and Difference

A GSRD therapist may think they know what it is to be or feel like a person from the same GSRD community. The phenomenon of countertransference is a well-known concept in psychotherapy, describing the therapist's material being evoked by the client's material. If therapists are unaware of their countertransference, they may risk imposing their experience and feelings onto the client (projection) as "truth". This takes away the opportunity for the client to share their own experience. Knowledge is different from experience. The client and the therapist may share how it is to be a GSRD individual in a specific country, but the individual's experiences may differ. Acknowledging the client's experience, which may or may not be similar to the therapist's, makes the client feel seen, heard and understood through their own experience.

DOI: 10.4324/9781003530848-16

Often in my supervisory role, I see the need for therapists to show that they know how the client feels under the guise of empathy when it is actually the therapist's need to feel useful as empathic professionals. This is a tremendous lost opportunity to be curious about the client. This seems to happen mostly in minority groups where the experiences seem to be similar. The need for cohesive, unified and joint communal feeling can sometimes be so great that therapists from minority groups, such as the GSRD community, can develop blind spots. Let's consider this dialogue:

Client: It's hard to be bisexual and a person of colour whilst there is such public unrest and overt racism.
Therapist: I know exactly what you mean, as a bisexual person myself. I was and have been very alert to this public unrest and racism. I may be white, but I share your fear.
Client: Oh really? Glad you feel the same.

In the above interaction, the therapist's attempt to empathise with the client resulted in them translating the client's "it's hard to be" to mean they share mutual fear. It's a lost opportunity to explore the client's meaning of "hard to be". Instead of the first round of interaction, let's see it differently:

Therapist: It really sounds hard for you, being both bisexual and a person of colour in such spaces. What is it like for you? What do you feel?
Client: At home, I have to hide from my family that I am bisexual. They don't understand, and then I am scared to be a POC out there and have to support my family too during these racist times.
Therapist: So, is hiding your sexuality and yet having to support your family during these racist events hard for you?
Client: Yes, it is. I am angry with them for not accepting me for who I am, and it seems the world doesn't accept the colour of my skin. Neither is my fault, and I am not choosing my sexuality or my skin colour.
Therapist: No, it's not your fault. Sexuality and your skin colour are parts of who you are. Is that important to you? Does the world need to accept your skin colour?
Client: No, not the world, as such, but I don't feel safe anywhere, outside or at home.
Therapist: As you said, feeling unsafe outside and at home must be hard. How are you coping, and what do you do to keep yourself safe?

The conversation's enquiry and curiosity can lead to understanding and exploring the client's hardship rather than the therapist's seemingly helpful empathy. This chapter will explore the importance of cultural competence and humility, as these are two components of GSRD therapy. Expanding the decolonising vision of well-being in psychotherapy for GSRD clients involves integrating culturally sensitive practices, recognising and addressing systemic oppression, and empowering clients within their cultural contexts.

It is impossible to know every culture, religion, or regional impact from countries of origin in depth to relate to clients. It's a blessing in disguise because it makes the therapist genuinely curious. On the other hand, not knowing the basic facts of the cultural differences of the main existing minority cultures in the UK would be considered the therapist's ignorance and incompetence. The client's job is not to teach the therapist about general cultural knowledge and societal implications. Still, it is for the therapist to keep learning about diverse populations and be attuned to the impact of societal oppression on the client's mental health, interacting in their own specific ways depending on the client's intersectionalities. The client's individual lived experience will be unique, and there will be cultural commonalities.

Cultural Competence and Humility

It is imperative for therapists to continuously educate themselves about the histories, cultures, and experiences of different LGBTQI+ communities, particularly those from marginalised racial and ethnic backgrounds. Psychosexual and relationship therapy is an essential area of clients' concerns because their sex lives, sexuality, and intimate relationships might be met with overt oppression. It is also necessary to understand that diverse sections of the LGBTQI+ population have their own sexual, erotic, and relational cultures and sub-cultures. In this, I would include that the therapist needs to know which countries criminalise people who are not heterosexual.

As mentioned above, it is vital to engage in self-reflection to recognise the therapist's biases and assumptions. Reflexive practice is essential in adopting a stance of cultural humility, acknowledging that clients are the experts on their own experiences. As Kim *et al.* (2003) noted, increasing one's cultural humility and understanding is expanding one's knowledge of the cultural positioning. Kim *et al.* (2003) also posited that improving one's culturally humble clinical practices takes more than cultural knowledge. Indeed, it takes the related self-work and related reflection in cultural awareness and culturally affirming clinical skills, including micro-skills. Clinical micro-skills are those specific skills that can be used by therapy providers, particularly psychosexual and relationship therapists, to enhance communication with clients in ways that lay the foundation for an effective therapeutic alliance (Miville *et al.*, 2011).

Affirmative and Anti-oppressive Practices

Using inclusive and affirming language that respects clients' gender identities, sexual orientations, and cultural backgrounds is the starting point for clients to feel validated and understood. Validating the client's unique experiences of GSRD, especially those related to systemic oppression, racism, and cultural marginalisation, goes beyond just being seen and heard. It makes the space safe for them to share their experience of oppression and its impact on memorisation. It is not just about listening to their story. Still, sometimes, clients need help from the therapist to address systemic oppression, which requires the therapist to understand how to work with an anti-oppressive framework. One of the things systemic changes can do is reduce barriers to mental health services for GSRD communities. In my opinion, one of the main parts of the anti-oppressive framework is for the therapist to work on the fear of their own biases (afraid of getting things wrong).

Decolonising Therapeutic Practices

The colonial impact on communities and individuals has had various faces. First, we need to be clear about what colonisation was about. It was not about supporting or helping inequality for sure. Colonisation occurred for various reasons, primarily driven by economic, political, and ideological motives. European powers, which started in the 15th century, sought to expand their territories to acquire resources and wealth. The discovery of new lands promised access to valuable commodities like spices, gold, and other natural resources, which were in high demand in Europe. Colonisation was also driven by the desire to establish trade routes and control key strategic locations, ensuring that European nations could dominate global trade. The competition among European powers fuelled a race to acquire and control as much territory as possible, establishing vast colonial empires. Much of it was driven by power and control.

Beyond economic motives, colonisation was justified through ideological beliefs, such as the notion of the "civilising mission". Europeans often viewed their cultures as superior and believed their duty was to spread Christianity, Western values, and "civilisation" to the people they encountered. This ethnocentric perspective dehumanised indigenous populations, portraying them as "savages" who needed to be "civilised" through European intervention. These justifications masked the exploitation, violence, and displacement that often accompanied colonisation as European powers imposed their control over foreign lands and peoples. The legacies of colonisation, including cultural dilution/deconstruction/contamination, economic exploitation, and political subjugation, continue to impact former colonies today. It is important to note that the desire to make therapeutic suggestions and interventions in the Western way, without checking out the implications with the GSRD and POC client, using positional power as a therapist, can replicate the colonial oppression.

The historical context of colonisation on race, culture, and religion shaped communities for the future. Narratives from the West often clashed with the Eastern openness of gender, sexuality, and relationship diversity. GSRD communities historically had more freedom, were well integrated, and even celebrated within their societies before colonial embarkment. The influences of Western values and beliefs sought to erase gender, sexuality, and relational freedom, replacing it with the Christian imperatives of heterosexuality, monogamy, and cisgenderism. Individually, a client with GSRD, race, religion, and culture intersectionalities may need to understand and address the historical and ongoing impacts of colonisation on clients' mental health and well-being.

The intergenerational trauma experience of colonisation has to be acknowledged and recognised by LGBTQI+ communities, particularly those from indigenous and other colonised cultures. It is, therefore, essential to remember to consider and incorporate non-Western therapeutic practices and healing traditions that resonate with clients' cultural backgrounds to address deep transgenerational trauma; for example, storytelling in community groups with similar experiences. Storytelling and testimonies create platforms for LGBTQI+ individuals to share their stories and experiences, particularly those from marginalised backgrounds, to highlight diverse perspectives and needs. Incorporating traditional indigenous and non-Western healing practices into sexual and relational health services gives clients an option and choice to access comforting and familiar methods. Another thing to remember is that some clients may wish to access safe spaces to speak their mother tongue. Language accessibility for non-English-speaking communities can be valuable because not all languages encompass Western terminologies. Conversely, there are words in languages that are associated with well-being that are not part of Western concepts of health. Adopting holistic approaches to health that consider physical, emotional, spiritual, and relational well-being provides the client with choices and agency for self-healing.

Whilst this approach sounds wholesome, in my experience, some clients with various intersectionalities strive to address issues with Western philosophy of work and Western medicalised healing traditions. They often downgrade the non-scientific methods of Eastern healing and of self-care or mental health. I often wonder if this is an impact of white supremacy. What I mean by that is the belief that the Western methods and the white skin culture are perceived as greater and better because they are powerful – for example, wanting whitening cream to change skin colour to be lighter rather than having darker skin or making fun of their traditions to fit in with the Western culture. Some GSRD clients from non-British communities hold on to their culture as part of their identity. Others leave their culture behind and just about cope with their GSRD identity and mental health. Therefore, understanding the context and sharing the impact with the client is key and is integral to the therapeutic alliance.

Diaspora and the Impact on GSRD

Diaspora, the dispersion of people from their homeland to different parts of the world, profoundly impacts GSRD individuals. When individuals from diverse cultures migrate, they bring distinct gender roles, sexual norms, and reproductive practices, which can challenge or enrich the dominant norms in the host societies. For instance, diasporic communities may introduce non-binary gender identities or different sexual practices that broaden the understanding and acceptance of gender and sexual diversity in the host country. This can lead to a more inclusive society where multiple genders and sexual identities are recognised and respected. However, the impact of diaspora on GSRD is not always positive; in some cases, migrants may face discrimination or pressure to conform to the host society's gender and sexual norms, leading to tensions and marginalisation. For example, some cultures allow polygamy and marriage within family relations. They may be perceived as illegal and/or incestuous relationships in the UK, but they are legitimate relationships if they marry before entering the UK. Some GSRD folks who are unable to come out in their host country may commit to heterosexual marriages and come to the UK on their own, seemingly for an economic endeavour to support their family, but also taking the opportunity to explore and embrace their gender and sexuality safely.

Moreover, the intersection of diaspora and GSRD is often complicated by legal, social, and cultural factors. In many cases, diasporic communities navigate complex legal landscapes where their traditional practices around gender and sexuality may be criminalised or stigmatised. For example, LGBTQ+ individuals from countries with restrictive laws might continue to face discrimination in their diasporic settings due to lingering prejudices from both their home and host cultures. On the other hand, diasporas can also act as advocates for GSRD by forming networks that support gender and sexual minorities and by promoting more progressive views within their communities and beyond. In this way, the diaspora can serve as a powerful force for both the preservation and transformation of gender, sexual, and reproductive diversity across the globe.

Community and cultural connections can be powerful for some. Connecting with culturally specific resources, support groups, and community organisations that affirm their identities and experiences can give people a sense of belonging and validate their identities. Some clients can connect with their culture in a different country, even though they experienced shame due to being different (LGBTQI+) in their country of origin. In a host country that has more LGBTQI+ rights, they can stay connected with their culture and precious childhood memories whilst at the same time benefiting from exploring their sexual orientations, gender identities and/or relationship diversities (Foskett et al., 2006).

One example of community feeling is when GSRD clients unite to cook their traditional meals together (sometimes with a facilitator in community-based services) and share their common and individual experiences and memories of their country of origin. It is a space of multi-layered healing of the internalised detachment and phobias – Group Nourish by the Clare

Project (Sussex, UK) https://clareproject.org.uk/nourish/. This meaningful time together encourages and fosters a safe and affirming space. Helping clients to engage with community, culture, and traditions where they will not be judged or made fun of is key. Food and cooking together form a way to nurture the self and each other. Eating together can regulate the self, and specific familiar traditional dishes can comfort cultural identities.

If colonialism is about power, strengths-based approaches to empower GSRD clients to stand firm in demanding their human rights and reclaiming their self-worth are the appropriate way forward. They can feel they have choices in life and control their lives. Another power is focusing on clients' strengths, resilience, and coping strategies developed within their cultural contexts.

Trauma-based theories encourage clients with traumatic experiences to stabilise and then identify the resources and resilience that have helped them survive thus far. Asylum seekers who are GSRD often have to mask any of their identities, which may be detrimental to securing a safe abode. For example, one of my gay African clients had a circumcision because he was advised to do so to reduce HIV transmission as his sexuality made him high risk (circumcision reduces the risk of HIV transmission by 50 to 60% (WHO, 2008), and this was routine advice for African men and especially for MSM). He was in one of the settlements that Muslim asylum seekers primarily occupied, and he was bullied as an effeminate Christian man. He was asked to prove that he was Muslim by showing his circumcision. We discussed how his GSRD intersectionality of being a gay black man and circumcised enabled him to stop being bullied by pretending to conform to the Muslim environment, which turned out to be a positive experience (making him feel safe). Empowering clients by validating their experiences, supporting their agency, and fostering self-determination gives them back their power.

The therapeutic relationship gets more profound and more meaningful when there is attunement with the client. The client can feel safe to become more vulnerable and explore wounds so that they can heal. Working collaboratively to set therapeutic goals that are meaningful and relevant to their cultural and personal contexts is an essential step in decolonising a GSRD's self-care and well-being. A client-centred approach, including parts theory (Schwartz, 1995) where the client's narrative, lived experiences and perspective are given the floor, the parts that feel broken and disbelieved build up to form a whole, whilst all the various parts provide a valuable context for their identity.

The therapist must be aware of vicarious trauma, their sense of self, culture and intersectionalities that play an essential role in the relationship with the GSRD client. Training and supervision are key for the therapist to explore their transference and countertransference, as well as their blind spots and biases that may have come into the therapeutic space. When there are racist events (for example, far-right riots across the UK), if the therapist and the clients are both POC and GSRD identified, both may go through their own traumatic experiences. Still, the therapist needs to separate their distress so the clients don't support the therapist. It is very healthy to share experiences and acknowledge differences and similarities, which may add a layer of bonding, empathy, attunement, and trust.

Participating in training programmes focused on decolonising therapy and cultural competence in LGBTQI+ mental health as professional development is key for therapists to maintain and enhance their competencies, knowledge, and skills. The therapist may seek specialist supervision and consultation from culturally competent professionals who can guide on working with GSRD and diverse LGBTQI+ clients.

By implementing these strategies, therapists can expand their decolonising vision of well-being and provide more effective, respectful, and empowering care for GSRD clients.

Non-Western Approaches to Self-care and Wellbeing

Supporting well-being through culturally appropriate non-Western approaches involves recognising and respecting traditional practices, beliefs, and holistic approaches to health that are integral to various cultures. Most culturally sensitive, non-Western ways to support well-being are not evidence-based but have been practised successfully through generations and handed down as well-established traditions. Some of these practices will be meaningful to GSRD people of all cultures as they could be part of "queering" healthcare, as so many LGBTQI+ people face discrimination in Western healthcare systems.

Traditional Healing Practices

- *Ayurveda*: Originating in India, it emphasises a balanced life, incorporating diet, herbal remedies, meditation, yoga, and detoxification practices to maintain health. It includes the chemical facets of herbs and spices.
- *Traditional Chinese Medicine (TCM)* includes practices like acupuncture, herbal medicine, tai chi, and qi gong. It focuses on balancing the body's energy (qi) to achieve health.
- *Indigenous healing*: Many indigenous cultures have holistic healing practices involving rituals, herbal medicine, spiritual ceremonies, and the guidance of healers or shamans.

Spiritual and Religious Practices

- *Meditation and Mindfulness*: Various meditation and mindfulness practices are rooted in Eastern religions and philosophies, such as Buddhism and Hinduism. They promote mental clarity, relaxation, and emotional balance.

- *Prayer, Chanting and Rituals*: Engaging in religious prayers, rituals, and ceremonies can provide comfort, community, and a sense of purpose.

Community and Social Support

- *Collective support*: Many non-Western cultures emphasise community and family support. Engaging with extended family and community networks can offer emotional and practical assistance. Sometimes, engaging in sports can also give a sense of collectiveness.
- *Community gatherings*: Participating in cultural and social gatherings, traditional festivals, and communal activities fosters a sense of belonging and support.
- *Concept of "Ubuntu" from Africa*: There are various definitions of "Ubuntu". The *African Journal of Social Work (AJSW)* provided the most recent definition (Mugumbate & Chereni, 2020). The journal defined *Ubuntu* as:

> A collection of values and practices that people of Africa or of African origin view as making people authentic human beings. While the nuances of these values and practices vary across different ethnic groups, they all point to one thing – an authentic individual human being is part of a larger and more significant relational, communal, societal, environmental and spiritual world.
>
> (p. vi)

"Ubuntu" is sometimes translated as "I am because we are" (also "I am because you are") or "humanity towards others". Ubuntu describes a set of closely related African-origin value systems that emphasise the interconnectedness of individuals with their surrounding societal and physical worlds. It is often meant in a more philosophical sense to mean "the belief in a universal bond of sharing that connects all humanity". It encompasses the interdependence of humans on one another and the acknowledgement of one"s responsibility to their fellow humans and the world around them. It is a philosophy that supports collectivism over individualism.

Cultural and Artistic Expression

- *Art and music therapy*: Traditional music, dance, and art forms can be used as therapeutic practices to help people express emotions, reduce stress, and connect with their cultural heritage. This is particularly conducive to neurodiverse people.
- *Storytelling*: Sharing stories and oral traditions can provide wisdom, moral guidance, and a sense of identity and continuity.

Nature-Based Practices

- *Nature Immersion*: Spending time in nature with trees, practising forest bathing (shinrin-yoku), or engaging in traditional agricultural activities (gardening/farming) can reduce stress and improve mental well-being.
- *Herbal Medicine*: Many cultures practise using locally sourced herbs and plants for medicinal purposes, which supports physical health and connects individuals to their natural environment.

Holistic and Integrative Approaches

- *Balance and Harmony*: Many non-Western cultures emphasise the importance of balance and harmony within the body, mind, and environment. Practices like feng shui in Chinese culture aim to harmonise living spaces with natural energy flows.
- *Diet and Nutrition*: Traditional diets that emphasise whole, natural foods and seasonal eating patterns, such as the Mediterranean or traditional Japanese diet, support physical health and cultural identity.

Rituals and Ceremonies

- *Healing Ceremonies*: Participating in traditional healing ceremonies, such as sweat lodges, purification rituals, or fasting, can support spiritual and emotional healing.
- *Life Cycle Rituals*: Engaging in rituals that mark significant life events, such as births, coming of age, marriages, becoming parents, retirement and deaths, provides structure, meaning, and communal support.

Mind-Body Practices

- *Yoga*: An ancient Indian practice that combines physical postures, breath control, and meditation to promote physical, mental, and spiritual well-being.
- *Tai Chi and Qi Gong* are Chinese practices that integrate slow, deliberate movements with breath control and meditation to enhance physical and mental health.

The Integration of Cultural Competencies in Healthcare

When healthcare practitioners can enhance trust and effectiveness by ensuring that healthcare services are culturally competent and can incorporate traditional practices and beliefs into treatment plans, if it is possible to have services tailor-made to the specific cultural needs of clients in therapeutic settings, there may be more adherence to treatment. For example, interpreters and cultural mediators can help bridge the gap between patients and health-care providers, ensuring clear communication and culturally sensitive care. Educating healthcare staff about cultural heritages and traditional practices fosters pride, identity, and connection to clients' roots. Programmes that empower individuals through cultural knowledge, skills, and community engagement promote well-being and resilience. Integrating these non-Western approaches into well-being practices can create a more holistic and culturally resonant support system for individuals from diverse backgrounds.

Conclusion

Decolonising the vision of well-being in emotional, psychosexual, and relational health for GSRD clients is an essential step towards creating more inclusive and affirming therapeutic practices. Traditional frameworks often impose a Western, heteronormative, and cisnormative lens on well-being, which can further marginalise and pathologise the diverse experiences of GSRD individuals. By embracing a decolonised approach, mental health professionals can challenge these dominant narratives, acknowledge the impact of colonial histories, and honour their clients' unique cultural, social, and relational contexts. This shift fosters a more holistic understanding of well-being and empowers GSRD individuals to reclaim their identities and relationships on their terms.

In moving towards this decolonised vision, therapists must engage in ongoing self-reflection and education, recognising their own biases and the limitations of traditional models. This involves adopting intersectional approaches that consider the interplay of various identities, including race, religion, ethnicity, gender, and sexual orientation, and how these intersect with systemic oppression. By centring the voices, fostering joy and agency, and acknowledging the experiences of GSRD clients, therapists can co-create healing spaces that are not only affirming but also transformative, supporting clients in their journey towards emotional, psychosexual, and relational health that is authentic and self-determined.

References

Davies, D., & Neal, C. (1996) *Pink therapy: A guide for counsellors and therapists working with lesbian, gay and bisexual clients.* Milton Keynes, UK: Open University Press.

Davies, D., & Neal, C. (2000) *Therapeutic perspectives on working with lesbian, gay and bisexual clients.* Milton Keynes, UK: Open University Press.

Foskett, T, Brophy, M., & Hurst, A. (2006) *Talking Spaces II: A research report about the first ten years of the PACE gay/bi men"s groupwork programme.* PACE. Available at: https://timfoskett.com/budcms/includes/kcfinder/upload/files/Talking%20Spaces%20II.pdf (Accessed: 20 May 2025).

Kim, B. S. K., Cartwright, B. Y., Asay, P. A., & D'Andrea, M. J. (2003) 'A revision of the multicultural awareness, knowledge, and skills survey-counselor edition', *Measurement and Evaluation in Counseling and Development*, 36(3), pp. 161–180. doi: https://doi.org/10.1080/07481756.2003.11909740

Miville, M. L., Redway, J. A. K., & Hernandez, E. (2011) 'Microskills, trainee competence, and therapy outcomes: Learning to work in circles', *The Counseling Psychologist*, 39(6), pp. 897–907. https://doi.org/10.1177/0011000011404438

Mugumbate, J. R., & Chereni, A. (2020) 'Editorial: Now, the theory of Ubuntu has its space in social work', *African Journal of Social Work*, 10(1), pp. v–xv.

Schwartz, R. C. (1995) *Internal family systems therapy*. New York: Guilford Press.

World Health Organization & UNAIDS (2008) 'Male circumcision: Global trends and determinants of prevalence, safety and acceptability'. Available at: https://iris.who.int/handle/10665/43749 (Accessed: 20 May 2025).

Part 3

Special Interests in GSRD Therapy

Chapter 14

Working with LGBTQ+ Youth

Cat Johnston and Maria Kindstedt

Introduction

LGBTQ+ youth are often the centre of community-based activism, social liberation, and fights for institutional change (Owen, 2020; Marshall, 2021). They offer us a glowing beacon of hope, providing new and exciting ways of being in the world. However, challenging the status quo is threatening to many. Challenging long-held beliefs about social roles and norms can feel uncertain and frightening. It is this fear and unknowability of expanding identities that puts queer youth at the centre of many moral panics throughout history and increasingly victims of state-sanctioned homophobia and transphobia (Gitari and Walters, 2020; Mendos, 2019).

Young people already navigating the challenges of adolescence are additionally faced with systemic oppression and barriers to support and healthcare, attempting to survive in a world not designed for them. Young people are particularly vulnerable to experiences of trauma and stress (Craig and Austin, 2017), are typically more impacted by their experiences, and require compassionate, informed support from therapists holding an intersectional, sensitive understanding of their world.

A key issue in working with LGBTQ+ youth is the implicit and explicit suggestion that they are unreliable narrators of their own lives and untrustworthy authorities of their experiences. We see this in research (McDermott and Roen, 2016), first-hand accounts (Cunningham *et al.,* 2024), and commonly heard condescensions such as: "You are too young to know you are gay"; "How could you know you are a lesbian if you have never had sex with another girl?"; "what if you change your mind?". Childism, this form of prejudice, becomes more concentrated towards neurodivergent youth who are also more likely than their neurotypical peers to openly identify as LGBTQ+ (Mendes and Maroney, 2019).

Compounding this lack of trust, adults often mistakenly believe LGBTQ+ youth are inherently troubled by their identity, that who they are is the cause of their distress (McDermott and Roen, 2016). The reality is that LGBTQ+ youth are subject to cisgenderism and heteronormativity every day in their

DOI: 10.4324/9781003530848-18

social environments (Roe, 2015), their school settings (Ferbezar *et al.*, 2024; Stonewall, 2017), and the world at large. Experiences of expectation, othering, and discrimination cause LGBTQ+ youth to be overrepresented across mental health and physical health concerns (Brännström *et al.*, 2019). Additionally, mistrust of health professionals makes LGBTQ+ youth less likely than their cisgender, heterosexual counterparts to seek support (The Trevor Project, 2023a; Stonewall, 2018). It is essential to recognise our trans youth as being most at risk across these concerns and currently most vulnerable in our society due to increased media and political focus (Mermaids, 2019; Houseal, 2024).

LGBTQ+ youth living in poverty experience increased risk due to the impact of discrimination in the context of increased instability (Tobar, 2018). For LGBTQ+ youth of colour, there is a consistent lack of representation across research and social narratives, increased risk of discrimination from peers and adults, and higher occurrences of not being believed about their own experience (Jones, 2024a; GSA Network, 2018). The unique harm faced by youth of colour is influenced by white supremacy and the specific expectations of gender expression through this lens (Jones, 2024b).

In this chapter, we combine our extensive experience working with gender and sexually diverse young people, blending differing cultural and clinical experiences to provide an overview of compassionate and practical support. We offer this in the context of a world where young people are increasingly identifying with diverse sexualities and genders (Jones, 2024a; ONS, 2023), yet continue to lack the acceptance and support necessary to thrive.

To set a shared understanding:

1. When referring to youth, we typically mean children, adolescents, and young adults up to 25 years old.
2. We believe there is no one cause of LGBTQ+ identities. There is no specific identifiable factor that causes people to be queer or trans.

Furthermore, if research ever does point to genetic, hormonal, developmental, social, environmental, or cultural factors that "cause" LGBTQ+ identities, this is not a reason for pathologisation as:

3. No identity or orientation is preferential, more valuable, or more valid than any other.
4. Young people know who they are and deserve to be believed when sharing their experiences and identities. Young people who do not yet "know who they are" but may be questioning and exploring equally deserve support and belief.
5. We use LGBTQ+ as an umbrella term but recognise and celebrate our community's ever-growing diversity of identities.

Practising a Commitment to Social Justice

Commitment to social justice must exist inside and outside of the therapy room. Recognising all forms of oppression as interlinked and understanding how social and economic systems impact different groups uniquely form this work's foundation. Without this, we risk excluding some of the most vulnerable from our support. We understand intersectionality (Crenshaw, 1989) as an active and ongoing process of awareness, curiosity, and critical thinking, not simply a tick-box exercise. This might involve (1) taking a critical approach to understand the formation of our clients' (and our own) beliefs and values; (2) active commitment to studying and understanding different perspectives on complex social problems (Collins and Bilge, 2016); (3) remaining curious about the unique constellations of our clients' identities.

While this is relevant to clients of all ages, the factors worth emphasising for young people include peer relationships (including online relationships), family relationships and parental circumstances, school, and feelings of responsibility and independence. There is added nuance for young people as they have less autonomy and control over decisions that directly impact their lives. It may be necessary to explore the involvement of other services or professionals who may be less informed or less affirming.

Staying informed on social discourse and understanding anti-oppressive practice allows us to have more insight and empathy for clients and understand the complexities of the world and social systems impacting their lives. It also provides language and scaffolding to navigate these conversations. Having a language to understand their unique positions of power and oppression can enable young people to connect with their community and feel part of a social movement, fostering hope and joy. These conversations can support young people in making sense of and beginning to externalise feelings of shame and distress, conceptualising that their identity is not the cause of these feelings but rather the social responses to their identity. Crucial in this dialogue is not taking on a position of expert or authority but collaborating in a process of consideration and re-consideration to enable them to make sense of their world without experiencing further loss of power. Radical educator and philosopher Paulo Freire (1973) describes this process as "problem-posing education", in which we can help our clients to critically understand their relationships with the world around them, "as a reality in process, in transformation" (p. 56). Approaching our work with this critical inquiry is inherently hopeful, offering possibility and potential.

Supporting young people in recognising the social norms or narratives they experience also creates space to imagine and identify alternative opportunities and choices. This process can invite joy, authenticity, and fears around change and visibility. When challenging social expectations, we can make room to explore anxieties about further alienation or stigma.

Within organisations, commitment to social justice might involve efforts to influence policy and procedure and campaign for more inclusive practices. What this involves will depend on the practitioner's context and level of safety. However, it could include advocating for more inclusive paperwork and language use, not making assumptions about parents, clarifying what names to use in session and what name to use when communicating with others, considering access for those who cannot be safely "out" to family, etc.

We are all responsible for our own learning and striving to keep updated with the ever-changing socio-political landscape. Those working solely in private practice may face a particular challenge in staying connected with a network of support. Working inside an organisation can also feel isolating and draining if you are the only LGBTQ+ practitioner or feel unsupported by colleagues. Practitioners without a community of support may fall behind or lack knowledge of contemporary language, theories, emerging politics, and policies, potentially impacting ethical maturity and capacity to work competently. Lack of community also increases the likelihood of burnout. Our work is challenging; we offer much of ourselves and hold a lot for our clients. To continue doing so, practitioner self-care, rest, and community connection are vital to working as trauma informed and committed to social justice.

Demonstrating Cultural Humility and Cultural Competence

Cultural humility with young people is paramount, as our clients may regularly experience adults in their lives as authority figures who enact their power or claim to know best. We offer an alternative and can empower our young people by allowing them to be experts in their own lives, providing reassurance that they know their identity best and can take control of what and how they share with us.

With this client group, cultural competence may involve maintaining up-to-date knowledge of legislation and guidelines for access to trans healthcare – particularly as this can change quickly and impulsively, school requirements (or lack of) for inclusive sex and relationship education, engaging with youth-focused literature and media, and continued training and development around specific presenting issues.

Many LGBTQ+ youth are exceptionally well-informed and embedded in ongoing campaigns for global equality, and are knowledgeable about the history of this movement. Practitioners taking an interest in this and engaging with the impact and legacy of LGBTQ+ rights have the potential to enhance therapeutic relationships and demonstrate, authentically, their own commitment to social justice. For LGBTQ+ therapists, this can potentially raise feelings from their youth and own activist engagement. Rather than focusing on generational differences and comparison, which can create feelings of judgement and a sense of hierarchy, we seek to connect with the shared motivation and desire for liberation.

We demonstrate our commitment to social justice through this humility and competence by not depending on our clients to bring relevant news into the therapeutic space. In response to events affecting our LGBTQ+ young people, we can sensitively bring this into the work and explore the feelings and impact arising. Directly acknowledging events that impact our clients allows us to understand their experience better and demonstrate our care, that we know not all young people are affected the same, and that we are invested in this social change. Cultural competence with LGBTQ+ young people may also take the form of appropriate therapeutic self-disclosure, particularly where we can model resilience and self-care in a challenging world.

We can be mindful of how we "police" our therapy sessions and what expectations we put on clients. Children and adolescents are constantly exposed to the weight of others' guidance, expectations, and demands, and this is compounded for our LGBTQ+ young people who additionally experience the expectations and assumptions of a cisnormative and heteronormative world. Depending on the context, LGBTQ+ young people may be expected to complete paperwork with binary gender options, to comply with rigid, goal-oriented "treatment plans" that are unable to take account of complexity and multiple intersections of identity, draw attention to themselves by leaving class to access school-based counselling, or to wait in a common area where they are visible to peers. We may not always have control over these factors, but we can be thoughtful about how they might impact our clients and what additional harm may be caused.

Working with young people also requires cultural *in*competence and the capacity to sit comfortably with this. Youth culture will always belong to the youth; it is not our place as adults to claim or appropriate that. For example, youth are at the forefront of linguistic development and new ways of communicating. While some language makes its way into everyday use, much remains informal slang – a way of identifying and connecting with peers, and attempting to use this language ourselves as adults is a quick way for our young clients to perceive us as inauthentic, misinformed, or even judgemental and condescending. Young people are susceptible to displays of inauthenticity (Cooper, 2025) and incongruent efforts to connect that risk our therapeutic relationship. We can connect with our young clients through cultural curiosity and by allowing them to share their world with us through language, pop culture, media, and fashion. Group Work can be a particularly connective space for this, as young people can relate to each other and explore shared interests.

Our work can benefit from cultural knowledge and understanding of the internet and social media, emphasising how this impacts our clients' experience of the world. The internet's greatest strength, removing barriers and providing access, can also be perceived as its most significant deficiency. LGBTQ+ young people face a significantly increased risk of cyberbullying and online harassment (GLSEN, 2013; Trevor Project, 2023a). Additionally, they may be more vulnerable to online grooming or sexual exploitation (Thorn, 2023; Capaldi *et al.,* 2024). Research indicates that LGBTQ+ youth of colour are most at risk of harm by digital stressors, which may be due to differences in gendered expectations and norms, alongside differing perceptions of safety online (Trevor Project, 2023b). Barriers in place with the intent to "protect" may limit the helpful information LGBTQ+ youth can access. Filters in schools and libraries may restrict access to any content haphazardly deemed "sexualised", including mentions of sex, sexual health, or sexual orientation. These barriers disproportionately impact LGBTQ+ young people without access to reliable internet at home, including those in care, rural communities, or living in poverty. Further, online algorithms and "safe" modes may limit and de-prioritise LGBTQ+ content, significantly impacting online representation (Myles *et al.,* 2023; Southerton *et al.,* 2021).

Overall, online spaces provide access to community, information, diverse stories, digital support services, and more accessible ways to engage with social justice and activism. Online platforms and games offer environments where young people play with different gender expressions in relative anonymity and safety. Our role is to support clients in identifying reliable sources of information, engaging critically with media, and sensitively yet soundly risk-assessing online relationships.

Understanding the Specific Adverse Effects of Oppression

For young people, the adverse effects of oppression are compounded by the inherent vulnerability of adolescence that comes from a lack of independence, combined with rapid and relentless biological, psychological, and social change. The teen years in particular require a sensitivity to challenge and change that must be taken into consideration to understand how minority stress and oppression impact this group.

Sometimes, as adults, we hold the general challenges of adolescence against LGBTQ+ young people. In a developmental period where the brain is rapidly rebuilding, the hormonal influx of puberty is influencing their entire system, and social relationships are fluctuating – young people are faced with questions and challenges to their identity, with expectations and pressures to find certainty and definitive language to describe their own experience. As therapists, we have a unique opportunity to offer a safe space for exploration and uncertainty, away from the incessant pressure of peers. Demonstrating a compassionate curiosity will be necessary, as any questions perceived as judgement or criticism will likely close down the relationship and opportunities for shared understanding.

We know many LGBTQ+ youth struggle in hostile home or school environments and that this has a significant impact on their well-being. However, even those in safer and more supportive contexts are subjected to stress and distress through incessant news reports and social media representations of the global hostility and persecution experienced by their community. LGBTQ+ young people are often acutely aware of their peers in other spaces being attacked, murdered, executed, prosecuted, and convicted simply for being who they are. The chronic stress from all of these factors becomes cumulative and traumatic for LGBTQ+ youth, impacting mental and physical health (Brännström *et al.*, 2019). We talk more about the outcomes of this trauma in the following section.

Being Trauma, Grief, and Shame Informed

Understanding trauma for LGBTQ+ youth requires acknowledging that our profession has been the perpetrator of serious harm (Stonewall, 2018). Long-term pathologising of LGBTQ+ identities continues to cast a shadow of mistrust and fear, which is further compounded by experiences of discrimination from professionals. Relatedly, anxiety around conversion practices (harmful attempts to change LGBTQ+ persons' sexual or gender identity to heterosexual and/or cisgender) remains a reality, with some young people having experienced this, or fearing it as something non-affirmative professionals may subject them to (Mallory *et al.*, 2019). Lack of knowledge or validation for a young person's expression can inadvertently cause increased internalised shame and stigma, negatively impacting their overall well-being. Even therapists who believe themselves to be inclusive and supportive of LGBTQ+ identities, without deeper learning and self-reflection, are at risk of perpetrating "accidental" conversion practices (Sale, 2019) through questions or reflections that imply doubt or aversion to how a client makes sense of and expresses themselves. Trans and asexual youth are most at risk of conversion practices, and therapists may need additional supervision or training to ensure they are working ethically with these clients and not communicating a preference for one identity (or expression) over any other. This work demands extensive inner work for the therapist to recognise their own beliefs and biases and be sensitively aware of their responses and competencies. We must show up as real humans with our own experiences. However, ultimately, we must be ready to connect with a young person's world and be present in their reality, not just as an outsider observing from our adult perspective. Working through an intersectional lens naturally aligns with this as it invites us to consider the unique and specific harms caused by systems of power and how these might impact our clients.

For many LGBTQ+ youth, experiences of trauma are the result of violence, discrimination, rejection, and microaggressions (Meyer, 2003). Across this population, rates of Adverse Childhood Experiences (ACES) are also higher and combined with lower levels of social support and barriers to professional services, these events can lead to significant distress and associated mental health concerns. Research in this area consistently shows LGBTQ+ youth are disproportionately represented across self-harm and suicidal ideation, with young girls, non-binary and trans individuals being most at risk (Jadva *et al.*, 2021). There is also an elevated occurrence of eating disorders among trans and gender diverse youth (Kramer *et al.*, 2024), often linked to gender dysphoria. Skills and competence with these presentations are necessary for anyone working with LGBTQ+ young people, to be particularly understanding of self-harm as a means of coping with and surviving distress. Attempts to stop self-harming behaviour without alternative means of coping or emotional regulation may cause further distress and could be considered unethical. Even with evidence-based approaches to self-harm (DBT, ERGT) and understandings of safe trauma therapy, there remains a need to understand the young LGBTQ+ person's triggers from a queer perspective, such as the impact of minority stress, internalised oppression, or gender dysphoria.

Working with trauma also links to working with shame. Trauma-related shame is often overlooked in PTSD treatment. However, CBT can be effective at reducing shame through repeated exposure to shameful memories and a supportive, accepting attitude of the therapist (Norling and Olsson, 2021). In adolescence, sensitivity to peer evaluation and constant self-evaluation make young people more vulnerable to shame. As shame is socially constructed (Leeming and Boyle, 2003), group work can be a potent antidote for LGBTQ+ youth. Not only do you break the isolation of shame and share feelings with others who might have similar experiences, but you also get social feedback and support from peers, which is vital during adolescence.

Working with grief and LGBTQ+ youth is sensitive, as children and adolescents often need to live in the moment and move forward. The grief experienced around (for example) not having accepting parents, having a more challenging path than cisgender and heterosexual peers, might not be manageable to navigate while embedded in all the other challenges of adolescence. Grief is often an experience that can be processed or felt on the other side of trials when in a safer space. Evidence-based practices for supporting young people with grief (TF-CBT, Multidimensional Grief Therapy) also need to be adapted to the particular needs of this client group and the nuances of their emotions.

Knowing Contemporary Sexology

For some therapists, exploring sex and relationships with young people will be the source of anxiety and feelings of incompetence, possibly eliciting worries about "appropriateness" (Luxmoore, 2016). Knowing that the majority of LGBTQ+ youth continue to report sexual health education as inadequate and unsuitable for their needs (Goldfarb and Lieberman, 2021; Haley *et al.*, 2019) and that they are more likely to seek sexual health information online (Flinn *et al.*, 2023), therapists are in a uniquely privileged position to have open, transparent conversations about young people's sexual experiences, feelings, and behaviours. Any indication of reluctance or unease in these discussions has the potential to communicate that this part of their life is not welcome in therapy and intensify feelings of shame. We can be sensitive to communicating that the whole spectrum of sexual feelings and experiences is okay to talk about in therapy, should our young people want to. There is an additional consideration of being cautious and sensitive with language for LGBTQ+ young people who are more likely than their non-LGBTQ+ peers to have experienced sexual exploitation and sexual abuse. Being mindful of the balance between caution and respect for individual comfort levels while not shying away from the subject may involve personal reflection and exploring our comfort with language around sex.

Research suggests LGBTQ+ students of colour feel especially let down by access to sex education and are at increased risk of stigma when accessing sexual health services (Roberts *et al.*, 2020). While social media and mainstream success of Netflix's *Sex Education* have allowed some young people to be more candid and well-versed in conversations about sex than previous generations (Allen, 2023), they continue to highlight the lack of inclusion for LGBTQ+ youth. Many of our young people are leaving compulsory education, having experienced no relevant sexual education and having no nuanced understanding of consent. The impact of religious and homophobic/transphobic campaigning has heavily influenced inclusive legislation and curricula (Jones, 2023; Morgan, 2023). Those with financial and social power continue to limit the well-being and educational rights of LGBTQ+ youth. We must not, as therapists, be passive to this reality and assume our young people are getting the information that they need.

Fictional media, particularly online fan fiction, can be a valuable tool for inviting young people to reflect on their feelings and desires, allowing them to separate fantasies and behaviours in a way that makes sense. For therapists to maintain their knowledge and capacity to converse with young people on these issues, accessing resources already aimed at an adolescent audience can be helpful. For example, Bish UK (bishuk.com) and Brook (brook.org.uk) are excellent, reputable, up-to-date resources in the UK that have already "translated" information into easy-to-understand and young person-friendly language. Similarly, YouTube channels like Sexplanations (youtube.com/sexplanations) and Watts the Safeword (youtube.com/wattsthesafeword) offer an even more expansive, inclusive insight into sex, relationships, and desire. It is worth noting here that online access for young people will vary depending on geography, and ongoing issues with LGBTQ+ or sexual health content being problematically flagged as "inappropriate" or "sexualised".

Integrating Core GSRD Theories

Theories referred to in this section contribute to a foundation for working with LGBTQ+ youth. While we cannot explore each of these in depth – and this is by no means an exhaustive list – we aim to offer an overview and highlight the application to work with LGBTQ+ youth.

1. *Minority Stress Theory* (Meyer, 2003; Meyer and Frost, 2013; Meyer, 2015), as explored earlier, provides an essential lens through which to approach work with LGBTQ+ youth, to understand and anticipate the kinds of stress, both acute and chronic, that our clients may be experiencing. This theory can be particularly important for adolescents as this is a critical developmental stage where long-term beliefs and identities are internalised and more fully integrated (Mustanski *et al.*, 2013). *Social Safety Theory* (Diamond and Alley, 2022) further expands on Minority Stress.

2. *Intersectionality* (Crenshaw, 1989; Crenshaw, 1991; Collins and Bilge, 2016) works alongside minority stress theory, offering a structure to consider multiple and overlapping identities and experiences of marginalisation. We cannot understand any one aspect of identity, or experience of marginalisation, on its own or even cumulatively like building blocks. Instead, we must consider complex systems that overlap and interact with each other in unique and changeable ways depending on the environment, social roles, and context. For young people, parental circumstances and identities naturally have a bigger impact on their sense of self, so this can be important to explore in therapy with an open mind. Identity can be very fluid for young people, making understanding their experience an ongoing, constant process.

3. *Coming In or Inviting In* (Beckett, 2010) offers an alternative to the traditional and cis-het centred notion of "coming out", recognising that not all LGBTQ+ individuals can share their identity safely. Inviting in challenges the idea of identity requiring some sort of confession, and grants the individual agency to choose who to let into this part of their life – a shift towards connection and trust over secrets and disclosure. For youth, this can feel like less pressure and expectation and offer empowerment and autonomy around who gets to know this part of them.

4. *Safe and Supportive School Environments* are consistently associated with improved well-being for LGBTQ+ youth (Day *et al.*, 2019; Kosciw *et al.*, 2020; Leung *et al.*, 2022). The presence of LGBTQ+ groups, visibility of LGBTQ+ or affirming staff, inclusive learning, and effective responses to homophobic and transphobic bullying can all be life-changingly positive for young people. An environment that offers non-dominant narratives and encourages diverse expression provides more opportunities for youth to live authentically and feel affirmed in their true self.

5. *One Supportive Adult* can be life-saving for LGBTQ+ youth. Striking research has repeatedly confirmed that those with at least one supportive adult in their life are 40% less likely to attempt suicide (Price *et al.,* 2023; Green *et al.,* 2021; The Trevor Project, 2019, 2023c). We can be that adult for our LGBTQ+ youth. We can help our clients identify who their supportive adults are, and we can educate others to take on this role.

Fostering Joy

Vital to supporting and empowering queer and trans youth in an increasingly hostile world is creating and holding space for reflection on joy, finding community, and experiences of gender euphoria. For the authors, this involves consistent use of compassion-focused approaches, reflections on strengths and resources, supporting young people to connect with their community, and facilitating connection and care within families where this work is possible and families are affirming.

Within the therapy room, fostering joy can be as simple as holding space for a young person to be authentically themselves, bringing the entirety of their experience, and not feeling they have to hide or censor parts of themselves. Creating space for young people to present and express in ways they may not otherwise have the opportunity to do so can be a profound part of therapy. Talking about a partner, being called by their chosen name, and dressing in affirming ways may not be safe for our young people in their wider world, but we can witness and celebrate this with them. Visibility, even in small ways, such as LGBTQ+ art, flags, badges, etc., can be significant to those who are used to feeling unseen.

Exploring what identity means and supporting young people to write their own "gender script" (Roche, 2020), to feel the freedom to make sense of whatever language feels right for them, can be wonderfully joyful and insightful. Embracing the fluidity of identity and allowing our clients to experiment with meaning and labels can enhance therapeutic connection and feelings of empowerment.

Exploring and enjoying positive queer representations in media – shows, movies, TV, literature – can offer rich material for reflection. Seeing themselves reflected in the wider world, particularly in depictions of characters or storylines that do not solely revolve around an individual's identity, can be transformative. Connecting with their own hobbies, relationships, and nurturing all parts of oneself allows queer and trans youth to live authentically, connect with their hopes and dreams, and not feel limited by how others may perceive or define them. Supporting young people to connect with the community, in whatever way feels accessible, can also form a vital part of therapeutic work. It is essential to be mindful of the many intersecting factors that will influence what is possible and what feels safe for each individual depending on location in the world, access to physical queer spaces, what internet censorship or limitations there may be, age, race, health etc. Sabah Choudrey (2022) invites us to reflect on these spaces critically, in collaboration with our clients, to identify what feels safer for them, which spaces align with their values, and where they feel truly seen and welcome.

Many young people rely on the comparative accessibility of online spaces, including social media, to connect and find their people. Seeking others with similar interests, or gravitating to those with whom we share experience, is an intrinsic and valuable part of socialising. Working with our clients to identify their own safe spaces and refuges from the heteronormative, cis-genderist world can both foster joy and offer us greater insight into their lived experience. Awareness of local pride and LGBTQ+ specific events and appropriately signposting to these, asking about attendance, or even letting a young person know you will be there yourself (see Davies, 2023) can invite excitement into the therapeutic space. Ask how it felt for a young person to attend Pride, let them share pictures of their most joyful outfits, celebrate their experiences and authentic expression.

Fostering joy is also a crucial intrapersonal process for the practitioner. Our work is often tricky and trauma-focused, and we also exist within the systems and power structures we are helping our youth navigate. The necessity of connection to community and supportive others is as applicable to professionals as it is to those we support.

References

Allen, L. (2023) 'What can the netflix series sex education teach school-based sexuality education?', *American Journal of Sexuality Education*, 19(4), pp. 398–416.

Beckett, S. (2010) 'Azima ila Hayati - An invitation into my life: Narrative conversations about sexual identity', in: Moon, L. (ed.) *Counselling Ideologies: Queer Challenges to Heteronormativity*. London: Routledge.

Brännström, R. Pachankis, J., Gillsund, S., Gornitzki, C., and Ekstrom. A.M. (2019) *The Health and Situation of Young LGBTQ People in Sweden: What Do We Know and Where Is More Research Needed?* FORTE: Swedish Research Council for Health, Working Life and Welfare. Available at: https://www.suicideinfo.ca/resource/the-health-and-situation-of-young-lgbtq-people-in-sweden-what-do-we-know-and-where-is-more-research-needed/ (Accessed: 25 May, 2025).

Capaldi, M., Schatz, J., and Kavenagh, M. (2024) 'Child sexual abuse / exploitation and LGBTQI+ children: Context, links, vulnerabilities, gaps, challenges, and priorities', *Child Protection and Practice*, 1. https://doi.org/10.1016/j.chipro.2024.100001.

Choudrey, S. (2022) *Supporting Trans People of Colour: How to Make your Practice Inclusive*. London: Jessica Kingsley Publishers.

Collins, P.H., and Bilge, S. (2016) *Intersectionality*. Cambridge: Polity Press.

Cooper, Y. (2025) *Black Male Sexuality: Race, Genre, and Class*. Cambridge: Cambridge University Press.

Craig, S.L., and Austin, A. (2017) 'Childhood and adolescence', in: Eckstrand, K.L., and Potter, J. (eds.) *Trauma, Resilience, and Health Promotion in LGBT Patients: What Every Provider Should Know*. Cham: Springer International Publishing, pp. 57–73.

Crenshaw, K. (1989) *Demarginalizing the Intersection of Race and Sex: A Black Feminist Critique of Antidiscrimination Doctrine, Feminist Theory, and Antiracist Politics*. Chicago. University of Chicago Legal Forum.

Crenshaw, K. (1991) 'Mapping the margins: Intersectionality, identity politics, and violence against women of colour', *Stanford Law Review*, 43(6), pp. 1241–1299.

Cunningham, E., Jamieson-Mackenzie, I., McMellon, C., McCallin, M., Eltiraifi, M., Smith, L., and Hepburn, K. (2024) '"Don't tell me how to tell my story": Exploring young people's perceptions around what it means to 'feel (mis)understood' by adults in supporting roles', *Children and Youth Services Review*, 156. https://doi.org/10.1016/j.childyouth.2023.107361.

Davies, D. (2023) 'Living and working within our communities', in: Neves, S., and Davies, D. (eds.) *Relationally Queer: A Pink Therapy Guide for Practitioners*. Oxon: Routledge.

Day, J.K., Ioverno, S., and Russell, S.T. (2019) 'Safe and supportive schools for LGBT youth: Addressing educational inequities through inclusive policies and practices', *Journal of School Psychology*, 74, pp. 29–43.

Diamond, L.M., and Alley, J. (2022) 'Rethinking minority stress: A social safety perspective on the health effects of stigma in sexually-diverse and gender-diverse populations', *Neuroscience and Behavioural Reviews*, 138, pp. 104720. https://doi.org/10.1016/j.neubiorev.2022.104720

Ferbezar, N., Kopinic, A., and Gavriloski Tretjack, M. (2024) 'Elements of minority stress and resilience in LGBTQ+ students' experience of education', *Journal of Homosexuality*, 72(3), pp. 520–543. https://doi.org/10.1080/00918369.2024.2326473

Flinn, C., Koretsidou, C., and Nearchou, F. (2023) 'Accessing sexual health information online: Content, reasons and practical barriers in emerging adults', *Youth*, 3(1), pp. 107–124. https://doi.org/10.3390/youth3010007

Freire, P. (1973), *Pedagogy of the Oppressed*. London: Clays Ltd.

Gitari, E.M., and Walters, M. (2020) *Hate Crimes Against the LGBT Community in the Commonwealth: A Situational Analysis*. London: Human Dignity Trust.

GLSEN (2013) *Out Online: The Experiences of Lesbian, Gay, Bisexual and Transgender Youth on the Internet*. New York: GLSEN.

Goldfarb, E.S., and Lieberman, L.D. (2021) 'Three decades of research: The case for comprehensive sex education', *Journal of Adolescent Health*, 68(1), pp. 13–27. https://doi.org/10.1016/j.jadohealth.2020.07.036.

Green, A.E., Price-Feeney, M., and Dorison, S.H. (2021) 'Association of sexual orientation acceptance with reduced suicide attempts among lesbian, gay, bisexual, transgender, queer, and questioning youth', *LGBT Health*, 8(1), pp. 26–31.

GSA Network (2018) *LGBTQ Youth of Colour: Discipline Disparities, School Push-Out, and the School to Prison Pipeline*. CA: GSA Network.

Haley, S.G., Tordoff, D.M., Kantor, A.Z., Crouch, K.M., and Ahrens, K.R. (2019) 'Sex education for transgender and non-binary youth: Previous experiences and recommended content', *Journal of Sexual Medicine*, 16(11), pp. 1834–1848.

Houseal, J. (2024) *Politicized Coverage is Failing the Trans Community*. Online: Centre for Journalism Ethics. Available at: https://ethics.journalism.wisc.edu /2024/01/30/politicized-coverage-is-failing-the-trans-community (Accessed: 2 November 2024)

Jadva, V., Guasp, A., and Brown, C. (2021) 'Mental health outcomes of transgender and gender diverse students in higher education: A UK study', *Transgender Health*, 6(2), pp. 101–110. https://doi.org/10.1089/trgh.2020.0041

Jones, J.M. (2024a) 'LGBTQ+ Identification in US now at 7.6%'. Available at: https:// news.gallup.com/poll/611864/lgbtq-identification.aspx (Accessed: 2 November 2024)

Jones, L. (2024b) '"You're not supposed to be gay, you're black"': Analysing race and LGBTQ+ youth identity through an intersectional lens', *Journal of Sociolinguistics*, 29, pp. 3–21. https://doi.org/10.1111/josl.12676

Jones, T. (2023) 'Religious freedom and LGBTIQA+ students', *Sexuality Research and Social Policy*, 20, pp. 1133–1151.

Kosciw, J.G., Clark, C.M., Truong, N.L., and Zongrone, A.D. (2020) *The 2019 National School Climate Survey: The Experiences of Lesbian, Gay, Bisexual, Transgender, and Queer Youth in our Nation's Schools*. New York: GLSEN.

Kramer, R., Aarnio-Peterson, C.M., Conard, L.A., Lenz, K., and Matthews, A. (2024) 'Eating disorder symptoms among transgender and gender diverse youth', *Clinical Child Psychology and Psychiatry*, 29(1), pp. 30–44. https://doi.org/10 .1177/13591045231184917.

Leeming, D., and Boyle, M. (2003) 'Shame as a social phenomenon', *Proceedings of the British Psychological Society*, 11(2), p. 295.

Leung, E., Kassel-Gomez, G., Sullivan, S., Murahara, F., and Flanagan, T. (2022) 'Social support in schools and related outcomes for LGBTQ youth: A scoping review', *Discover Education*, 1, 18. https://doi.org/10.1007/s44217-022-00016-9

Luxmoore, N. (2016) *Horny and Hormonal: Young People, Sex, and the Anxieties of Sexuality*. London: Jessica Kingsley Publishers.

Marshall, D. (2021) *Queer Youth Histories*. London: Palgrave Macmillan.

Mallory, C., Brown, T.N.T., and Conron, K.J. (2019) *Conversion Therapy and LGBT Youth*. The Williams Institute, UCLA School of Law. Available at: https:// williamsinstitute.law.ucla.edu/wp-content/uploads/Conversion-Therapy-Update -Jun-2019.pdf (Accessed: 2 November 2024).

McDermott, E., and Roen, K. (2016) *Queer Youth, Suicide, and Self-Harm: Troubled Subjects, Troubling Norms*. London: Palgrave Macmillan.

Mendes, E.A., and Maroney, M.R. (2019) *Gender, Identity, Sexuality, and Autism: Voices from Across the Spectrum*. London: Jessica Kingsley Publishers.

Mendos, L. (2019) *State Sponsored Homophobia*. Geneva: ILGA.

Mermaids (2019) *Research Into Newspaper Coverage of Trans Issues*. Leeds: Mermaids Press.

Meyer, I.H. (2003) 'Prejudice, social stress, and mental health in lesbian, gay, and bisexual populations: Conceptual issues and research evidence', *Psychological Bulletin*, 129(5), pp. 674–697.

Meyer, I.H. (2015) 'Resilience in the study of minority stress and health of sexual and gender minorities', *Psychology of Sexual Orientation and Gender Diversity*, 2(3), pp. 209–213.

Meyer, I.H., and Frost, D.M. (2013) 'Minority stress and the health of sexual minorities', in: Patterson, C.J., and D'Augelli, A.R. (eds.) *Handbook of Psychology and Sexual Orientation*. Oxford: Oxford University Press.

Morgan, R.J. (2023) *Gender Heretics: Evangelicals, Feminists, and the Alliance Against Trans Liberation*. London: Pluto Press.

Mustanski, B., Kuper, L., and Greene, G.J. (2013) 'Development of sexual orientation and identity', in: Tolman, D.L., and Diamond, L.M. (eds.) *Handbook of Sexuality and Psychology*. Vol. 1. Washington: American Psychological Association.

Myles, D., Duguay, S., and Flores-Echaiz, L. (2023) 'Mapping the social implications of platform algorithms for LGBTQ+ communities', *Journal of Digital Social Research*, 5(4), pp. 1–30.

Norling, M., and Olsson, J. (2021) *Treating Trauma-related Shame: A Systematic Literature Study*. Student publication for Master's degree, Lunds Universitet.

Office for National Statistics (ONS) (2023) *Sexual Orientation, UK: 2021 and 2022*. Newport: UK Statistics Authority.

Owen, G. (2020) *A Queer History of Adolescence: Developmental Pasts, Relational Futures*. Georgia: University of Georgia Press.

Price, M.N., and Green, A.E. (2023) 'Association of gender identity acceptance with fewer suicide attempts among transgender and nonbinary youth', *Transgender Health*, 8(1), pp. 56–63.

Roberts, C., Shiman, L.J., Downling, E.A., Tantay, L., Masdea, J., Pierre, J., Lomax, D., and Bedell, J. (2020) LGBTQ+ Students of colour and their experiences and needs in sexual health education: 'You belong here just as everybody else'. *Sexuality, Society and Learning*, 20(3), pp. 267–282.

Roche, J. (2020) *Gender Explorers: Our Stories of Growing Up Trans and Changing the World*. London: Jessica Kingsley Publishers.

Roe, S.L. (2015) 'Examining the role of peer relationships in the lives of gay and bisexual adolescents', *Children and Schools*, 37(2), pp. 117–124.

Sale, J. (2019) *Are you an Accidental Conversion Therapist?* Contemporary Institute of Clinical Sexology. Available at: https://www.theinstituteofsexology.org/blog/are-you-an-accidental-conversion-therapist (Accessed: 2 November 2024)

Stonewall (2017) *School Report*. Cambridge: University of Cambridge.

Stonewall (2018) *LGBT In Britain - Health*. London: YouGov.

Southerton, C., Marshall, D., Aggleton, P., Rasmussen, M.L., and Cover, R. (2021) 'Restricted modes: Social media, content classification and LGBTQ sexual citizenship', *New Media and Society*, 23(5), pp. 920–938.

The Trevor Project (2019) *Accepting Adults Reduce Suicide Attempts Among LGBTQ Youth*. Hollywood: The Trevor Project.

The Trevor Project (2023a) *2023 US National Survey on the Mental Health of LGBTQ Young People*. Hollywood: The Trevor Project.

The Trevor Project (2023b) *LGBTQ Youth of Colour in Online Spaces*. Hollywood: The Trevor Project.

The Trevor Project (2023c) *Acceptance from Adults is Associated with Lower Rates of Suicide Attempts Among LGBTQ Young People*. Hollywood: The Trevor Project.

THORN (2023) *LGBTQ+ Youth Perspectives: How LGBTQ+ Youth are Navigating Exploration and Risks of Sexual Exploitation Online*. Available at: https://info

.thorn.org/hubfs/Research/Thorn_LGBTQ+YouthPerspectives_June2023_FNL
.pdf (Accessed: 22 May 2025).

Tobar, K. (2018) *Ending the 'Closet to Poverty Pipeline' for LGBTQ Youth.*
Available at: https://generocity.org/philly/2018/06/28/ending-closet-poverty
-pipeline-lgbtq-youth-kee-tobar/ (Accessed: 2 November 2024)

Chapter 15

The Spectrum of Family
Navigating the Challenges and Triumphs of Queer Parenting

Daniel Morrison

Introduction

In recent years in the UK, we have moved a long way away from a limited heteronormative definition of family as two cisgender heterosexual parents and their 2.4 biological children towards a more progressive and expansive view of what children need to grow up healthy, happy and resourced. Few people now would argue that unmarried parents or stepparent families are inherently damaging to children, although this view still persists in some circles. Yet of the vast spectrum of diverse family structures, some are still prioritised or marginalised, seen as more or less desirable or acceptable.

The axes of identities and circumstances intersect in complex ways and include race, class, socioeconomic status, location, disability and neurodiversity, among many other elements. Here we take a brief overview of some of the ways in which queer families differ and some of the challenges faced in parenting where orientation, gender diversity and relationship structure diverge from the societal norm. Despite focusing on queer identities, we hold this exploration within the framework of other relevant factors; not all queer families are the same, not all lesbian couples or polyamorous families will share experiences, many different threads exist which impact the specifics, and every story is unique.

In all these situations, the fundamental questions are the same. Are the child's basic needs met reliably? Do they have a felt sense of ok-ness? Are they held in safety and connection within the family system, whatever that system looks like? Are they respected and listened to; do they have space to grow into who they are without fear? Are they loved?

We all have a relationship with parenting in some way. Some of us are parents through birth, biology, adoption or step-parenting. We have all been parented in some way. Those who are not parents have a relationship with that situation, whether they have chosen to go against the world's expectations, whether the circumstances haven't arisen for them to become parents, or whether they wanted children but haven't been able to. All of these circumstances can be causes of grief, anger, distress, shame and trauma. In the

DOI: 10.4324/9781003530848-19

therapy room, there may be anger and grieving to be witnessed, heard and held. Therapists must be trauma, grief and shame-informed to meet this in their clients.

The spectrum of queer families and the specific problems they face is vast. This chapter is a brief overview of some of the major issues to be aware of, beginning with a look at what a queer family is, how it might be created, and the impacts of neurodiversity and other intersections. There follows a look at polyamorous families, possible presenting issues in therapy, and some brief case studies.

What Is a Queer Family?

A queer family is a system beyond a traditional heteronormative framework. For this chapter exploring queer parenting, it is a family which includes one or more children. It may consist of one or more adults who identify as LGBTQ+ in some way, non-binary or gender expansive. It may include one parent, two parents or more than two parents, collaborative co-parenting with friends or chosen family, polyamorous or ethically non-monogamous relationships. A queer family may be formed through sex if the parents have the necessary gametes or through sperm donation, IVF, surrogacy, adoption or fostering.

A queer family might be two cis gay men who adopted their children. It might be a lesbian couple, one cis and one trans, with their child. It could be a cis lesbian couple who carried one baby each and used a sperm donor for IVF. It could be a collective of three non-binary parents who raise their children co-operatively: a single lesbian mother, a gay trans man who birthed his children and his cis gay partner. A queer family might also be cis het parents raising queer children, which is beyond the scope of this chapter.

Some queer families are more visibly queer than others, and this significantly impacts their experiences, the questions they are asked and the ways they are read and met in the world. A same-sex couple is visibly queer, and people often ask a couple who they read as cis lesbian or gay about IVF or adoption or assume that these are how their children began. This puts a gay or lesbian couple where one is trans in the position of having to out that person or sidestep the question and allow an incorrect assumption to stand. A bisexual person in a relationship which is read as heterosexual might find their queerness invisible, leading to isolation, marginalisation and difficulty finding belonging in queer or straight parenting friendships and social circles. Trans and non-binary people may be visibly or invisibly queer in both directions; they may be read as their assigned or true gender, meaning their relationships may be read as queer or straight, and this may vary over time and in different circumstances.

The question of whether to be open about queerness is ongoing when some or all aspects are invisible, and this constant coming out is a significant additional stressor. Questions of whether, when and how to come out to children and wider families, and how to integrate the knowledge of the structure of the family into the community are constant where queerness is invisible. Other types of relationship diversity, such as polyamory or kink-identified relationships, may be even more marginalised and, therefore, invisible. Visible queerness carries its own challenges of more open discrimination or bias and microaggressions such as inappropriate questions or assumptions.

Navigating microaggressions from schools, other parents and extended family presents significant challenges for queer families. Reflecting on these experiences in therapy raises essential questions about effective strategies for handling situations well. This might involve an openness to discussing with friends and supportive family, finding spaces to express the hurt and be heard and validated in the feelings arising. Many queer parents are isolated socially and have limited support from family, and microaggressions can come from within the available support networks. There can be a choice between confronting the issue and risking isolation or being silent to preserve connections.

When children reach an age where they're interacting with other children and their families, they may experience their own microaggressions and need to learn to navigate them. Queer parents may aim to create an open and communicative relationship where children can name and explore these issues. Parents being open in front of children about ways they manage difficult conversations might help provide context, talking about the difference between curiosity and hostility. This process helps children understand the broader social dynamics and modelling resilience and strategies for dealing with discrimination. Open dialogue and emotional validation are important ways in which queer parents equip their children with essential skills, and are mirrored and modelled in turn in the therapeutic relationship.

Beyond all these considerations, queer families, like all families, are about the relationships and connections that build them, the love and care between people, and the container of safety and belonging that nurtures their children, however they came into being.

Case Study

Jason and Noam are dads to Kim (6), who they adopted a year ago. They had fostered Kim for two years before that. They're also foster dads to Lior (2) and Hannah (9) and have fostered three other children over the fifteen years of their relationship. 'We decided to foster as we've both always wanted to be dads,' says Noam, 'and we've never regretted it, although it's challenging sometimes. The hardest part is saying goodbye to a child you've grown to love.' He is a full-time dad, and Jason works and spends as much time as he can with the children. 'I can't imagine my life now without children in it. The process of becoming foster parents is long and complicated; there's a lot of training and meetings and all kinds of things, and then adoption is another huge set of hoops to jump through. And while it's going on, you're just doing the everyday things, getting the washing done, feeding the kids, and managing all the things that come up. It was almost surreal when the adoption came through, and Kim didn't understand what it meant. It felt like something changed; he was ours, and it was permanent and official. In a way, everything changed, and in another way, nothing changed at all; we just carried on with life.'

Strengths of Queer Families

Queer families have been shown to have stronger parent-child relationships in terms of attunement, warmth and communication (Golombok *et al.*, 2014; Bos *et al.*, 2007). This may come from a higher level of intentionality in queer families, as prospective parents are unlikely to become pregnant by accident or without a lot of thought and decision-making around whether, when and how to have children. This process supports a style of parenting that challenges traditional norms in other ways and may result in a more engaged and conscious approach to parenting.

Queer parents and families embody and promote an acceptance and celebration of diversity, and this lived experience can extend to an openness to difference in other areas. Studies show that children raised in queer families have a greater understanding and acceptance of differences in race, class, disability and socioeconomic status (Tasker and Golombok, 1997; Golombok *et al.*, 2003). They are likely to hear adults and be involved in open discussions about navigating the world, addressing marginalisation and celebrating queer pride. Such conversations leave children well-equipped to critically engage with societal norms and question the status quo, promoting their resilience and adaptability development.

While children of queer parents are no more likely to identify as queer when they are adults than are the children of heterosexual parents, they are often more inclined to challenge restrictive gender norms and societal expectations. Their perspective and openness can support an ability in them to think critically about their own behaviour, abilities, identity and lifestyle choices. There is often more willingness to transgress gender norms in same-sex couples or families with transgender or non-binary parents. Children grow up without gender stereotypes, or at least with a healthy challenge to those norms which could limit their behaviour and choices. They see the division of labour in the family as being based on preference and necessity rather than gender, and this benefits them regardless of their own identity.

Therapists can be aware of these and other potential strengths of queer families, taking and maintaining a strongly affirmative stance and fostering joy and pride in the benefits children gain from being brought up in a queer family.

Case Study

Emma and Kate are a cis lesbian couple and parents to Jack (4). Emma's parents are actively involved in childcare and helped with the cost of accessing IVF. 'We were very lucky that they were willing and able to help with the cost of it,' says Emma. 'We found a private fertility clinic that reduces the cost if you donate any spare eggs. That was a big decision to make since there's no guarantee it will work. There's a chance that we might not have got pregnant, but someone else would be pregnant with Kate's eggs. That was a strange thought, but it was the only way we could make IVF affordable.' Assisted reproductive technology (ART) and cosmetic surgery are the two big private commercial medical industries in the UK, and donations to offset some of the cost are often available. 'Once I was pregnant, especially when Jack was born, I enjoyed the idea that I'd helped out other people. I'd like to have another baby, and we're saving up. You think that IVF is just one thing, but there are so many decisions to make and then so much waiting; it's a whole process and takes years. And we were lucky, it worked on our first cycle.' Jack was born by emergency caesarean after a long labour, and both women had difficult experiences in the hospital. 'We both wanted to breastfeed, and most of the staff at the hospital didn't know that was possible for a non-birthing mother,' says Emma. 'We had to explain it a few times, but they didn't stop us from trying. I'm glad we knew about that because Kate was out of it for a while after the surgery.' Queer parents may experience challenges when navigating the healthcare system, and non-birthing mothers can often feel excluded from the conception, pregnancy and birth (Greenfield, 2022).

How Do Queer Families Begin?

Queer individuals, couples, throuples and polycules face unique challenges and opportunities when considering parenthood, influenced by biological, social and systemic factors. Some have the gametes needed to reproduce through sex within their relationship, and others need assisted reproductive technology (ART). Queer families may navigate co-parenting arrangements where donors might have varying levels of involvement, necessitating clear agreements to avoid legal complications.

Transgender and non-binary people may conceive using their own gametes even after hormone therapy. Testosterone is not a contraceptive, although it can affect fertility, and trans men who have a uterus can conceive and carry a child, although pregnancy may trigger gender dysphoria. Gamete storage, according to WPATH criteria (Coleman *et al.*, 2022), should be offered before hormone therapy begins and offers options for future use, but the process can involve physical and emotional challenges.

Lesbian couples might use sperm donors for intrauterine insemination (IUI) or in vitro fertilisation (IVF), including reciprocal IVF, where one partner's egg is carried by the other. However, IVF accessibility through the NHS may be limited due to heteronormative criteria, requiring expensive private IUI treatment first.

Gay men may use surrogacy, either with a gestational surrogate or traditional surrogacy using the surrogate's own egg. In the UK, altruistic surrogacy is legal but not commercial surrogacy, complicating access and requiring legal parental orders. The cost can be enormous, and there is discrimination and bias within the surrogacy industry, making it difficult for gay men to find willing surrogates ethically.

Adoption and fostering are alternative pathways, but again queer prospective parents may face additional challenges. Some adoption agencies refuse due to religious objections, which are legal in some states and countries, while international adoption laws often exclude LGBTQ+ people. Research highlights significant barriers queer people face in fostering or adopting children (Goldberg and Sweeney, 2019).

Often, the barriers to healthcare are insidious and invisible. Some doctors will be well-informed queer allies or queer themselves, but experiences of microaggressions and bias are common for queer people accessing healthcare. Much of the medical system still operates under heteronormative assumptions, leaving LGBTQ+ people feeling unwelcome and misunderstood. The uncertainty creates additional barriers to access, as medical appointments carry a potential for distress and harm.

Case Study

Jodie and Charlotte are a polyamorous lesbian couple and parents to Hebe, aged 6, and Hoagy, aged 3. 'We got pregnant in the good old-fashioned way,' says Jodie, 'but we have a lot of people assuming that we didn't, and that can lead to some tricky moments.' The area they live in is known for queer families and particularly lesbian parents. They have found they're easily accepted, and both children are friends with other children who have two mums. 'It's not really an issue, I don't suffer from it,' says Charlotte, 'and I think in some ways it's easier for me because I can decide in the moment whether I want to out myself as trans, do I like this person, does it feel like we could have an interesting conversation or is it just a passing comment, sort of thing.' For Jodie, it's more difficult. 'It's not my story,' they say, 'not my decision to out Charlotte but then I'll have people wanting to talk, oh, my sister had IVF, or a lesbian couple who are in that really tough process or want to be. Then because Hebe looks Chinese and Hoagy looks Caucasian, they'll often assume that I carried Hoagy and Charlotte carried Hebe, and that's not true either.' Queer families can face complex legal challenges at every stage of parenthood. For Charlotte and Jodie, it took over two years for Hoagy to have a birth certificate. 'We fought for two years to try to get Charlotte on there as second parent, but it wasn't possible,' says Jodie. 'In the end we were forced to use the F word, but I put her occupation down as full-time mother, which is something. We had to. We couldn't register Hoagy for school or nursery; we couldn't get any benefits for him.' The case of Mccornall v Registrar General, 2020 established that trans parents must be recorded on the birth certificate as their assigned gender at birth, even if they have a gender recognition certificate.

Intersectionality

Intersectionality as a framework for understanding overlapping systems of oppression and privilege profoundly shapes the experiences of families. The interplay of identities such as class, queerness, race, single parenthood and neurodivergence creates complex dynamics which influence access to resources, social acceptance and community support in many ways. One of the core components of GSRD therapy is practising a commitment to social justice, and therapists can do that by holding a strong anti-racist, feminist, and queer affirmative space for clients.

Class intersects significantly with queerness in parenting experiences. Some queer parents report feeling more excluded based on their working-class background than their queerness. Middle-class parenting circles may be more accepting of queerness but less aware of class exclusion, compounding structural barriers such as access. 'I've found people pretty accepting of me as a lesbian mum,' says Charlotte, 'but I guess I feel more on the outside of these groups, yoga mummies and those things. I don't want to say middle class, but they're very yoghurty, you know, they're lovely, but they're not the kind of people I'd usually hang around with'. Parents who must work or have less financial flexibility may not be able to participate in groups and are therefore excluded from the support networks these spaces foster. Single parents are often challenged by the assumption that they are less capable or lacking in stability, as well as the presumption of reliance on a partner's income or support. This stigma can be amplified in spaces that prioritise economic privilege or normative family structures. Neurodivergence and disability, visible or invisible, compound exclusion due to a lack of understanding or accommodation of different needs.

Parents of colour often face additional marginalisation in predominantly white parenting spaces, where cultural norms and expectations may exclude their experiences. The intersection of race with class, queerness and disability can heighten systemic barriers to accessing healthcare, education and community resources and add to the isolation and the emotional burden of advocating for themselves and their children in a system which fails to recognise or accommodate needs.

Children who grow up in multiply marginalised families may develop greater empathy, tolerance for difference and social awareness. They may also face challenges in navigating norms that don't reflect their family's structure. Similarly, marginalised parents often emphasise resilience, adaptability and critical awareness of inequality in their parenting, and they may also suffer the consequences of social isolation and minority stress.

Minority stress is the chronic and ongoing stress faced by people who belong to marginalised groups arising from social stigma, discrimination and prejudice. Queer families face challenges in maintaining emotional, societal and physical safety. It is important to balance a realistic assessment of the difficulties with the recognition of family strengths and resilience. The stress is real and present, and therapists can do harm by minimising or dismissing experiences. At the same time, essential work with clients involves building strategies to manage and navigate these stressors. Community building supports clients in finding online or in-person support, which fosters a sense of belonging and reduces isolation where it is available and accessible. Promoting and supporting open communication within the family system equips children and parents to respond constructively. Therapists can centre resilience practices developed in the family, like celebrating diversity, cultivating queer pride and framing challenges as opportunities for growth, without minimising the challenges experienced. A good understanding of the adverse effects of oppression is essential.

Neurodivergent Families

There is a significant correlation between neurodivergence and queerness (Strang *et al.*, 2014). Often, the route for adults to obtain diagnosis or self-diagnose is through seeking assessments or support for their children and realising that they share traits. This kind of delayed diagnosis or understanding can bring mixed emotions. There can be relief and self-compassion arising, and there can be grief or anger over the unmet needs of their childhood. Some parents come to realise that their own parents are similarly undiagnosed and that they were brought up being taught how to mask rather than how to manage. This can leave parents in a dual process of meeting their child's needs while simultaneously addressing and grieving their own unmet needs through inner parenting.

Growing up as an undiagnosed neurodivergent person in a neurotypical world is inherently traumatising, in the gradual accumulation of microaggressions and subtle or not-so-subtle messages of wrongness. Increased societal awareness has improved the likelihood of early diagnosis for children now, sometimes allowing them to access support and interventions if their parents have the resources to seek this out and it's available. Neurodivergent parents who may have experienced this marginalisation may be particularly attuned to creating an environment that values openness, understanding and accommodation for children's different needs. Similarly, queer parents who are not themselves neurodivergent may also bring this understanding due to their lived experiences of being marginalised and othered due to their queerness.

Openness and curiosity about difference, empathy and validation of their child's experiences, all support an ability to be active in advocacy, pushing for systemic change in education, healthcare and social support systems.

The need to be an active advocate in this way is a drain on resources for parents, emotionally and physically. The therapy room may be where they can receive support, be less strong for a time and be seen in vulnerability, question whether they are making the right choices for their child and acknowledge the cost of this work of parenting. Therapists can support the grieving and anger arising from the unmet needs of child parts that were never diagnosed or supported. Internal Family Systems (Schwartz, 1995) or a plural approach to therapy offer frameworks to hold and process the pain of these young parts, fostering self-compassion and healing. There is also the recognition of the wider cultural context, that the internal family of the individual reflects the family system within which they parent, which in turn reflects the wider community and systemic marginalisation. This individual, collective and cumulative trauma can result in internalised shame.

Both queerness and neurodivergence often lead people to seek out and create intentional communities online or in person. This can result in unique supportive networks that challenge traditional family norms, or the lack of availability and emotional impact of trying to create such a community can be a factor in social isolation. Ayesha is a bisexual autistic woman and single parent to Luna, 7. 'My biggest issue has always been isolation. I feel very alone with her,' she says. 'I live in a rural area, it's very white around here, and it's important to me to be visibly queer. I worry that I'm impacting Luna by the way I present, but the idea of changing how I look to fit in is intolerable. And I know I shouldn't have to, and I feel resentful that I even consider it, but sometimes I feel so alone I'm just desperate. I've tried the kids' groups and the school gate thing, and people aren't often actually hostile, but there's just this drifting away: they'll say hello and then chat with each other, and I'm always on the outside. It feels impossible to find a space where all the different parts of me can be seen and accepted. There's an autistic group in town, but you can't bring children; there are parenting groups, but everyone's complaining about their husbands all the time and so on. There isn't a place for me, and that hurts.'

More than Two Parents

Children may have more than two parents in many circumstances, such as stepparents in blended families. They may also have other parental figures, adults in their lives who fill some of the role of parent, some or all of the time. A situation where there are only two parents is a standard that is not seen as the ideal circumstance for children in many other cultures and periods of time. Children benefit from having adults in their lives who care about them and meet their needs in different ways, and parents benefit from having the support of other adults, wider family and community.

However, there is specific stigma around families where there are more than two parents who are in a relationship with one another. Parents may feel pressured to conceal their relationship dynamics from teachers, medical professionals or their community out of fear of this bias, and there may be judgement and lack of understanding. Since ethically non-monogamous (ENM) families are not recognised or protected in the UK, there are risks in engaging with the legal system or social services. This can impact disputes around residency and contact, education or medical issues, and estate planning. Maria Pallotta-Chiarolla (2006) studied the impact of heteronormative and mononormative culture on the lives of children from polyamorous families and calls for more research in the area. She suggests that the low rate of discrimination experienced by her research participants may reflect the invisibility and silencing of polyamorous families, with many choosing not to disclose the nature of their relationship beyond the immediate family or close people or being unable to be open about this safely.

Dr Elizabeth Sheff found that children from polyamorous families generally thrive and benefit from a more extensive network of supportive adults (Sheff, 2020). Adults who can navigate the practical and emotional complexities of managing multiple relationships while parenting tend to have strong communication and conflict-resolution skills. They tend to prioritise healthy relationships and intentionally put time and energy into developing and maintaining connections with depth and authenticity. Sheff found that 'Young adults who have grown up in polyamorous families report that they have practised the communication and negotiation skills that allow them to defuse conflicts with roommates and establish supportive relationships that provide emotional intimacy wherever they live.'

Case Study

Thomas is a gay trans man and birth parent to three boys, now teenagers. He came out to them when they were 6, 8 and 11 and transitioned over the next few years. 'There was a lot of testosterone in the house,' he remembers. 'Going through puberty simultaneously with your kids is sometimes fun and sometimes tricky. We had lots of loud music, long hikes and occasional big rows. They knew what was going on though; they were old enough to understand, and I could talk to them about big, sudden, angry feelings and having too much energy and needing to move. In a way, it helped us connect, especially with my eldest.' His children have related to his transition in different ways over the years. 'I'm not sure my youngest even noticed. I've never asked them to change what they call me; they've made up their minds about that. They've had fun trying out different variations – the youngest went through phases of mixing up Mummy and Daddy, calling me Muddy or Dummy, which he found hilarious, and Mister Mummy for a while, which I think was my favourite. Now they all just use my name, or sometimes Mum. The only thing I asked was that they didn't call me Mum if we were in men's toilets in public.'

In the Room: Queer Parents in Therapy

Queer parenting can be a key issue in one-to-one therapy with individuals considering parenting or already part of queer families. It may well come into relationship therapy with queer partners, and systemic and family therapists may work with the entire queer family. This latter can enable a holistic approach that allows therapists to address both the individual struggles of queer parents, the relational structures affecting their family dynamics, and the societal and cultural factors that shape internalised oppression and active discrimination. One-to-one and relationship therapists may also benefit from such a systemic framing of queer parenting. They may consider referrals to systemic family therapists if working with the whole family would be beneficial.

The specific issues brought into the therapy room by queer parents will be many and varied, but there may be broad similarities based on their identities and whether their queerness is visible or invisible, whether they are read accurately or otherwise. As an example, gay fathers may meet with suspicion in some areas due to tropes associating gay men with paedophilia or may be celebrated disproportionately in others due to misogyny and the assumption that women will be primary caregivers. Lesbian mothers may face prejudice around hypersexualisation or doubt about the stability of their family. Trans people may experience different incorrect assumptions based on how they are read, and bisexual parents may struggle for visibility and acceptance in both queer and heterosexual circles.

Thomas, a gay trans man, noticed this difference in how he was treated as a parent, having had the experience of being read as both a woman and a man over the course of his transition. 'One of the first ways I knew I was passing was how people talked to me. I'd be in the park and someone would say, oh, it's so great to see you taking them to the park. Or we'd be out and someone said, you're so lovely with them, it's good to see. It was confusing at first and then I realised and I was furious. I've always taken them to the park, I've always interacted with them in the same way; I was never congratulated for it when people saw me as female. Especially being seen as a single mum, or a single lesbian mum, I'd get looks, you know, I felt disapproval. One of my children would have meltdowns in public, he'd run and hide, and what he needed was for me to be a barrier between him and the world and not make him interact until he was ready. So there were moments when he'd be hiding behind a bin, crying, and I'd be stood with my back to him on my phone or something, because he needed to know I was there but not pushing him. The reaction to that changed; I really noticed it, from side-eye when people saw a mum ignoring a distressed child to smiling when they saw a dad not 'giving in to a tantrum.' It was so weird the way the picture changed with how I looked. I didn't realise when I was read as a woman, it was only when it changed that I saw it. I think that's a particular gift of being trans, that you see those invisible things when they change.'

Therapists can acknowledge layered identities and intersectional oppression by recognising how race, disability, class or neurodivergence compound experiences of discrimination or othering in families. Shame arising from internalised homophobia or transphobia may be a common issue. Isolation or lack of support from the family of origin is more common for queer parents. The issue of coming out is constant and varying and is compounded when children reach an age where they understand that their family is different. They then need support to navigate coming out in their own way, to be prepared for possible bias while fostering pride and resilience in their family.

Parents may have their own concerns about the effect of their queerness or family structure on their children. They can be reassured that there is now a significant body of long-term research which consistently shows that children of queer parents are just as well-adjusted, successful and happy as those from heterosexual families, and are more empathic and accepting of diversity. This research shows similar outcomes for children of lesbian mothers (Golombok, 2000; Golombok et al., 2003; Patterson, 1992), gay fathers (Goldberg, 2010; Golombok et al., 2014) and trans and non-binary parents (Hafford-Letchfield et al., 2019).

Children benefit from attuned and reliable care, strong relationships with caregivers, open communication, freedom and celebration of who they are as individuals. The sexual orientation, gender identity, number and relationship structure of their parents are far less relevant than connection, safety and love.

References

Bos, H. M. W., van Balen, F. and van den Boom, D. C. (2007) 'Child adjustment and parenting in planned lesbian-parent families', *American Journal of Orthopsychiatry*, 77(1), pp. 38–48. https://doi.org/10.1037/0002-9432.77.1.38

Coleman, E., Radix, A. E., Bouman, W. P., Brown, G. R., de Vries, A. L. C., Deutsch, M. B., … Arcelus, L. (2022) 'Standards of care for the health of transgender and gender diverse people, Version 8', *International Journal of Transgender Health*, 23(S1), S1–S259. https://doi.org/10.1080/26895269.2022.2100644

Goldberg, A. E. (2010) *Lesbian and gay parents and their children: Research on the family life cycle.* American Psychological Association.

Goldberg, A. E. and Sweeney, K. (2019) 'LGBTQ parent families', in Sanders, M.R. and Morawska, A. (eds.) *Handbook of parenting and child development across the lifespan.* Springer, pp. 743–760.

Golombok, S. (2000) *Parenting: What really counts?* London, Routledge.

Golombok, S., Mellish, L., Jennings, S., Casey, P., Tasker, F. and Lamb, M. E. (2014) 'Adoptive gay father families: Parent-child relationships and children's psychological adjustment', *Child Development*, *85*(2), pp. 456–468. https://doi .org/10.1111/cdev.12155

Golombok, S., Perry, B., Burston, A., Murray, C., Mooney-Somers, J., Stevens, M. and Golding, J. (2003) 'Children with lesbian parents: A community study', *Developmental Psychology*, *39*(1), pp. 20–33. https://doi.org/10.1037/0012-1649 .39.1.20

Greenfield, M. (2022) 'What about partners? Lesbian partners' experiences of fertility clinics with Bev Turner-Matthews, season 1 episode 3, Pride in Birth'. Available at: https://pod.co/pride-in-birth (Accessed: 23 May 2025)

Hafford-Letchfield, T., Cocker, C., Rutter, D., Tinarwo, M., McCormack, K., and Manning, R. (2019) 'What do we know about transgender parenting? Findings from a systematic review', *Health & Social Care in the Community*, *27*(4), pp. 1111–1125. https://doi.org/10.1111/hsc.12759

Pallotta-Chiarolli, M. (2006) 'Polyparents having children, raising children, schooling children', *Lesbian and Gay Psychology Review*, *7*(1), pp. 48–53.

Patterson, C. J. (1992) 'Children of lesbian and gay parents', *Child Development*, *63*(5), pp. 1025–1042. https://doi.org/10.2307/1131517

Schwartz, R. C. (1995) *Internal family systems therapy*. London, Guilford Press.

Sheff, E. (2020) 'Children in polyamorous families', *Psychology Today*. Available at: https://www.psychologytoday.com/gb/blog/the-polyamorists-next-door/201704/ children-in-polyamorous-families-age-dependent-experiences (Accessed: 23 May 2025).

Strang, J. F., Kenworthy, L., Dominska, A., Sokoloff, J., Kenealy, L. E., Berl, M., Walsh, K., Menvielle, E., Meagher, H., Iglesias, J. E., Luong-Tran, C., Didehbani, N. and Wallace, G. L. (2014) 'Increased gender variance in autism spectrum disorders and attention deficit hyperactivity disorder', *Archives of Sexual Behavior*, *43*(8), pp. 1525–1533. https://doi.org/10.1007/s10508-014-0285-3

Tasker, F. and Golombok, S. (1997) *Growing up in a lesbian family: Effects on child development*. London, Guilford Press.

Chapter 16

Queer Spirituality in Counselling and Psychotherapy

Matt Cormack

Introduction

How do spirituality and GSRD intersect? How can this be present in the therapy room? How do we as practitioners work with these issues?

This chapter provides insight into the potential interaction between GSRD identities and spirituality. Few counselling training programmes explore faith in depth, and some courses do not discuss this topic. For gender, sexual, and relationship diverse communities, the connection with faith and spirituality can be far more nuanced than is often acknowledged. Practitioners need to consider these nuances to work with clients ethically when addressing spiritual issues. This chapter will explore the intersections of faith and spirituality within a GSRD context to support practitioners working with these communities. There will be a discussion of the impact of conversion practices. This chapter will explore the effects of accepting and celebrating GSRD identities. Finally, there will be some experiential exercises that provide opportunities to explore or reflect.

It is essential to exercise caution when defining spirituality, faith, and religion. Across the world, these can vary greatly, with differing ideas of what defines each. Any definition has the potential to be limited by that person's experience and research, which could inadvertently exclude other belief systems. Faith might be defined as a strong belief in a particular deity, practice, or philosophy, whereas religion could be described as following a specific system of beliefs and/or practices. However, some definitions of what constitutes a religion have been used to invalidate people from minoritised faiths by suggesting their beliefs are not a real religion or faith, so it must be tentative. With that in mind, a loose definition of spirituality may be: 'Spirituality relates to matters of the spirit and may include the acknowledgement, sense, or belief that there is something greater than ourselves. It may involve feeling a connection to a greater whole with a cosmic or divine aspect to which we are all linked.'

DOI: 10.4324/9781003530848-20

Positionality

I must consider my positionality in writing this chapter, as my experience will inevitably influence my approach. I am an autistic, queer person from a working-class background in Scotland. I have been practising my faith for 18 years.

I served on the BACP Spirituality Division for three years, during which I wrote journal articles, delivered CPD network groups on spirituality, and represented the division at various events. I have been involved in interfaith work in Scotland for years. This has included attending events organised by people of various faiths, engaging in constructive conversations, and identifying commonalities. I have regularly spoken about faith and mental health at events. I currently represent the Scottish Pagan Federation on the Scottish Government's Faith and Belief Representative Group, where faith representatives meet regularly to engage with the Scottish Government and discuss issues relating to faith communities.

Why Is it Essential for Practitioners to Consider?

The most straightforward answer is that it might come up. If practitioners have explored spirituality in a GSRD context, they will be better prepared to facilitate those explorations with clients. We don't live in a vacuum. It has been widely accepted by most, if not all, psychotherapy theories that our experiences and the things we are exposed to influence our lives. This may be represented by conditions of worth within person-centred therapy, defence mechanisms in psychodynamic therapy, or maladaptive coping strategies within CBT. All of these, although slightly different, stem from our shared experiences. The Ethical Framework requires us to work within our competence (BACP, 2018). Other professional bodies have similar expectations for practitioners. Therefore, we cannot work with clients around spirituality if we have not gained an understanding of what may arise. In particular, practitioners need to consider that there have been numerous interactions between different faiths and beliefs, as well as queer identities, across the world throughout time. These continue to play out today, having a direct impact on our clients.

Conversion Practices

It is necessary to acknowledge that some religious-focused ideas and practices are harmful experiences for the GSRD populations, such as conversion practices. Conversion practices (sometimes called conversion or reparative therapy) are different methods with the aim or intention of suppressing or changing a person's sexuality or gender identity. They connect to the idea that being cisgender and heterosexual are the default or preferred way to be. Many conversion practices have been linked to faith groups. However, we must be aware that no one faith is entirely for or against these practices. As with most things, there is diversity within religions and how they view conversion practices. According to the UK Government (2021), no robust data are available on the number of people in the UK who have experienced conversion practices. However, they do highlight a study suggesting that 2% have undergone conversion practices and a further 5% have been offered conversion practices. It further highlights that people of colour have experienced higher rates of conversion practices. It is essential to note that there is no credible evidence to support the effectiveness of conversion practices. The Independent Forensic Expert Group (2020) conclude that conversion practices have no medical or scientific validity.

Furthermore, they highlight that they could be considered a form of torture. We know that conversion practices harm the individuals who undergo them (Goodwin, 2022; Green *et al.*, 2020; Independent Forensic Expert Group, 2020; Ozanne Foundation, 2018). Many people who experience conversion practices are left with trauma that they may carry with them for years or their whole lives. This can substantially impact how a GSRD person relates to the world, others, or themselves. It may make gender-affirming care or relationships more difficult due to internalised ideas about what is and is not acceptable. Some people who have experienced conversion practices may not consciously acknowledge that these practices have contributed to their difficulties. If practitioners are not trained to notice this, it may go unaddressed in therapy. Stonewall (2020) indicates that gender-diverse survivors of conversion attempts are significantly more likely to attempt suicide. Green *et al.* (2020) add that LGBT+ young people who have survived conversion practices are twice as likely to have had multiple suicide attempts. This makes the lived experience of conversion practices a significant risk factor for GSRD people that practitioners may want to consider asking about as part of their risk assessment or initial session.

When writing this chapter, conversion practices were still legal in the UK. There has been a promise to ban this at Westminster, and the Scottish Government has finished a consultation on a ban. No legislation has been passed to date. While that is yet to happen, these conversations happening more publicly will likely lead to more people recognising they may be queer and experiencing conversion practices. In Scotland, the LGBT Centre for Health and Wellbeing (2024) have launched a service supporting survivors of conversion practices. Across the UK, there is the National Conversion Therapy Helpline that exists for people who have been through conversion practices (Galop, 2024). It is increasingly likely that we will see clients who have been impacted.

Faith and GSRD People

While we must acknowledge the harm that some GSRD people have experienced, practitioners need to have an awareness of queer spirituality for the exact opposite reason as well. There will be clients who find strength, community, and a sense of belonging in their belief systems. This is across different faiths, so we must never assume that a person's faith and identity conflict. Bonelli *et al.* (2012) explain that faith can be helpful in the recovery from depression. While this is not specific to queer individuals, understanding it is beneficial. There is a possibility of us making the error that no faith or belief will accept queer people, which is simply incorrect. Many queer people, therapists included, have been harmed by faith or religion and may carry anger or pain. However, as therapists, if we are not aware of our countertransference, it may impact our work with clients in subtle ways that could shut down the discussion and become a block to therapy. Practitioners should be curious about clients' responses to faith and religion issues, as this can offer crucial insight into our feelings. These may then need to be unpacked in personal therapy or supervision. Similarly, it is necessary to be cautious when inviting clients to discuss their faith or beliefs, such as stating that all religions are the same or that all are abusive, as this may result in missing some valuable exploration opportunities. If we carry these biases surrounding faith into the therapy room, we risk alienating clients who might find this a source of comfort.

We may also encounter clients for whom faith is essential, but they may not yet be conscious of this or may not yet feel safe exploring it with us. Reeves (2015) suggests that by using the word suicide, we enable clients to discuss it openly. I wonder if a similar thing might happen if we use the words 'faith,' 'belief,' or 'spirituality.' How many practitioners ask about a client's beliefs in their initial session?

As we begin to unpack spirituality and GSRD within therapy, it is helpful to understand our relationship or feelings surrounding spirituality initially. By reflecting on our responses, we can be better equipped to support clients who bring spirituality into our work. It reduces the likelihood of countertransference in the room, although this is always worth exploring within supervision. So, what is present for you when thinking about spirituality?

Visualisation Exercise

This is an optional exercise to help you notice some of your own feelings towards spirituality. I have often used this exercise in group work and found it effective for exploration. It is a visualisation exercise, although for some people, visualisation may not be possible. I want to acknowledge this and highlight that reflecting through journaling or other methods is equally valid.

Find a place where you can be undisturbed for a few minutes and get comfortable. Either soften your gaze or close your eyes. Lift your hand with the palm facing upwards. Visualise in your hand spirituality. Imagine what kind of shape it is, considering the textures or colours. How much does it weigh in your hand? Does it have any noise or smell? Is it alive? Be curious about various aspects of spirituality in your hands. What would you like to do with it? Take a moment to do what you need to with the spirituality in your hand. Afterwards, imagine whatever was in your hand disappearing and then gently bring your awareness back into the space you are in.

You may want to journal about your response or discuss it with your supervisor, in personal therapy, or with peers. This exercise may be helpful in client work to support a client in beginning to explore their ways of connecting with spirituality. However, this exercise, like any creative endeavour, also has the potential to quickly evoke deep or complex emotions within a client. It would be recommended to seek out training to work creatively with clients and to be cautious when working with people who have experienced trauma.

Community

Being a part of a community can bring a sense of belonging and connection. For many people, their faith or belief group provides this. We recognise the importance of connection for people's mental health, a concept reflected in the current literature (Kok & Fredrickson, 2013).

Faith or religion can create strong communities that provide significant support to one another. Communal worship and celebrations, such as Beltane, Christmas, or Diwali, provide opportunities for communities to come together with a shared purpose. Many life rites may be included here, including marriages and funerals, which allow people to celebrate or mourn with others. For many, their spiritual path may provide a place for them to spend meaningful time with others.

It is worth considering the implications for practitioners of being part of a particular community on how it may affect our clients. Clients may internalise the messages about what is and is not acceptable from their faiths or communities. For those embraced by their community, this may be a protective factor when addressing issues in therapy, as they may have a robust support network. However, for those who are not accepted, this may contribute to experiences of shame. Etherson (2023) suggests that shame may be a mechanism to protect ourselves from not fitting in. Through making us feel bad, we change our behaviour to be accepted.

We also need to understand that every community is unique and not interchangeable. It would be a mistake to suggest moving to another group that may be more GSRD inclusive. This would risk invalidating the client's experiences and relationships. While finding a queer-friendly space may be rich in offerings, it is not a replacement for the relationships or community that a person may have had.

Leaving

While many people can reconcile their beliefs with their identity, others will struggle to do so. Some of these clients may choose to leave a belief group either before or sometimes during therapy. As practitioners, we can support our clients in exploring this, as they may want to reflect on what leaving a group would mean for them. However, practitioners should exercise extreme caution when advising a client to leave a community, group, or family. This has the potential to cause harm to a client. It could irreparably rupture the therapeutic alliance. It is also not a decision for us as practitioners to make. We can facilitate exploration of a client's options, but we cannot tell them what to do. This may evoke complex emotions in us as practitioners, particularly when a client remains in a painful situation. Practitioners could consider being congruent with clients about remaining in a harmful situation, but this should be carefully reflected on to ensure the therapist's feelings are not taking precedence. Clients might choose not to leave at this time for several reasons. Here, the focus might shift to providing resources, signposting, or supporting a client with resilience or self-care. Supervision may be beneficial in these situations to help you navigate them effectively.

If you are working with a client who is considering or has recently left, these themes may be useful for exploration and discussion. Has the client thought about what it will feel like to leave? Some clients may not have had the space to safely explore their feelings about leaving. Even though they may choose to leave a situation that is harmful for them, this may still raise feelings of loss or grief, because it is the end of a previous relationship. For some clients, this may evoke a sense of mourning for what they once had. There are different models to work with loss therapeutically. I often gravitate to Worden's four tasks of grief (Worden, 2010). These tasks are:

1. To accept the reality of the loss.
2. To allow yourself to experience the pain of grief.
3. Adjusting to an environment where the person/group/belief is no longer present.
4. Find an enduring connection to what or who is gone, while continuing with your life.

I believe it can be applied to work with a spiritual context quite organically (Cormack, 2021).

This may facilitate discussion about remaining in contact with people after leaving. The client may completely remove themselves without further contact or desire to stay in contact with certain people. Some groups will have no problem with this; however, others may actively advise their communities to stop speaking to someone who has left. The client may experience this as abandonment. However, there may also be practical considerations for the client to consider, particularly if relocation is involved.

Another aspect to consider is whether the client has a place to stay or access to other support. This could be isolating for the client, or they may be losing support networks. This may be a risk factor for suicidal ideation, so it may be necessary to explore additional support the client could link with. Are there places that you can signpost your client to? There will be some resources at the end of this chapter, but you may want to explore other options tailored to your client.

There may be an aspect of dual processing for the client in therapy (Worden, 2010). They may move between celebrating and affirming their identity and distressing over what they have given up. How do you, as a clinician, hold that space that allows for both of these to be explored without judgement? We may need to discuss this in our supervision to ensure that we don't inadvertently create a therapy space that is unaccepting for clients to express their longing for what they have left behind.

In particular, we need to have cultural awareness and humility. Our own experiences of community and family relationships may vastly differ from those of our clients. Many clients who leave a faith community may also be leaving a portion, or sometimes even all, of their family. This may raise significant feelings of sadness, shame, or distress for the client, who may need to be attended to gently in therapy. Resources for these clients can be valuable as they may want to find people of their faith who are accepting or have similar experiences. However, these are not a replacement. Joining a new community to replace one they have recently left will not heal that pain. It could harm the therapeutic relationship if we suggest going from one group to another. Our clients have likely formed deep bonds with many in these communities, which will require empathy and time.

Trauma

As previously mentioned in this chapter, clients can come with trauma from their experiences with faith. Goodwin (2022) offers a systematic review highlighting the impact of spiritual trauma for many LGBT+ people, which can lead to poor mental health, internalised stigma, and increased risk of suicidality. Skidmore (2023) suggests that self-compassion is a vital factor in resilience from spiritual trauma for LGBT+ people. As practitioners, we can support clients in developing self-compassion by offering empathy and understanding of their experiences. Clients who have suffered spiritual trauma may find it difficult to provide themselves with compassion or may offer it to a point and then return to previous internalised ideas of shame. The process may be comparable to peeling an onion, where some layers can be removed, but this takes time and needs to be done carefully. It may take some clients a long time to acknowledge and begin to unpack the impact of religious or spiritual trauma. Over time, you may notice more introjected values or conditions of worth that continue to affect a client. If you create a formulation for clients, this may evolve repeatedly as the client trusts you with more of their story.

An aspect of spiritual trauma that we should acknowledge as much as possible is the fear of divine retribution, that a God or Goddess will punish them for being GSRD. This fear may be potent and have implications for a person living authentically. This may inhibit a person from expressing their gender identity or sexuality. It may lead to distress when a client engages with these, which may cause them to repress their desires or identity. This, in turn, may contribute to clients feeling low or utilising self-harming behaviours. It may linger with clients, even long after they have left an environment like this. It is also possible for this to affect some GSRD people who aren't spiritual or religious through media messaging and other forms. Working with clients around these issues requires a trauma-informed approach. It may involve building a good therapeutic alliance and establishing tools for emotional regulation before being able to unpack the underlying trauma. Every client will be different and must go at their own pace.

It is possible, particularly if the person is from a minoritised belief system, that there may be additional aspects that arise when unpacking trauma in therapy. The impact of colonisation may come into the therapy space. Laxmi Narayan Tripathi explains that before colonisation, Hijras were considered divine beings with the power to bless (Women in the World, 2017). Colonisation led to legislative changes that have marginalised and harmed the Hijra community, which continues today. If we look at Turtle Island, we see further signs of the harm of colonisation in how indigenous people have been treated. Geo Neptune highlights that, before colonisation, many First Peoples identified as having another gender, and in 1990, it became known as Two-Spirit (Them, 2018). Colonisation led to the beliefs of First Peoples being oppressed and silenced. We cannot and should not ignore the atrocities that have resulted from colonisation. Some of this harm, however, is also being continued today through appropriation. This happens even within queer spaces unintentionally with some people claiming the identity of Two-Spirit or other identities while not being connected to these cultures. Sollod (2005) even highlights how some concepts introduced into therapy may stem from different cultures. As practitioners, we have an ethical responsibility to work within our area of competence and must ask ourselves if we have the necessary training to address this type of trauma. If you feel unsure, support from your supervisor or seeking additional training may be helpful.

Celebration

Throughout this chapter, there has been a focus on painful or traumatic experiences with spirituality. However, queer spirituality can also bring joy and celebration. This is often missing from conversations about GSRD people and spirituality.

Their spiritual beliefs or religion may affirm a person's GSRD identity. Some clients may fear being rejected by their faith, but are instead accepted for who they are. Others may search for a spiritual path that resonates with them and find joyous communities to be a part of.

Clients may also have affirming spiritual experiences, such as receiving a message or communication from a deity to which they feel connected. It may even be a sensation of feeling the divinity within them. A client might want to share an event like this in therapy. However, people from some faiths may fear judgement or pathologisation from a therapist. What thoughts come to your mind about a client sharing a spiritual experience?

All of these possibilities provide opportunities for a client to integrate their spirituality and GSRD identity into their organismic self, feeling more congruent with the world. Super and Jacobson (2011) highlight that moving away from dichotomous thinking around spirituality and sexuality may support clients with integration.

The act of sex itself can be a positive expression of queer spirituality. Across many cultures, we see links between sex and spirituality. Worshipping a partner, whether in a regular or one-off relationship, can be a spiritual experience that meets a person's emotional or spiritual needs. It may be that a client considers having sex with others a spiritual, or even transcendent, experience. Dean (2009) describes cruising as a form of spiritual ritual. For some who engage with kink, worshipping a partner, or partners, through domination or submission may be a spiritual offering which leads to profound experiences during sex. This can be further connected to sex magic rituals, which have existed since antiquity and continue today in some Pagan and Spiritual groups, where there has been explicit consent (Prower, 2018; Penczak, 2003). Many therapists don't talk about sex or spirituality, so there is a need for spaces for people to explore both in combination. It is worth reflecting on how we feel about sex and spirituality, and consider how comfortable we are with exploring this to minimise the possibility of countertransference.

Ritual forms a part of many people's lives. Significant moments are often marked with rituals, whether that is a graduation, a birth, or a wedding. Most rituals in Western society are portrayed through a cis-heteronormative lens. We rarely get to see a queer throuple having a handfasting ceremony. Navigating the world of queer spirituality with a client may include unpacking these societal expectations. Still, it may also be an opportunity to reclaim rituals or facilitate creativity by developing our own. In addition to being a therapist, I am a Pagan celebrant and can perform legal weddings for couples of any gender. These weddings can take almost any form the clients would like, transforming into a spiritual expression of their love and joy. Anderson (2005) and Goodwyn (2016) argue that therapy can be a ritual. This opens up the possibility of integrating GSRD identities as both a therapeutic and spiritual experience for clients; however, further research would be valuable in this area.

Table 16.1 Meaning of original rainbow flag colours

Pink	Sexuality
Red	Life
Orange	Healing
Yellow	Sunlight
Green	Nature
Turquoise	Art/Magic
Blue	Harmony/Serenity
Violet	Spirit

Within the GSRD, and especially the queer community, we also have our rituals. Coming out, pride marches, and remembrance days all form part of queer spirituality rituals. Interestingly, there are references in ancient Mesopotamia to a ritual involving Inanna that potentially changed a person's gender (Academus Education, 2021). Pride can be another expression of queer spirituality. This can be a truly spiritual experience, being united with thousands of other queer people who share our community's thoughts. The first Pride march I ever attended had a minute of silence to honour members of our rainbow family that we have lost. This included the people we have lost as a result of violence, the AIDS epidemic, homophobia, biphobia, transphobia, or suicide. This was immediately followed by a minute of noise. The noise represented our collective determination to continue to make change in this world, that we would not be silent. This parallels some spiritual rituals where ancestors are honoured before making oaths or promises for the future.

Continuing the theme of Pride, Gilbert Baker created the original rainbow flag with eight colours, each with its meaning (see Table 16.1) (Grovier, 2016).

Rainbow Poem Exercise

This is another exercise that may be useful for you in noticing your connection to these different aspects of the Pride flag. Reflecting on this chapter and the eight original colours of the Pride flag, take some time to consider which colours you are drawn to, and which ones feel more distant. Allow yourself some time to consider what each of the eight colours means for you at this moment. Write a single sentence that represents how you feel about each of these.

For example, Pink – sexuality might be 'My connection to pink is vibrant and joyful.'

Once you have written your eight sentences, take your time to read them aloud in order of the flag. Be curious about what you notice in your words and your response to your rainbow poem. You may want to journal your response or discuss it with your supervisor, a therapist, or peers. If you prefer to use paint, collage, or another form of expression, then you can adapt this exercise to suit your way of working.

Queer spirituality may be impossible to completely define or encapsulate; particularly as it may take other forms than what may be perceived to be faith or religion. This chapter has only given a glimpse of what is possible and how that may be presented in the therapy room. Queer spirituality has the potential to be profoundly positive for those who feel a connection to it and decide to engage with it. It may be affirming for someone's GSRD identity to find a space of acceptance and celebration. Queer spirituality has the potential to be healing for people who have experienced religious trauma. At its core, queer spirituality is a form of not only accepting or embracing gender, sexual, and relationship diversity within spirituality but also recognising the divine brilliance and beauty that shines within queer people.

Resources

- Galop National Conversion Therapy Helpline: 0800 130 3335 https:// galop.org.uk/
- Hidayah LGBTQI+, a Queer Muslim charity: https://hidayahlgbt.com/
- House of Rainbow, supporting LGBTIQ+ people of colour: https://www .houseofrainbow.org/
- Imaan, an LGBTQI Muslim Support charity: https://imaanlondon.word-press.com/
- Keshet UK, supporting Jewish LGBT+ people: https://www.keshetuk.org/
- LGBT Health and Wellbeing LGBT+ Helpline: 0800 464 7000 https:// www.lgbthealth.org.uk/
- Metropolitan Community Church, an inclusive Christian church: https:// www.mccchurch.org/
- Naz and Matt Foundation, supporting LGBTQI+ people and their parents: https://www.nazandmattfoundation.org/about/
- Sarbat, support for LGBT+ Sikhs: https://www.sarbat.net/
- Scottish Pagan Federation, supporting Pagans in Scotland: https://scot-tishpf.org/
- Quest, pastoral support for LGBT+ Catholics: https://questlgbti.uk/

References

Academus Education. (2021) *Ancient Mesopotamian Transgender and Non-Binary Identities*. Available at: https://www.academuseducation.co.uk/post/ancient -mesopotamian-transgender-and-non-binary-identities (Accessed: 28 September 2024).

Anderson, M. (2005) 'Psychotherapy as ritual: Connecting the concrete with the symbolic', in Moodley, R., & West, W. (eds.) *Integrating Traditional Healing Practices into Counselling and Psychotherapy*. London: Sage, pp. 282–291.

Bonelli, R., Dew, R., Koenig, H., Rosmarin, D. and Vasegh, S. (2012) 'Religious and spiritual factors in depression: Review and integration of the research', *Depression Research and Treatment*, 2012, p. 962860. doi: 10.1155/2012/962860.

British Association for Counselling and Psychotherapy (BACP) (2018) *BACP Ethical Framework*. Available at: https://www.bacp.co.uk/events-and-resources/ethics -and-standards/ethical-framework-for-the-counselling-professions/ (Accessed: 24 September 2024).

Cormack, M. (2021) 'The ritual in endings', *Thresholds*, pp. 8–11.

Dean, T. (2009) *Unlimited Intimacy*. Chicago/London: The University of Chicago Press.

Etherson, L. (2023) 'Shame containment theory - A new approach to shame', *Attachment*, 17(2), pp. 141–154.

Galop (2024) *Conversion Therapy Helpline Update*. Available at: https://galop.org .uk/news/conversion-therapy-helpline-update/ (Accessed: 28 September 2024).

Goodwin, M. (2022) 'The impact of religious trauma on the LGBTQ+ community: A systematic review'. Available at: https://ir-api.ua.edu/api/core/bitstreams /2ed055d9-bb8f-4b9a-a576-384b5c02f50d/content (Accessed: 28 September 2024).

Goodwyn, E. (2016) *Healing Symbols in Psychotherapy*. Oxon: Routledge.

Green, A., Prince-Freeney, M., Dorison, S., and Pick, C. (2020) 'Self-reported conversion efforts and suicidality among US LGBTQ youths and young adults', *American Journal of Public Health*, 110(8), pp. 1221–1227. https://doi.org/10 .2105/AJPH.2020.305701

Grovier, K. (2016) *The History of the Rainbow Flag*. Available at: https://www .bbc.com/culture/article/20160615-the-history-of-the-rainbow-flag (Accessed: 28 September 2024).

Independent Forensic Expert Group (2020) *Statement on Conversion Therapy*. Available at: https://pdf.sciencedirectassets.com/273591/1-s2.0-S1752928X20X00047/1-s2.0 -S1752928X20300366/main.pdf?X-Amz-Security-Token=IQoJb3JpZ2luX2VjEPr %2F%2F%2F%2F%2F%2F%2F%2F%2F%2FwEaCXVzLWVhVhc3QtMSJIME YCIQDhyChWoaRrdjxjybNMpmrjdX6vceGtY%2BF8n95d5NWb8gIhALv p8avKwD (Accessed: 28 September 2024).

Kok, B. E. and Fredrickson, B. L. (2013) 'Wellbeing begins with "we"', in Cooper, C.L. (ed.), *Wellbeing*. https://doi.org/10.1002/9781118539415.wbwell042

LGBT Health and Wellbeing (2024) *Conversion Practices Support*. Available at: https://www.lgbthealth.org.uk/services-support/conversion-practices/ (Accessed: 28 September 2024).

Ozanne Foundation (2018) *Faith and Sexuality Survey*. Liverpool: Ozanne Foundation.

Penczak, C. (2003) *Gay Witchcraft*. San Francisco: Weiser Books.

Prower, T. (2018) *Queer Magic*. Woodbury: Llewellyn.

Reeves, A. (2015) *Working With Risk*. London: SAGE.

Skidmore, S. (2023) 'Self-compassion as a protective factor against religious and sexual identity struggles among religious and post-religious sexual minorities'. Available at: https://www.tandfonline.com/doi/full/10.1080/09515070.2024.2332623?fbclid =IwY2xjawFkto1leHRuA2FlbQIxMQABHRXzfyJBbfLGQf3_FJS8cnt9eaVHTJq CJ2RUGO_xVwhtHy5Z8RudijwVtA_aem_r1a0_ckj0yHP_XQcnmdbTw#abstract (Accessed: 28 September 2024).

Sollod, R. (2005) 'Spiritual and healing approaches in psychotherapeutic practice', in Moodley, R., & West, W. (eds.), *Integrating Traditional Healing Practices into Counselling and Psychotherapy*. London: Sage, pp. 270–281.

Stonewall (2020) *2020 'Conversion Therapy' and Gender Identity Survey*. Available at: https://www.stonewall.org.uk/system/files/gict_report_-_final.pdf (Accessed: 28 September 2024).

Super, J., and Jacobson, L. (2011) 'Religious abuse: Implications for counselling lesbian, gay, bisexual, and transgender individuals', *Journal of LGBT Issues in Counselling*, 5(3–4), pp. 180–196. doi: 10.1080/15538605.2011.632739.

Them (2018). *What Does "Two-Spirit" Mean?*. Available at: https://www.youtube.com/watch?v=A4lBibGzUnE (Accessed: 28 September 2022).

UK Government (2021) *Conversion Therapy: An Evidence Assessment and Qualitative Study*. Available at: https://www.gov.uk/government/publications/conversion-therapy-an-evidence-assessment-and-qualitative-study/conversion-therapy-an-evidence-assessment-and-qualitative-study#who-undergoes-conversion-therapy-and-why (Accessed: 19 December 2024)

Women in the World (2017) *What Is a Hijra?*. Available at: https://www.youtube.com/watch?v=Z4tuHJey1i4 (Accessed: 28 September 2024).

Worden, W. (2010) *Grief Counselling and Grief Therapy*. 4th ed. London: Routledge.

Chapter 17

Queer Ageing and Endings

Christian Schulz-Quach and Margo Kennedy

Introduction

Ageing and end-of-life experiences are universal human phenomena, yet they are profoundly shaped by individual identity, societal structures, and cultural contexts. The normative frameworks typically applied to ageing and dying—anchored in traditional life milestones and biological family structures—frequently fail to account for the lived realities of GSRD individuals; they often neglect the effects of societal marginalisation, queer isolation in older age, the importance of chosen families, and how GSRD individuals face mortality, grief, and meaning-making.

This chapter draws upon our decades-long experiences as two queer clinicians working in mental health, cancer, palliative, and hospice care, as well as our personal encounters with loss and grieving, to examine the complexities of ageing and endings in GSRD communities. Our own existential encounters and our losses have shaped us into the therapists we have become, and we believe that an important starting point for any reflection on ageing and endings is an articulation of one's own positionality and narrative towards these topics (Schulz-Quach, 2018a, 2018b). Central to our perspective is a concept we call *"queer loneliness"*, which emerges not only from the existential confrontation with mortality but also from the intersubjective effects of societal exclusion, ageism, and the possible erosion of social networks in later life.

And still, while these experiences of loneliness and isolation are critical, they are not the whole story. As we have come to experience and observe firsthand, GSRD communities also demonstrate remarkable resilience and the capacity to cultivate joy, even in the face of life-limiting illness, approaching death, grieving lost opportunities or processing life's losses and regrets. Some of the most profound and creative forms of endings, mourning and grieving we have witnessed in our work have been within GSRD communities. The presence of chosen family—a network of non-biological, deeply affirming relationships—often plays a vital role in mitigating loneliness and fostering a sense of belonging. Chosen families provide not only emotional

DOI: 10.4324/9781003530848-21

and practical support but also can shape a space in which GSRD individuals experience dignity, authenticity, and connection including in their final years and moments of living. Some of the most impactful and lasting contributions to the development of the modern hospice and palliative care movement originate from queer spaces, such as Casey House in Toronto in Canada (Chiotti & Joseph, 1995)

Our thinking seeks to provide therapists, within and outside of formalised healthcare, with one possible approach towards understanding the psychosocial and existential needs of ageing GSRD individuals and those among us whose lives end earlier than we might have expected. By highlighting the importance of chosen family and community in end-of-life care, we advocate for more inclusive, affirming practices that honour the full complexity of GSRD ageing. Ultimately, we aim to contribute to the broader discourse on equity and dignity in ageing and endings, advocating for care environments that enable all individuals to navigate the profoundly human experiences of ageing and dying with support, connection, and affirmation ... and in some cases with a true sense of fulfilment and joy!

Deconstructing Developmental Theories through Queer Theory and Intersectionality

Traditional developmental theories often conceptualise human growth as a linear, universal progression through predefined stages. These models prioritise the progression of identity formation, intimacy, and generativity, largely through the lens of cis-heteronormative milestones (Miller, 2022). By integrating queer theory and intersectional identities theory, we are advocating for a developmental framework that embraces the diversity of GSRD experiences. Such a model would recognise the complexity of identity formation, the fluidity of life milestones, non-binary positionalities on gender, sex and relationship diversity as well as the central role of chosen families in fostering well-being. Such an inclusive framework challenges traditional developmental theories and underscores the resilience and agency within GSRD communities, offering a path towards more equitable and affirming practices in mental health and end-of-life care (Koffman et al., 2023).

Developmental Theories of Ageing and Their Normative Assumptions

Conventional developmental frameworks, such as Erikson's stages of psychosocial development, are predicated on life pathways that align with heteronormative expectations—such as heterosexual pair bonding, biological parenthood, and early-life identity resolution. These models often fail to account for those whose life trajectories diverge due to their gender, sexual, or relational identities. For GSRD individuals, milestones such as coming out or living authentically are deeply personal experiences that can take place at any point across the lifespan (Floyd & Bakeman, 2006). These processes are often influenced by a complex interplay of societal, relational, and individual factors, including shifts in cultural acceptance, evolving personal circumstances, or health-related challenges (Kahn, 1991). Coming out, for instance, may not be a singular event but rather an ongoing negotiation, shaped by the safety and inclusivity of one's environment (Spornberger MA, 2016). For some, external changes such as progressive social attitudes or affirming community spaces can create new opportunities to live more openly, even later in life. Research has highlighted how older GSRD individuals may embrace their identities more fully in response to life transitions, such as retirement or the passing of unsupportive family members, which reduce fear of rejection or societal repercussions (De Vries et al., 2019). These late-life transitions often occur in response to significant life events, such as the loss of a long-term partner, retirement, or serious illness, prompting reflection on authenticity and fulfilment. For those who come out later in life, these transitions can offer a profound sense of liberation and self-congruence (Fabbre, 2015). However, they may also bring challenges, such as navigating family dynamics, confronting ageism within queer communities, and dealing with societal prejudice and personal grief about lost opportunities and unlived lives (Ogden, 2014; Scott, 2020). Additionally, many GSRD individuals who never felt safe to come out may carry the burden of unresolved identity conflicts, leading to existential isolation and diminished well-being in later years. These later-life milestones challenge assumptions that identity development is confined to early adulthood and underscore the fluidity of self-expression over time (Weststrate & McLean, 2010).

However, we believe it is equally critical to acknowledge the enduring barriers many GSRD individuals face. Systemic oppression, such as discriminatory laws, workplace stigmatisation, or lack of familial support, may inhibit a person's ability to disclose or express their authentic selves. For others, deeply rooted fears of rejection or societal backlash may create an internalised sense of vulnerability, perpetuating a state of concealment. For some, this prolonged internal conflict, sometimes referred to as *identity incongruence*, can lead to significant psychological distress, including feelings of alienation, depression, or unfulfilled potential (Cahill et al., 2003, p. 86; Haviland et al., 2021). While we acknowledge that not all GSRD individuals experience identity concealment as harmful, for those who experience an inability to align outward behaviours with internal identities, it often represents a source of chronic tension. This is more prevalent in GSRD individuals from ethnocultural groups holding strong homophobic values and generations who have grown up under radically different societal and cultural conditions. The radical change of what it means to live openly as an out and open queer person within the past fifty years highlights the need for inclusive frameworks that move beyond rigid timelines of identity development (Odets, 2019). Instead, we believe there is value in adopting models that use intersectional frameworks and recognise identity as a lifelong, contextually driven process, deeply influenced by societal attitudes, personal safety, and advocacy work (Worthen, 2023).

Intersecting Identities and the Ageing Experience

The experiences of ageing and end of life are profoundly shaped by the social locations and intersecting identities individuals hold (Bratt et al., 2018). These identities are dynamic and may shift based on factors both within and outside of one's control, such as health, illness, or changing social and financial circumstances. The interplay of these identities creates unique combinations of advantages and challenges, which must be understood within a broader socio-cultural context to address the diverse needs of ageing populations effectively (Fabbre, 2015; Yarns et al., 2016). Intersectionality underscores the necessity of considering these overlapping identities when developing more inclusive developmental models.

Social Constructions of Ageing across Cultures

Cultural attitudes towards ageing vary significantly and can shape how individuals experience later stages of life. For instance, many white Western societies often associate ageing with stigma, loss of value, and social invisibility, reinforcing experiences of ageism and marginalisation. In contrast and as an example from our own context, many Indigenous communities in Canada and globally view elders as sources of wisdom and leadership, conferring respect and social status on ageing individuals (Changfoot et al., 2022). These cultural distinctions highlight the importance of situating discussions about ageing within specific historical and social frameworks rather than assuming universal experiences.

There remains a significant gap in research addressing the experiences of transgender and non-binary individuals as they age, reflecting the persistence of cis-heteronormative and ageist assumptions in gerontology and healthcare. These assumptions often present older adults as a homogenous group, devoid of sexual or gender diversity, and exclude trans and non-binary people from narratives of ageing altogether (Witten, 2014). As a result, transgender and non-binary older adults face compounded marginalisation—frequently navigating exclusion from "normative" ageing spaces, mainstream GSRD communities, and gerontological research itself (Fabbre, 2015, p. 75). Histories of discrimination further exacerbate the challenges faced by transgender and non-binary older adults. The intersection of transphobia, racism, and ageism creates barriers to accessing inclusive community support and healthcare services, leaving many trans and non-binary elders without adequate systems of care (Silverman & Baril, 2023; Walker et al., 2023). These overlapping forms of marginalisation underscore the need for intersectional approaches to ageing that account for the complexity of GSRD identities and provide accessible and inclusive care services.

The Role of Community and Chosen Families in Promoting Well-Being in Ageing

As we have pointed out, community support plays a vital role in the well-being of older adults, particularly those navigating the intersectionality of marginalised identities. The research on this topic clearly highlights that exclusion from communities—whether mainstream or queer-specific—has significant implications for mental health, access to resources, and overall quality of life in ageing (Cahill et al., 2003; De Vries et al., 2019; Pang et al., 2019). When considering community, we often refer to attachment theory in our clinical work and formulations by emphasising the importance of secure and meaningful connections throughout life. For many GSRD individuals, chosen families serve as the primary source of these connections (Kim & Feyissa, 2021; Milton, 2024). During illness and other challenging life events, chosen families provide critical emotional and practical support, fostering resilience and dignity (Jackson Levin et al., 2020). These affirming relationships become particularly vital during end-of-life care, when chosen family members can accompany their dying family members, providing an opportunity for facing their final life stage with a sense of belonging and legacy. Inclusive community initiatives can help foster environments that validate and affirm diverse identities (Jeste et al., 2016). For example, programmes designed to support chosen families or promote intergenerational connections within GSRD communities are essential in creating a sense of belonging and combating the loneliness that many GSRD elders experience (Oswald & Cooper, 2024).

A Queer Critique of "Positive Ageing"

When we examine the meanings ascribed to ageing in Western society, it is essential to consider the socially constructed context of ageing and gender within cis-heteronormative narratives. Ageing is often framed as a process of decline, characterised by the loss of agency, independence, productivity, and cognitive and physical abilities. Healthcare systems often reinforce ageism, starting with assessments that rely heavily on two demographic descriptors: gender and age. These categories are frequently laden with assumptions—for example, conflating gender with biological sex or associating age with comorbidities and functional decline—biases that are not always aligned with an individual's actual health or abilities. Ageism, deeply ingrained in cultural consciousness, manifests in ideas about what is considered *age-appropriate* behaviour or appearance.

The concept of *successful* ageing, popularised by Rowe and Kahn's model in the late 20th century, aimed to shift the focus of ageing discourse from decline to growth (Martinson & Berridge, 2015). Their framework emphasised three components: low risk of disease and disability, maintenance of high mental and physical function, and continued engagement in life. While this model has been influential, it has also been critiqued for creating yet another limited definition of what it means to age well (Sandberg & Marshall, 2017). It fails to consider the intersecting impacts of race, gender, sexuality, socioeconomic status, and access to quality healthcare. As a result, the *success* it promotes is largely unattainable for individuals marginalised by structural inequities.

For an example, in transgender and non-binary individuals, the binary foundation of "successful ageing" excludes their lived realities. The framework privileges youthfulness, cisnormativity, whiteness, able-bodiedness, and middle-classness, leaving little room for diverse expressions of ageing. Expectations tied to gender and societal ideals of success further marginalise GSRD older adults, disregarding the compounded effects of ageism and systemic discrimination on their well-being (Fabbre, 2015). Queer theory provides a transformative framework for rethinking dominant narratives around ageing and failure, offering new ways of understanding the ageing process that challenge exclusionary societal norms. Central to this perspective is the recognition that traditional concepts of *successful ageing* often perpetuate binary, heteronormative, and cis-normative ideals. These ideals prioritise youthfulness, reproductive success, and adherence to rigid gender roles, positioning those who deviate from these norms as *failures*. For many transgender and non-binary individuals, as well as other GSRD elders, these exclusionary frameworks marginalise their identities, histories, and lived experiences.

Failure, within a queer framework, is not something to overcome but rather a starting point for transformation. Jack Halberstam (2011), in *The Queer Art of Failure*, positions failure as a rejection of societal norms and a tool for dismantling oppressive systems. For ageing individuals in GSRD communities, failure can disrupt the binary categorisations of *successful* versus *unsuccessful* ageing. It opens the door to creative reimagining of what it means to age—embracing queer ways of being that resist normative scripts about productivity, independence, and reproduction (Mulqueen, 2013). We believe that there is a transformative and therapeutic potential in this perspective and the accompanying potential for shame and vulnerability. Shame is often a companion to failure, particularly for GSRD individuals whose identities or ageing processes deviate from societal expectations. However, queer theorists argue that shame can also be a source of strength and creativity (Liu, 2017; Morrison, 2015, p. 23). Morrison's exploration of queer shame reinterprets it not as a purely negative affect but as a space for resistance and self-affirmation. By confronting and reframing shame, ageing GSRD individuals can transform it into a catalyst for agency, community building, and empowerment.

Community spaces, such as queer elder networks, chosen families, or intergenerational initiatives, could provide support for this process, if and where they exist (Miller, 2023). These spaces would allow GSRD individuals to share stories, celebrate their unique journeys, and find solidarity in the commonalities of their experiences. By foregrounding the diversity of ageing experiences, these communities would thereby resist the exclusionary logic of mainstream ageing narratives and affirm the value of queer perspectives on ageing (Fabbre, 2017). Queer ageing could, from our perspective, thus be understood as an act of resistance—an affirmation of the unique beauty, creativity, and strength that emerges when individuals and communities reject the constraints of normative expectations. Instead, the focus would be on the power of resilience, offering a vision of ageing that celebrates diversity, adaptability, and the rich complexity of queer lives.

Existential and Queer Loneliness in GSRD Individuals

We have so far approached queer ageing and endings from a developmental perspective. In this section, we would now like to turn to the psychology of ageing and endings, which often involves contemplation or lived experiences of some level of loss. In this context, loneliness is a pervasive and multifaceted phenomenon, with profound existential dimensions that often resonate deeply within GSRD populations, as demonstrated in queer art, writing, and cinema (Maguire, 2023). For our communities, loneliness is not merely an individual psychological experience but an intricate interplay of social, cultural, and existential factors (Boot-Haury & Cusick, 2023). In our experience, it intertwines with the long-term specific traumata and grieving that many members of the GSRD community who are of older age today have carried for their whole lives (e.g. systematic and political discrimination, incarceration, AIDS crisis) (Odets, 2019). GSRD individuals reaching old age today are the pioneers of a world that we sometimes repress from collective memory and whose societal advances and consequences we too often take for granted. We would like to examine the existential and queer dimensions of loneliness in GSRD individuals, drawing on key theoretical and empirical contributions to elucidate the complexities of this lived experience.

Conceptualising Queer Loneliness

Queer loneliness, as explored in Nunoda's work on *unconsummated queer loneliness,* emerges as a state of unresolved longing that challenges normative paradigms of intimacy and relationality. This form of loneliness destabilises conventional binaries of connection and disconnection, occupying a liminal space where intimacy often remains elusive or unfulfilled (Nunoda,

2023). Unlike conventional understandings of loneliness, which centre on the absence of social ties, queer loneliness reflects a deeper existential dissonance—we suggest that this is rooted in the systemic marginalisation of cis-heteronormativity. For example, Grimmer's qualitative investigation into queer experiences in Berlin underscores the relational and spatial dimensions of queer loneliness in this regard (Grimmer, 2020). It is deeply intertwined with the search for community and belonging within a queer context. Queer loneliness is not just about being physically alone but also about feeling emotionally and socially disconnected, even within spaces that are supposed to be inclusive and supportive. Grimmer explores how queer loneliness is influenced by various factors, including the myth of the queer city, the complexities of identity formation, and the challenges of navigating community norms and expectations. It is experienced through feelings of unbelonging, exclusion, and the struggle to find spaces where one's whole self is accepted and valued. Queer loneliness is also linked to the disappointment and hurt that come from unmet expectations of community and connection. She emphasises that this type of loneliness is not just a negative emotion to be overcome but a part of everyday life that can inform personal growth and community building. It is seen as a counter to the ideal of the *happy queer* and is acknowledged as a valid and significant aspect of queer existence. (Grimmer, 2020, p. 9) Urban centres, often idealised as havens for queer community and belonging, paradoxically can exacerbate feelings of isolation through mechanisms of exclusion and unmet expectations. We believe that this concept is helpful in highlighting the tension and fragility that is inherent in queer community structures, wherein inclusivity is often counterbalanced by dynamics of othering and internalised hierarchies.

Existential Dimensions of Loneliness

From an existential perspective, loneliness is integrally tied to fundamental human concerns, including meaning, freedom, isolation, and mortality. In the context of GSRD individuals, these concerns are further amplified by the intersectionality of marginalised identities. Boot-Haury and Cusick's thematic analysis of asexual and transgender individuals reveals that existential tensions, such as the polarity between connection and isolation, are central to their lived experiences (Boot-Haury & Cusick, 2023). This duality underscores the struggle for authentic self-expression within societal structures that often invalidate or marginalise non-normative identities. Moreover, Morrison's exploration of the *dignity of queer shame* situates queer loneliness within a broader affective and existential framework. Shame, a pervasive affect in queer lives, is reinterpreted not as a deficit but as a site of potentiality and creative resistance (Morrison, 2015, p. 9). Through this lens, loneliness can become a fertile ground for therapeutic inquiry, which we have experienced as helpful in prompting individuals to confront and reconstruct their identities in the face of systemic marginalisation and personal estrangement.

We believe the experience of loneliness among GSRD populations cannot be fully understood without considering the structural and relational contexts in which it unfolds. Empirical studies on older lesbian, gay, and bisexual individuals highlight the compounded effects of minority stress, social isolation, and the erosion of traditional support networks. In juxtaposition to what we proposed earlier, the reliance on chosen families while framed as a resilience mechanism can reveal its limitations in providing consistent and enduring support, particularly in the face of societal and institutional exclusions. The urban mythos of queer-friendly spaces, as articulated by Grimmer, illuminates the paradoxical realities of seeking refuge in urban environments. While cities like Berlin are constructed as loci of queer belonging, they can also perpetuate cycles of exclusion and disillusionment, reflecting broader societal dynamics of privilege and marginalisation within queer communities. We are highlighting this phenomenon, as from our point of view this duality encapsulates a central existential tension for GSRD individuals: the simultaneous aspiration for belonging and the inevitability of estrangement.

Ian Hodges' work on queering psychoanalysis provides a critical framework which we have found helpful for reinterpreting these existential concerns within GSRD populations (Hodges, 2011). Queer theory challenges the cis-heteronormative foundations of psychoanalysis, highlighting how annihilation anxiety in queer individuals is intricately tied to societal and relational structures. The existential dread of erasure is not merely personal but deeply contextual, shaped by the systemic marginalisation of queer identities. Within queer spaces, the pervasive avoidance of ageing and endings can be understood through the lens of annihilation anxiety. These spaces, often focused on youth and vitality, may reflect an unconscious defence against the confrontation with mortality and the associated fear of invisibility. Hodges underscores how queer communities, while offering critical sites of belonging, can paradoxically contribute to the isolation of ageing members. The erasure of queer elders mirrors the societal rejection they face, perpetuating a cycle of existential and queer loneliness.

Practical Implications: Harnessing the Power of Community and Connection

Addressing existential and queer loneliness in GSRD individuals requires more than clinical intervention; in our view it calls for a compassionate, community-centred approach. At the heart of this effort is our recognition that GSRD communities have long been sources of creativity, resilience, and healing. Even in the face of systemic discrimination, our communities have historically come together to build spaces where connection, visibility, and solidarity can flourish. Practitioners have an opportunity to honour and amplify these efforts by drawing on the rich tapestry of community-driven initiatives and resources.

While community initiatives provide crucial support, we acknowledge that systemic changes are necessary to address the root causes of queer loneliness. GSRD practitioners can advocate for policies that dismantle barriers and promote intersectional inclusivity in healthcare, housing, and social services. By doing so, we believe that we can play our part in creating a society where GSRD individuals can thrive at every stage of life. From our perspective, queer joy takes many forms. It can be bold, radical, and defiant, standing in opposition to systems of oppression, or it can be found in quiet, simple moments of connection with chosen family, loved ones or in therapeutic spaces. In our experience, both expressions are deeply rooted in resilience—the ability to navigate adversity with creativity, strength, and authenticity. Queer communities have long exemplified the power of finding joy and building connection even in the face of profound challenges, creating spaces of love, solidarity, and healing.

Queer(ing) Grief through the Lens of Intersubjective Systems Theory

We think it is time to talk about grief. In this third section, we are approaching the topic through the perspective of Robert Stolorow's *intersubjective systems theory* as we believe that it provides a compelling framework for exploring the unique dimensions of queer grief, emphasising the relational contexts in which grief is experienced and processed (Stolorow, 2013). When considering queer grief, we introduce the concepts of *disenfranchised grief*, *moral distress*, *minority stress theory*, and *fragilification* to provide insights into how we understand how grief is both lived and resisted within queer spaces. Moreover, we have formulated the notion of *queering grief* as a challenge to normative paradigms of mourning, in the hope of opening new pathways for collective and transformative mourning practices.

Disenfranchised Grief: The Marginalisation of Queer Mourning

Disenfranchised grief occurs when societal norms deny or diminish the legitimacy of an individual's grief (Smelser, 2023). For GSRD individuals, this form of grief is pervasive, as their losses often remain unrecognised or invalidated. Examples include the loss of chosen family members, estrangement from biological families, or mourning non-conventional relationship structures (Corns, 2022). Additionally, grief related to systemic oppression—such as mourning opportunities lost to discrimination—can be disenfranchised by a society that marginalises queer experiences. For instance, in death rituals, families might refuse to recognise a deceased individual's queer identity or relationships, thereby disenfranchising the grief of surviving queer partners and communities. Stolorow's intersubjective systems theory highlights how such relational disconfirmation intensifies grief, deepening feelings of isolation and existential despair. We find that Stolorow's concept of *fragilification* provides a useful lens here. Fragilification suggests that the trauma of relational disconfirmation leaves individuals more vulnerable to emotional collapse in future losses (Stolorow, 2023). For GSRD individuals, repeated experiences of disenfranchised grief can create an ongoing sense of emotional precarity. However, it is crucial to approach this concept tentatively. While some may experience heightened vulnerability, others may develop significant resilience, finding strength and solidarity within their communities to navigate disenfranchised grief.

Moral Distress and the Compounding Role of Minority Stress and Strength

Moral distress arises when individuals are unable to act in accordance with their ethical values due to external constraints (Morley et al., 2019). In the context of queer grief, moral distress frequently emerges in institutional or relational settings that invalidate queer identities and relationships. For example, a queer individual may feel morally distressed when unable to publicly mourn a lost partner due to fear of societal judgement or familial rejection. In our view, the concept of *moral distress* in queer grief is compounded by *minority stress*, which encompasses the chronic stress associated with living in a stigmatising society. Minority stress includes external forces such as discrimination and violence, as well as internalised stressors like internalised homophobia or shame. These stressors can intensify the grief experience, as queer individuals must navigate both the pain of their loss and the added burden of societal oppression.

For example, a queer person mourning the death of a partner may face institutional barriers that deny the legitimacy of their relationship, amplifying feelings of helplessness and invisibility (Pinel et al., 2022).

At the same time, we also found interesting contemporary studies looking at expanding minority stress theory combined with ecological systems theory that conceptualises the interplay between systems and individual-level variables in terms of protective factors mediating stress and emphasising *minority strength* (Perrin et al., 2020). This research is exploring ways specific factors related to personal and collective strengths in minority populations work in combination to create resilience and positive mental and physical health. We found this work valuable in helping us to understand the strengths of GSRD populations and the process by which important variables combine, coalesce and interrelate, becoming personal and collective strengths for GSRD populations that can be applied to grief and end-of-life therapeutic work.

Queering Grief: Challenging Normative Frameworks of Mourning

Queering grief involves disrupting and reimagining normative paradigms of mourning, which often centre on heteronormative and cis-normative assumptions. Traditional grief models tend to emphasise linear processes of acceptance and closure, often neglecting the fluid and collective dimensions of queer mourning. Queer grief, by contrast, resists closure and instead embraces mourning as an ongoing, relational, and transformative process (Ah-Fat, 2024; Craven & Peel, 2014). Collective mourning practices, such as those seen during the HIV/AIDS crisis, illustrate the queering of grief. The AIDS Memorial Quilt, for instance, serves as a collective act of resistance against societal erasure, transforming individual losses into a shared narrative of remembrance and activism (Blair & Michel, 2007). The Trans Day of Remembrance (TDOR) holds profound significance within queer grieving, serving as both a memorial and a communal act of resilience. Observed annually on 20 November, TDOR honours the lives of transgender individuals lost to violence, systemic neglect, and discrimination, while also acknowledging the ongoing injustices faced by trans communities worldwide (Lamble, 2008). Its relevance in queer grieving lies in its dual role as a space for collective mourning and a site of visibility for lives that might otherwise be erased. By naming and remembering those who have been lost, TDOR resists the societal erasure that so often compounds grief within marginalised communities. It transforms mourning into an act of defiance against the forces that perpetuate harm and celebrates the strength, dignity, and humanity of transgender lives. For queer individuals and allies, TDOR is not only a time to reflect on loss but also an opportunity to commit to the ongoing work of advocacy, solidarity, and creating spaces where trans people can thrive. Through Stolorow's existential-contextual lens, such practices function as intersubjective systems that validate grief, hold pain, counteract isolation, and create spaces for mutual healing (Stolorow, 2016, 2018).

Annihilation Anxiety and Relational Trauma

In this context, we believe that the concept of *annihilation anxiety*, the fear of existential erasure, is deeply relevant to queer grief. This anxiety, which extends beyond the fear of death, centres on the dread of erasure and invisibility. Annihilation anxiety speaks to the deep-seated fear of being obliterated not just physically but socially and existentially (Whitestone, 2022). When grieving individuals encounter disconfirming responses from family, institutions, or even queer communities, their mourning process can be disrupted, leading to profound emotional suffering. The emotional weight of grief, especially when compounded by disenfranchisement, moral distress, and minority stress, can feel overwhelming and unbearable when faced alone.

The Emotional Weight of Addressing Annihilation Anxiety

Confronting mortality and annihilation anxiety is inherently overwhelming, particularly when done in isolation. The emotional burden of facing these anxieties can feel intolerable, leading to avoidance. For many, the prospect of grappling with existential fears of erasure and invisibility triggers profound despair. Without relational or communal support, individuals may find it impossible to bear the weight of such confrontation, retreating into denial or avoidance. We believe it is important to clarify that this avoidance is not a failure of resilience but rather an indication of the immense emotional demands involved in facing existential givens. The therapeutic encounter thus can become a crucial space for gradually approaching these anxieties within a safe, relational context. By fostering a sense of connection and shared meaning, therapy can offer GSRD clients an opportunity to address avoidance and begin to process fears and possibly develop an existential attitude (Vos et al., 2015).

In our existential-relational perspective, we sometimes speak of the *contextualised self* as a way of understanding how mortality salience and annihilation anxiety are experienced relationally. Existential-relational psychoanalysis posits that the self is inherently intersubjective, shaped by and through relationships. For GSRD individuals, whose relational contexts can be fraught with stigma and exclusion, the confrontation with mortality and erasure becomes a profoundly relational experience. We have argued that annihilation anxiety arises within these relational contexts, making the therapeutic space a crucial site for reconstituting relational meaning. In this space, clients can explore their fears of mortality and erasure within a framework of acceptance and affirmation. The clinician's role involves not only facilitating the exploration of death anxiety but also addressing the societal and relational dynamics that compound the fear of invisibility. Existential-relational psychoanalysis, particularly as articulated by Robert Stolorow, emphasises the inevitability of existential angst as individuals grapple with the finitude of life. Stolorow's *world-collapse* theory posits that the confrontation with mortality disrupts one's ontological security, exposing the fragility of subjective experience on an individual and collective level, respectively (Stolorow, 2014).

Terror Management Theory: Navigating Mortality Salience in the Context of Social Oppression

Through our own conversations and work, we believe that terror management theory (TMT) offers a helpful framework for understanding the existential anxieties that arise from the awareness of mortality. According to TMT, individuals cope with existential anxiety by adhering to cultural worldviews and bolstering self-esteem, which provide a sense of symbolic immortality.

For GSRD individuals, however, mortality salience is often heightened by systemic oppression, including discrimination in healthcare and the erasure of their identities in later life stages, which relates to threats to self-esteem and held worldview beliefs. The existential fears experienced by GSRD individuals are often (but not always) compounded by the lack of traditional legacy structures, such as biological lineage or conventional family narratives. This absence can lead to existential isolation, especially for those who have lived in incongruence with their identities due to societal pressures.

TMT and Symbolic Immortality through a GSRD Lens: Applied Examples for Therapeutic Practice

Robert J. Lifton's concept of symbolic immortality, which relates to TMT and describes how individuals seek continuity and meaning in the face of existential anxiety, offers a helpful framework for exploring existential concerns within the GSRD community (Lifton, 1973; Lifton & Olson, 2004). We have used Lifton's five modes—biological, creative, spiritual, experiential, and natural—in formulating existential concerns in our GSRD clients and patients. In therapeutic practice, we find that these modes can help frame discussions around identity, legacy, and connection, offering pathways for clients to find meaning and continuity despite the challenges they may face.

Biological Mode: Redefining Generativity through Diverse Family Structures

Biological continuity, traditionally tied to genetic reproduction, takes on expanded meanings within the GSRD community. Pathways to parenthood—such as surrogacy, adoption, and co-parenting—can allow GSRD individuals to experience generativity, often later in life due to earlier barriers like legal restrictions or financial constraints. For instance, a gay couple becoming parents via surrogacy in their 50s might fulfil long-held desires for family and connection, experiencing a sense of purpose and continuity through caregiving and nurturing.

In therapy, discussions about generativity can extend beyond traditional parenting to include the caregiving roles within chosen families, mentorship, and broader acts of legacy-building. A transgender woman mentoring a younger trans individual through their transition, for example, embodies biological generativity by fostering continuity within the GSRD community.

Creative Mode: Activism, Art, and the Preservation of Queer Histories

Creativity often provides a way for GSRD individuals to leave enduring legacies. Whether through writing, art, activism, or the creation of affirming community spaces, these acts ensure that their lives and identities contribute to the collective memory of queer histories. As discussed above, the AIDS Memorial Quilt, for instance, exemplifies a shared creative effort that honours lives lost while preserving narratives of resilience and solidarity. Therapeutically, exploring creative legacies can provide clients with a sense of purpose and connection to a broader community. A non-binary client who organises a community art exhibit celebrating diverse gender identities might find meaning in their contributions to both their personal identity and the visibility of the wider GSRD community.

Spiritual Mode: Affirming Identity through Rituals and Community

Spiritual continuity is often found in rituals and practices that affirm identity and foster connection. Queer-affirming spiritual spaces, LGBTQIA+ faith groups, and rituals such as Pride parades provide existential grounding and celebrate the enduring significance of queer lives. These practices are particularly meaningful for those who have been excluded from traditional religious or cultural ceremonies. In therapy, clients can be encouraged to create their own rituals that reflect their values and affirm their identities. For instance, a non-binary individual might create an annual "rebirth day" ceremony to honour the anniversary of their name change and gender affirmation. The ritual could include lighting candles, reciting affirmations, or inviting close friends and chosen family to participate in celebrating their journey of self-discovery and authenticity. Such practices not only offer spiritual comfort but also create opportunities for connection, fostering a sense of belonging and continuity that affirms their place within both their community and their broader life narrative.

Experiential Mode: Building Bonds through Shared Memories

The experiential mode emphasises the importance of relationships and shared memories in creating continuity. For GSRD individuals, chosen families often become the cornerstone of these connections, offering spaces of safety and care that transcend time. For example, a group of queer elders might gather to document their collective experiences through storytelling and shared photographs, preserving their history for future generations. Therapeutically, exploring the significance of these bonds can help clients recognise the enduring presence of their relationships. Group therapy or community-based interventions can also create new opportunities for shared experiences, reinforcing the sense of continuity within a supportive network. In addition, it is our experience that fostering intergenerational connections within queer communities can help address the avoidance of ageing and endings. We think intergenerational initiatives—such as shared storytelling or mentorship programmes—create opportunities for mutual understanding and solidarity. These connections can offer spaces for existential reconciliation, allowing younger and older queer individuals to engage in collective meaning-making and affirm their shared histories.

Natural Mode: Connection to the Environment and Life Cycles

For many GSRD individuals, connection to nature offers a sense of belonging within the broader cycles of life. Acts like gardening, environmental activism, or simply spending time outdoors provide ways to experience continuity through the natural world. A queer individual planting a garden in memory of a lost loved one, for instance, might find solace and meaning in watching the garden grow, symbolising the enduring impact of their relationship. Therapeutically, clients can be encouraged to explore their relationships with nature as a grounding and meaningful practice. Nature-based rituals, such as planting trees or participating in community clean-up projects, can offer ways to connect with something larger than themselves and create legacies that extend beyond the individual.

Our approach to integrating existential-relational psychoanalysis with queer frameworks reflects our way of thinking about mortality salience and annihilation anxiety in GSRD clients. This approach offers ways to explore the interplay between identity, societal exclusion, and deeply personal existential fears. While this is but one of many ways of thinking about existential concerns, we find that models like this can help in identifying which ways of addressing existential anxieties appear most meaningful and most achievable for a client in their individual circumstances and contexts. It also allows for conversations around contributors to deep-seated existential anxieties when expected or anticipated life projects did not come to fruition or were interrupted due to separation, life events or rupture.

Satisficing Death

Finally, in our exploration of queer ageing and endings, we find the concept of *satisficing death*, as articulated by Lampe (2024), to be an insightful framework that resonates with the realities of GSRD individuals. It challenges traditional ideals of a *good death*, often shaped by privilege—assumptions of familial support, financial stability, and affirming care (Lampe, 2024). For transgender elders and others within GSRD communities, these ideals may feel unattainable due to the discussed systemic inequities and pervasive marginalisation. In our view, *satisficing death* offers a more realistic and empowering way to think about end-of-life experiences, emphasising the balance between existential concerns and structural constraints.

This concept acknowledges that marginalised individuals often focus on meeting basic needs, such as safety, dignity, and identity preservation, rather than striving for conventional markers of a *good death*. In our work, we see how fears of medical erasure, misgendering, and exclusion influence

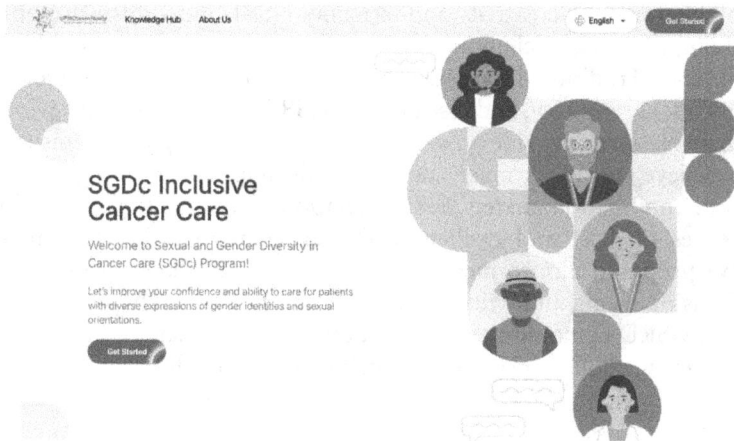

Figure 17.1 www.pmchosenfamily.com is a learning platform for healthcare providers educating on communication strategies around pronouns, gender identity, sexual orientation, and relationship diversity.

end-of-life planning for many transgender elders. Their strategies—such as detailed advance care planning, reliance on chosen family as healthcare proxies, and informal networks to ensure their wishes are respected—reflect the pragmatism central to the concept of satisficing death. Rather than compromises, we understand these strategies as acts of resilience and self-determination. *Satisficing death* reframes these efforts as creative ways to navigate structural barriers, aligning with our broader view that end-of-life care must account for marginalisation while fostering relational and existential safety. This concept also challenges clinicians, caregivers, and policymakers to rethink universalised frameworks of the *good death* and instead develop practices tailored to the diverse realities of GSRD individuals.

Resources like our pmchosenfamily.ca learning platform (Figure 17.1), the *Planning for My Care* guide and the *Proud, Prepared, and Protected* initiative by the Canadian Virtual Hospice exemplify how the process of satisficing death can be supported through practical tools that centre dignity and identity. By shifting the focus from unattainable ideals to achievable acts of agency, *satisficing death* provides a path for affirming end-of-life experiences while transforming how queer communities approach ageing and endings as collective acts of care, resilience, and recognition.

Conclusion

From our perspective, ageing, and endings are profoundly human yet shaped by the intersecting identities, systemic marginalisation, and societal norms

GSRD individuals navigate. In this chapter, we have explored these complexities, highlighting the creativity and resilience GSRD individuals demonstrate in building meaning, reclaiming joy, and fostering connection amidst isolation and loss. Traditional frameworks often overlook the central role of chosen families, community, and resistance in GSRD lives, yet we have witnessed how these elements provide powerful counterpoints to systemic erasure.

We believe therapists must adopt an affirming, inclusive approach that addresses annihilation anxiety, fosters relational safety, and honours diverse experiences of grief and resilience. The existential-relational frameworks we have proposed aim to meet these needs while challenging exclusionary paradigms of ageing and dying. Ultimately, we hope this chapter affirms the ability of GSRD communities to reimagine ageing and endings on their own terms, offering dignity, meaning, and belonging even in life's most vulnerable moments.

References

Ah-Fat, A. (2024). When grief arrives: An oral history of grief and death within queer, trans and black, Indigenous and people of colour communities. *International Journal of Narrative Therapy and Community Work, 2*, 51–63.

Blair, C., & Michel, N. (2007). The AIDS memorial quilt and the contemporary culture of public commemoration. *Rhetoric and Public Affairs, 10*(4), 595–626

Boot-Haury, J. W., & Cusick, K. M. (2023). Intersectional asexual and transgender and gender diverse identity and existential concerns: A thematic analysis. *The Humanistic Psychologist.* https://psycnet.apa.org/record/2024-37958-001

Bratt, C., Abrams, D., Swift, H. J., Vauclair, C.-M., & Marques, S. (2018). Perceived age discrimination across age in Europe: From an ageing society to a society for all ages. *Developmental Psychology, 54*(1), 167.

Cahill, S., Battle, J., & Meyer, D. (2003). Partnering, parenting, and policy: Family issues affecting Black lesbian, gay, bisexual, and transgender (LGBT) people. *Race and Society, 6*(2), 85–98.

Changfoot, N., Rice, C., Chivers, S., Williams, A. O., Connors, A., Barrett, A., Gordon, M., & Lalonde, G. (2022). Revisioning aging: Indigenous, crip and queer renderings. *Journal of Aging Studies, 63*, 100930.

Chiotti, Q. P., & Joseph, A. E. (1995). Casey house: Interpreting the location of a Toronto AIDS hospice. *Social Science & Medicine, 41*(1), 131–140.

Corns, D. L. (2022). *Disenfranchised grief in queer companionship and chosen family.* https://scholarworks.lib.csusb.edu/etd/1509/

Craven, C., & Peel, E. (2014). Stories of grief and hope: Queer experiences of reproductive loss. In M. F. Gibson (Ed.), *Queering maternity and motherhood: Narrative and theoretical perspectives on queer conception, birth and parenting* (pp. 97–110). Bradford, Ontario: Demeter Press.

De Vries, B., Gutman, G., Humble, Á., Gahagan, J., Chamberland, L., Aubert, P., Fast, J., & Mock, S. (2019). End-of-life preparations among LGBT older canadian adults: The missing conversations. *The International Journal of Aging and Human Development, 88*(4), 358–379. https://doi.org/10.1177/0091415019836738

Fabbre, V. (2017). Queer aging: Implications for social work practice with lesbian, gay, bisexual, transgender, and queer older adults. *Social Work*, 62(1), 73–76.

Fabbre, V. D. (2015). Gender transitions in later life: A queer perspective on successful aging. *The Gerontologist*, 55(1), 144–153.

Floyd, F. J., & Bakeman, R. (2006). Coming-out across the life course: Implications of age and historical context. *Archives of Sexual Behavior*, 35(3), 287–296. https://doi.org/10.1007/s10508-006-9022-x

Grimmer, C. (2020). *On longing and belonging: The promise of queer community in Berlin: A qualitative study of queer loneliness and community building in Berlin.* https://www.diva-portal.org/smash/record.jsf?pid=diva2:1514794

Halberstam, J. (2011). *The queer art of failure.* New York: Duke University Press. https://doi.org/10.1515/9780822394358

Haviland, K., Burrows Walters, C., & Newman, S. (2021). Barriers to palliative care in sexual and gender minority patients with cancer: A scoping review of the literature. *Health & Social Care in the Community*, 29(2), 305–318. https://doi.org/10.1111/hsc.13126

Hodges, I. (2011). Queering psychoanalysis: Power, self and identity in psychoanalytic therapy with sexual minority clients. *Psychology and Sexuality*, 2(1), 29–44. https://doi.org/10.1080/19419899.2011.536313

Jackson Levin, N., Kattari, S. K., Piellusch, E. K., & Watson, E. (2020). "We just take care of each other": Navigating 'chosen family'in the context of health, illness, and the mutual provision of care amongst queer and transgender young adults. *International Journal of Environmental Research and Public Health*, 17(19), 7346.

Jeste, D. V., Blazer II, D. G., Buckwalter, K. C., Cassidy, K.-L. K., Fishman, L., Gwyther, L. P., Levin, S. M., Phillipson, C., Rao, R. R., & Schmeding, E. (2016). Age-friendly communities initiative: Public health approach to promoting successful aging. *The American Journal of Geriatric Psychiatry*, 24(12), 1158–1170.

Kahn, M. J. (1991). Factors affecting the coming out process for lesbians. *Journal of Homosexuality*, 21(3), 47–70. https://doi.org/10.1300/J082v21n03_03

Kim, S., & Feyissa, I. F. (2021). Conceptualizing "family" and the role of "chosen family" within the LGBTQ+ refugee community: A text network graph analysis. *Healthcare*, 9(4), 369. https://www.mdpi.com/2227-9032/9/4/369

Koffman, J., Shapiro, G. K., & Schulz-Quach, C. (2023). Enhancing equity and diversity in palliative care clinical practice, research and education. *BMC Palliative Care*, 22(1), 64. https://doi.org/10.1186/s12904-023-01185-6

Lamble, S. (2008). Retelling racialized violence, remaking white innocence: The politics of interlocking oppressions in transgender day of remembrance. *Sexuality Research and Social Policy*, 5(1), 24–42. https://doi.org/10.1525/srsp.2008.5.1.24

Lampe, N. M. (2024). Satisficing death: Ageing and end-of-life preparation among transgender older Americans. *Sociology of Health & Illness*, 46(5), 887–906. https://doi.org/10.1111/1467-9566.13741

Lifton, R. J. (1973). The sense of immortality: On death and the continuity of life. *The American Journal of Psychoanalysis*, 33(1), 3–15. https://doi.org/10.1007/BF01872131

Lifton, R. J., & Olson, E. (2004). Symbolic immortality. In A. C. G. M. Robben (Ed.), Death, mourning, and burial: A cross-cultural reader (pp. 32–39). Blackwell Publishing.

Liu, W. (2017). Toward a queer psychology of affect: Restarting from shameful places. *Subjectivity, 10*(1), 44–62. https://doi.org/10.1057/s41286-016-0014-6

Maguire, G. (2023). The queer art of feeling: Futurity, Fin de siglo, and new queer realism. *JCMS: Journal of Cinema and Media Studies, 63*(5), 263–283.

Martinson, M., & Berridge, C. (2015). Successful aging and its discontents: A systematic review of the social gerontology literature. *The Gerontologist, 55*(1), 58–69.

Miller, L. R. (2023). Queer aging: Older lesbian, gay, and bisexual adults' visions of late life. *Innovation in Aging, 7*(3), igad021.

Miller, P. H. (2022). Developmental theories: Past, present, and future. *Developmental Review, 66*, 101049.

Milton, D. C. (2024). *An exploration of chosen family relationships with transgender and nonbinary people of color* [PhD Thesis, Oklahoma State University]. Available online: https://search.proquest.com/openview/8ccec9d44b3b0869c8b 9d152aa6b3ff7/1?pq-origsite=gscholar&cbl=18750&diss=y

Morley, G., Ives, J., Bradbury-Jones, C., & Irvine, F. (2019). What is 'moral distress'? A narrative synthesis of the literature. *Nursing Ethics, 26*(3), 646–662. https://doi .org/10.1177/0969733017724354

Morrison, M. (2015). Some things are better left unsaid: "The" dignity of queer shame. *Mosaic: A Journal for the Interdisciplinary Study of Literature, 48*(1)17–32.

Mulqueen, T. (2013). Succeeding at failing and other oxymorons: Halberstam's the queer art of failure. *Theory & Event, 16*(4). https://muse.jhu.edu/pub/1/article /530506/summary

Nunoda, E. S. (2023). *Unconsummated/Queer loneliness* [PhD Thesis, University of Toronto (Canada)]. Available online: https://search.proquest.com/openview/1b0 e1fa907603ab49293524536c0be0a/1?pq-origsite=gscholar&cbl=18750&diss=y

Odets, W. (2019). *Out of the shadows: Reimagining gay men's lives.* Farrar, Straus and Giroux. https://books.google.com/books?hl=en&lr=&id=ILhuDwAAQBAJ &oi=fnd&pg=PT220&dq=walt+odets+out+of+the+shadow&ots=0a-2-jESak &sig=9iaW7xQ-WYOYhK7bebykg2OizLU

Ogden, T. H. (2014). Fear of breakdown and the unlived life. *The International Journal of Psychoanalysis, 95*(2), 205–223. https://doi.org/10.1111/1745-8315 .12148

Oswald, A. G., & Cooper, L. (2024). Addressing equity and justice in age-friendly communities: Considerations for LGBTQ+ older adults of color. *The Gerontologist, 64*(7). https://academic.oup.com/gerontologist/article-abstract/64 /7/gnae050/7676507

Pang, C., Gutman, G., & De Vries, B. (2019). Later life care planning and concerns of transgender older adults in Canada. *The International Journal of Aging and Human Development, 89*(1), 39–56. https://doi.org/10.1177/0091415019843520

Perrin, P. B., Sutter, M. E., Trujillo, M. A., Henry, R. S., & Pugh, M. (2020). The minority strengths model: Development and initial path analytic validation in racially/ethnically diverse LGBTQ individuals. *Journal of Clinical Psychology, 76*(1), 118–136. https://doi.org/10.1002/jclp.22850

Pinel, E. C., Helm, P. J., Yawger, G. C., Long, A. E., & Scharnetzki, L. (2022). Feeling out of (existential) place: Existential isolation and nonnormative group membership. *Group Processes & Intergroup Relations, 25*(4), 990–1010. https:// doi.org/10.1177/1368430221999084

Sandberg, L. J., & Marshall, B. L. (2017). Queering aging futures. *Societies*, 7(3), 21.

Schulz-Quach, C. (2018a). The nakedness of the dead body: The meaning of death to healthcare professionals working with the dying. *Existential Analysis*, 29(2), 301–323.

Schulz-Quach, C. (2018b, January 22). "What is the meaning of death to you?" Metasynthesis of the lived experience of health care professionals who experience the death of others in a professional context | Request PDF. *ResearchGate*. https://www.researchgate.net/publication/343376788_What_is_the_meaning_of_death_to_you_Metasynthesis_of_the_lived_experience_of_health_care_professionals_who_experience_the_death_of_others_in_a_professional_context

Scott, S. (2020). The unlived life is worth examining: Nothings and nobodies behind the scenes. *Symbolic Interaction*, 43(1), 156–180. https://doi.org/10.1002/symb.448

Silverman, M., & Baril, A. (2023). "We have to advocate so hard for ourselves and our people": Caring for a trans or non-binary older adult with dementia. *LGBTQ+ Family: An Interdisciplinary Journal*, 19(3), 187–210. https://doi.org/10.1080/27703371.2023.2169215

Smelser, Q. K. (2023). Identity and loss: Where intersectionality and disenfranchised grief converge. In Blocker Turner & Stauffer (Eds.), Disenfranchised grief (pp. 24–41). Routledge. https://www.taylorfrancis.com/chapters/edit/10.4324/9781003292890-3/identity-loss-quinn-smelser

Spornberger MA, R. E. (2016). Coming out late: The impact on individuals' social networks. Available online: https://scholarworks.gsu.edu/gerontology_theses/40/

Stolorow, R. D. (2013). Intersubjective-systems theory: A phenomenological-contextualist psychoanalytic perspective. *Psychoanalytic Dialogues*, 23(4), 383–389.

Stolorow, R. D. (2014). Undergoing the situation: Emotional dwelling is more than empathic understanding. *International Journal of Psychoanalytic Self Psychology*, 9(1), 80–83.

Stolorow, R. D. (2016). Pain is not pathology. *Existential Analysis*, 27(1), 70–74.

Stolorow, R. D. (2018). *Emotional disturbance, trauma, and authenticity: A phenomenological-contextualist psychoanalytic perspective*. In K. Aho (Ed.), *Existential Medicine: Essays on Health and Illness*. Lanham: Rowman & Littlefield, pp. 17–25.

Stolorow, R. D. (2023). Emotional trauma and the fragilification of being. *Trauma Psychology News*. Available online: https://www.academia.edu/110573746/Emotional_Trauma_and_the_Fragilification_of_Being

Vos, J., Craig, M., & Cooper, M. (2015). Existential therapies: A meta-analysis of their effects on psychological outcomes. *Journal of Consulting and Clinical Psychology*, 83(1), 115.

Walker, R. V., Powers, S. M., & Witten, T. M. (2023). Transgender and gender diverse people's fear of seeking and receiving care in later life: A multiple method analysis. *Journal of Homosexuality*, 70(14), 3374–3398. https://doi.org/10.1080/00918369.2022.2094305

Weststrate, N. M., & McLean, K. C. (2010). The rise and fall of gay: A cultural-historical approach to gay identity development. *Memory*, 18(2), 225–240. https://doi.org/10.1080/09658210903153923

Whitestone, S. B. (2022). *A qualitative examination of discrimination after death: The distortion and erasure of transgender and other marginalized post-mortem identities.* University of California, Santa Barbara. https://search.proquest.com/openview/6bbe43790a4a95e7bbd237001301c417/1?pq-origsite=gscholar&cbl=18750&diss=y

Witten, T. M. (2014). End of life, chronic illness, and trans-identities. *Journal of Social Work in End-of-Life & Palliative Care, 10*(1), 34–58. https://doi.org/10.1080/15524256.2013.877864

Worthen, M. G. (2023). Queer identities in the 21st century: Reclamation and stigma. *Current Opinion in Psychology, 49*, 101512.

Yarns, B. C., Abrams, J. M., Meeks, T. W., & Sewell, D. D. (2016). The mental health of older LGBT adults. *Current Psychiatry Reports, 18*(6), 60. https://doi.org/10.1007/s11920-016-0697-y

Conclusion

Dominic Davies, Silva Neves, and Antonio Prunas

We hope this book will help guide therapists in delivering effective and ethical therapy with gender, sex, and relationship diversity (GSRD) clients. GSRD therapy can be practised in diverse ways and fully integrated into other modalities. In the introduction, we mentioned that this book is the culmination of decades of experience with key practitioners in the Pink Therapy community, building on the shoulders of giants in the field. We are also keen to look into the future. This book is by no means the final destination in our understanding of therapeutic work with GSRD clients. We look forward to seeing new, talented therapists and researchers with innovative ideas on expanding our knowledge of queering the psychotherapy field. As the web of Pink Therapy alumni and other like-minded organisations spreads around the world, we are excited to see a better future for the field of psychotherapy, but even more importantly, for the wellbeing of our GSRD clients in accessing safer therapeutic spaces. By reading this book, you are already part of the GSRD movement, and we thank you for it.

DOI: 10.4324/9781003530848-22

Index

addiction treatment 2
affirmative therapy 1, 2, 4, 69–71, 75, 80, 109
ageism 43, 239, 241–244
AIDS epidemic 42, 235
Alcoholics Anonymous (AA) 2
amatonormativity 43, 55
anodyspareunia 22, 43, 125
anti-oppressive practice 24, 39, 45, 49, 178, 185, 199
attachment theory 243

BACP 1, 227
Bartlett et al. (2009) 2
BDSM/Kink 44
biopsychosocial perspective 23
biphobia 43, 90, 100, 235
body image 43, 128, 131–142
body image dissatisfaction 131, 135
Borgogna et al. (2021) 43

cisgenderism 72, 156, 187, 197
cisnormativity 11, 13, 20, 39, 43, 91, 244
clinical formulation 23, 24, 106
coming out 4, 40, 45, 53, 70, 101, 134, 163, 171, 206, 214, 224, 235, 240
compassionate inquiry 130
complex PTSD 41
conversion therapy 1, 2, 21, 71, 73, 89, 151, 228, 236
Craig and Austin (2017) 197
Crystal Meth Addicts Anonymous (CMA) 2
cultural awareness 185, 232

cultural competence 25, 39, 43, 64, 108, 118, 133, 170, 172–176, 178, 184, 185, 190, 200, 201
cultural humility 20, 25, 39, 49, 108, 110, 118, 170, 172–176, 178, 185, 200

Davies, Dominic 1, 20, 37, 38, 87, 181, 261
depathologisation 92
Diamond and Alley (2022) 16, 74, 206
diaspora and GSRD 188
discrimination 16, 17, 21, 25, 44, 45, 52, 73, 79, 82, 101, 106, 126, 133, 135, 136, 141, 151, 160, 179, 188, 190, 198, 203, 215, 218, 220, 222–224, 242, 244, 245, 247–250, 252
disenfranchised grief 248–249
Drescher, Jack 3
Droubay and White (2024) 42
Dunlop (2022) 39, 43, 98, 106, 107, 110

Eckstrand and Potter (2017) 45
empathy and unconditional positive regard 41
Erikson's stages of psychosocial development 240

Fabbre (2015) 241, 242, 244–245
faith and spirituality 226
First Peoples 233
fostering joy 34, 44, 45, 96, 104, 118, 170, 171, 174–176, 193, 207–208, 216
Foucault 10, 94

Fredrickson and Roberts (1997) 131
French et al. (1996) 134
Frost and Meyer (2023) 41

gay community 16, 17, 43, 121, 133
Gender, Sex and Relationship Diversity
    (GSRD) 9
gender-affirming surgery 41
gender counselling 2
gender dysphoria 14, 22, 45, 72, 140,
    147, 204, 217
gender expansive 214
gender identity 9–11, 21, 27, 28, 55–60,
    62, 74, 79, 90, 128, 135, 136, 138,
    141, 158, 203, 224, 227, 233, 255
gender non-conforming people 2
Gestalt therapy 116–119, 121, 124–126
Grabski (2023) 4, 22, 43
Grief therapy 204
group therapy 12, 168–178, 181–182,
    253

harm minimisation approaches 2
Hawkins, Rima 50, 183
Heartstopper 41
heteronormativity 11, 13, 38, 39, 43,
    72, 74, 91, 98, 156, 197, 246
heterosexuality 2, 11, 56, 147, 187
Higher Power 2
Hijra community 233
HIV stigma 43
homophobia 31, 41–43, 54, 73, 74, 77,
    90, 100, 108, 116, 118, 122, 146,
    156, 161, 164, 197, 224, 235, 249
Hughes and Hammack (2019) 43
hypermasculinity 43
hypersexuality 43

IFS therapists 130
IFS therapy 130, 140, 142
Internal family systems 128, 221; *see
    also* IFS therapy
internalised homophobia 73, 74, 156,
    161, 224, 249
internalised stigma 21, 156, 158,
    160–162, 164, 232
intersectional identities theory 240
intersectionality 20, 25, 43, 50, 64, 73,
    96, 132, 180, 189, 199, 206, 219,
    240, 242, 243
intra-community minority stress 43, 77
Izzard (2000) 76–78

Jungian perspective 145

Kahn (1991) 241, 244
Kim and Feyissa (2021) 243
King et al. (2008) 23, 98
Koffman et al. (2023) 240
Krayer et al. (2008) 131

Laxmi Narayan Tripathi 233
lesbian women 128, 131, 133–134
Lyne, Simon (2023) 41

Maslow's hierarchy of needs 44
McClain and Peebles (2016) 131
McDermott and Roen (2016) 197
McDermott et al. (2008) 77
medical and surgical gender health
    care 2
Merino et al. (2024) 131
Meyer (2003) 22, 41, 43, 73, 92, 98,
    160, 203, 206
microaggressions 54, 73, 126, 203, 215,
    218, 220
Milton (2024) 243
minority strength 249
minority stress 17, 18, 20–23, 43, 44,
    51, 53, 62, 69, 70, 73–75, 77, 79,
    80–82, 92, 98, 126, 131, 132, 141,
    160–162, 173, 202, 204, 206, 220,
    247–250
minority stress theory 22, 44, 69, 206,
    248, 249
mirror ball encounters 167, 182
mononormativity 20, 39, 43, 156
moral distress 248–250

Neal, Charles 2–3
neurodivergence 53, 168, 219–221,
    241
Neves, Silva 37, 38, 50, 261
non-monogamous individuals 43

objectification theory 131
Ogden (2014) 241
Owens et al. (2003) 133–134

Pachankis et al. (2020) 17, 43, 77
parenting 31, 213, 214, 216, 217,
    219–223, 252
peer-led self-help groups 2
Perrin et al. (2020) 249
Pinel et al. (2022) 249

Pink Therapy 1–3, 37, 49, 53, 56, 75, 80, 87, 261
Pollock, Karen 86
polyamory 3, 92, 170, 215
post-trauma stress symptoms 40
Prause et al. (2015) 2
precarious manhood theory 43
psychoanalysis 70, 75–77, 81, 119, 121, 147, 148, 247, 251, 254

queer ageing 239, 245, 254
queer ageing and endings 239, 245, 254
queer communities 34, 181, 241, 247, 248, 250, 253, 255
queer critique of "Positive Ageing" 243
queer grief 248–250
queer identities 89, 213, 227, 247, 249
queer mourning 248, 250
queer spirituality 226, 228, 233–236
queer theory 11, 240, 244, 247

racial and sexual stereotypes 43
relational disconfirmation 249
religious trauma 236
Rogers (1961) 44
Rohleder (2020) 78
Rothblum (1994) 134

self-compassion 220, 221, 232
Self-Discrepancy theory 131
sex addiction 42
sex education 34, 41, 42, 52, 63, 171, 205
sexual and gender minorities 12, 70
sexual orientation 9, 11, 12, 25, 26, 28, 50, 55, 58, 90, 122, 185, 188, 193, 202, 224, 255
shame-induced depression 41

Silverman and Baril (2023) 243
social comparison theory 131
social justice 20, 24, 25, 27, 38, 39, 43, 69, 70, 81, 101, 103, 110, 118, 152, 153, 170, 172, 174–176, 199, 200–202
social norms 12, 134, 136, 199
social safety theory 44, 206
Sollod (2005) 233
spiritual trauma 232–233
Spornberger (2016) 241
stigma 10, 11, 16, 17, 20, 21, 43, 44, 51, 53, 74, 98, 109, 132, 156, 158, 160–162, 164, 188, 199, 203, 205, 219, 220, 222, 241, 242, 241
Stolorow's *intersubjective systems theory* 248–249
systemic oppression 23, 45, 185, 186, 193, 197, 241, 248, 252

therapeutic alliance 64, 109, 118, 162, 185, 187, 231, 233
therapeutic neutrality 72
therapist self-disclosure 20
therapy with trans and gender non-conforming people 2
trans clients 32, 45, 72, 125
transgender individuals 21, 128, 131, 135, 246, 250
trans joy and grief 41
transnormativity 12–13
trauma-informed approach 64, 141, 233
Two-Spirit 153, 233

UKCP 1
unconditional positive regard 28, 33, 41

WHO (2019) 1, 22, 41, 99, 189

For Product Safety Concerns and Information please contact our EU
representative GPSR@taylorandfrancis.com
Taylor & Francis Verlag GmbH, Kaufingerstraße 24, 80331 München, Germany

9 781032 868806